**Developing Translanguaging Repe**

# Critical Approaches in Applied Linguistics

Edited by
Netta Avineri

**Volume 1**

# Developing Translanguaging Repertoires in Critical Teacher Education

Edited by
Zhongfeng Tian and Nicole King

**DE GRUYTER MOUTON**

ISBN 978-3-11-162078-7
e-ISBN (PDF) 978-3-11-073560-4
e-ISBN (EPUB) 978-3-11-073569-7
ISSN 2629-3536

**Library of Congress Control Number: 2023931403**

**Bibliographic information published by the Deutsche Nationalbibliothek**
The Deutsche Nationalbibliothek lists this publication in the Deutsche Nationalbibliografie; detailed bibliographic data are available on the internet at http://dnb.dnb.de.

© 2024 Walter de Gruyter GmbH, Berlin/Boston
This volume is text- and page-identical with the hardback published in 2023.
Cover image: RiniSlok/iStock/Getty Images Plus
Typesetting: Integra Software Services Pvt. Ltd.

www.degruyter.com

# Note from the series editor

In the volume *Developing Translanguaging Repertoires in Critical Teacher Education* edited by Zhongfeng Tian and Nicole King, the authors highlight the central role of educators' translanguaging knowledge, skills, and dispositions in creating more equitable learning environments for diverse learners. The chapters demonstrate how translanguaging is a dynamic tool for deep relationship building, negotiation, and dialogue among educators and learners, in regional contexts across the United States. Collectively they explore when and how translanguaging can be fostered in the service of social justice, through a critical examination of histories of colonization, educator positionalities, and racialization processes. As the chapters highlight, curricula are negotiated opportunities for individual and collective identity formation. And educators' language policies are critical sites for redressing past and present injustices, with a focus on cultivating equitable spaces for teaching, learning, and becoming at multiple scales.

Netta Avineri
Middlebury Institute of International Studies at Monterey
January 2023

# About the book series

The *Critical Approaches in Applied Linguistics* book series focuses on methods of inquiry, approaches, theories, concepts, and topics in applied linguistics that are critical in nature – that is, geared toward interrogating the relationship between language and the (re)creation of present and possible worlds. The field of applied linguistics has traditionally focused on 'real world issues'. In recent years, there has been a socially-oriented turn that considers issues including language policy, language assessment, language acquisition, discourse, and other topics from a critical perspective. This critical approach not only describes social issues but recognizes societal inequities and seeks to intentionally address them. The series has a social change and social justice orientation to allow editors, authors, and readers to engage in critical dialogue about relevant topics from an applied linguistics perspective.

The books in the series take interdisciplinary approaches to focus on key topics (e.g., language and education; language, race, and racism; heritage language socialization; heritage and indigenous language education) using a range of methodological approaches (e.g., critical discourse analysis, participatory action research, narrative inquiry, ethnographies, case studies). This book series

https://doi.org/10.1515/9783110735604-202

provides a distinctive forum for scholars and practitioners to engage with these approaches and topics to move towards social action around the world. Early career scholars are especially encouraged to submit proposals to the series.

# Preface

We embarked upon this collaboration to take a critical look at the tensions, conversations, reflections, and ideological examinations necessary for TESOL, bilingual, and world language teachers, teacher educators, and researchers to begin to take up and to continue to develop translanguaging repertoires. The contributions detail the situatedness and context-driven nature of the pathways to embracing and enacting translanguaging repertoires as transgressive acts of teaching and learning that confront and reinvent critical teacher education. All of the contributions embrace the political act that is teaching as they share their experiences preparing teacher candidates and working with current teachers to create a more just world. The multifaceted shifts and transformations detailed by the contributions all reflect the tensions of teaching critically and multilingually in educational systems with structural, historical, social boundaries on language and language teaching.

We wrote this book for teachers, teacher educators, and language scholars in the fields of TESOL, bilingual education, and world language. However, as we are all teachers of language and content, teacher educators in a variety of content areas may find this book helpful. Additionally, this book is intended for graduate students in a variety of language fields and applied linguists who are interested in critical language learning, critical applied linguistics, and critical heritage language learning and teaching.

This book is a continuation of the work of Ofelia García and her conceptualization of translanguaging as a pedagogy for social justice and as a theory of language that affirms and leverages the assets of those traditionally marginalized and minoritized. Each page of this volume was made possible by her thoughts, ideas, and support. We would also like to thank Peter Sayer for his example of narrative knowledging to expand upon the words of the authors. A team of support at de Gruyter Mouton helped to bring this volume from a scheduled colloquium at American Association for Applied Linguistics (AAAL) into an edited volume; thank you Netta Avineri, Natalie Fecher, Kirstin Boergen, and Katrin Stein. We also have a very special thank you to all of the contributors and to the external reviewer whose hard work and thoughtful reflection made this volume possible. In addition, without the careful copyediting eye and diligent work ethic of Jessica McConnell, we could not have brought this volume to the finish line. Finally, we are grateful to the many teachers, teacher educators, and teacher candidates who willingly and generously shared their journeys towards translanguaging repertoires.

Zhongfeng Tian  
Newark, NJ, USA

Nicole King  
Rochester, NY, USA

# Foreword: Re-Seeing translanguaging in teacher education and research

This book invites us to *re-see* and *re-evaluate* translanguaging pedagogical practices in the hands, minds, and hearts of students of teaching – those being educated to teach bilingual children and those already teaching them. In many ways the book is a call to "start with the teachers," as Hadjioannou says in her chapter in this volume.

Tian and King are not simply advocating here for the teachers' use of translanguaging practices in teaching bilingual students. The "critical teacher education" that they espouse in this book develops the teachers' translanguaging stance so that teachers can open up translanguaging spaces in their lesson design and shift their teaching to follow the bilingual students' translanguaging corriente. But the main focus of the book is on the Why. Why are the translanguaging actions of teachers of bilingual students important? Over and over again, the chapters in this book show us how language is intimately tied to questions of power and control. Developing the repertoire of translanguaging practices of teachers is important because it ensures that language, the main medium of education, is used by teachers in ways that opens possibilities for ALL students, and especially for racialized bilingual students.

Bilingual students and their families are often blamed for their academic failure. Emergent bilingual students are said to be disengaged, uninterested, slow. Their families, many times immigrants with different school-system experiences, are criticized for not being involved, for not reading to their children. Other times the teachers are blamed for the bilingual students' failure to meet standards. But in this book the responsibility is moved up a notch. University faculty who are teacher educators, as well as researchers, are asked to assume responsibility for the lack of understanding about the coloniality of language and the language hierarchies that keep power in the hands of a few and produce the failure of others. The transformation that this book is calling for is not simply about pedagogical practices in classrooms; it is about the role of teacher educators, as well as academic researchers.

The role of teacher educators in developing a critical preparation program for teachers working with emergent bilinguals is most important. In most states in the United States teachers must be certified to teach emergent bilinguals either as English as a Second Language or bilingual teachers. The teaching of language – English in TESOL programs, and English and the additional language in bilingual programs – plays a very important part in these teacher education programs. Sometimes more attention is paid to teaching language than to teaching bilingual

https://doi.org/10.1515/9783110735604-204

students. And yet, very few teacher education programs are critical of this definition of language – of language as an external sociopolitical construction that is named English, Spanish, Russian, Vietnamese, etc. There is very little attention paid to the role that language has had in processes of colonization, as language, as well as race and gender are used as categories of exclusion. The emphasis in many teacher education programs is on making sure that emergent bilingual students "get" the language, "have" it, in ways that are comparable to those of middle-class white monolingual students. Much time is spent in language teaching methodology, without questioning the role of language itself in the racialization of bilingual students.

Few TESOL or bilingual education programs center the bilingual students' "doing" language – languaging. And until very recently, translanguaging, which centers bilingual students' languaging entre mundos, in the borderlands in which they live, had received scant attention in ESL and bilingual education teacher preparation programs.

The authors in this book question "deeply rooted assumptions and normative practices" (Hadjioannou) and "acknowledge practices permeated by monoglossic ideology" (Musanti) in teacher education programs. They reflect on this in a teacher education course in Spanish for bilingual teachers in a Hispanic serving institution at the border (Musanti), a practicum course for teacher education (Ceballos-Zapata and Kim), a pre-service teacher course in Southwest Texas (Henderson et al.), a TESOL course in Southeast U.S. (Pontier and Tian), courses for in-service ESL and bilingual teachers in Pennsylvania (Hadjioannou), a cohort of in-service teachers pursuing teacher licensure in English language Learners and Dual Language Bilingual Education in Indiana (Wright et al.), and the experience of a sheltered ESL high school teacher in rural North Georgia (Khote).

Developing the pre-service and in-service teachers' translanguaging stance is slow and takes place over time. To do so requires teachers and students to be engaged in "continuously interpreting and reinterpreting" (Ceballos-Zapata and Kim). The chapters in this book give us a sense of how teacher educators work with those preparing to be teachers, as their stances "shift through time and space" (Henderson et al.). Translanguaging practices in the classroom are both "liberating and challenging" (Pontier and Tian), and it is sometimes painful, so it is important that students are accompanied by teachers who can listen and support "difficult conversations" (Pontier and Tian) and the "tension" (Wright et al.) that translanguaging brings.

The work with teachers to develop a translanguaging stance must be culturally grounded and must be supported by teacher educators. An example of this is the construction of meaning in the dialoging and journaling between a professor, Ceballos-Zapata, and his pre-service teacher, Kim, based on Pansori, a Korean form of narrative song. In Pansori, the student copies the "master's voice," but then sets out to seek their unique voice. Kim, the pre-service teacher, describes her observations of students as she and her professor reflect on Kim's experiences through the lens of Pansori. Ceballos-Zapata and Kim conclude: "Let the students go to perfect their own unique voice," to "develop their own artistry." Multilingual students need to be nurtured as "agentive, creative artists," and to do so, the boundaries between categories and the control over the organization and pacing of the lesson must be weak, as Khote reminds us.

A book like this is important because it disrupts the complacency in the academy that frames teaching and research with concepts that have become so naturalized that we don't question them. There are more and more studies of English language acquisition, of bilingualism, without questioning "What is English?" What is bilingualism?" The chapter by Pontier and Tian raises a most important question: "Who gets to control what type of languaging we're supposed to use?" Is English what white monolinguals speak? What Black adolescents use? What do bilingual Latinx students do? Why is English in school closely defined as what white monolingual middle class students do? Why is it that white monolingual students have that privilege? And how about bilingualism? How are racialized bilinguals perceived as they perform their bilingualism? In what ways is the sequential bilingualism of elite bilinguals different from the simultaneous bilingualism of most colonized bilinguals? Why is the elite bilingualism that results from schooling considered superior to the ways in which racialized bilinguals perform their bilingualism in the family? Rarely are these questions, related to what Flores and Rosa call raciolinguistic ideologies, considered in teacher education programs. This book gives examples of programs in which these questions are being considered, transforming teacher education for minoritized bilinguals as a political act.

This book makes an important contribution not only to teacher education, but also to academic research. The authors of the chapters are themselves teacher educators, and in studying their own educational settings they move academic research closer to the ground, revealing voices that are not often heard in academic research, including their own. We not only "re-see" the act of teaching; we "re-see" the teacher educators/researchers themselves, as they transform research itself. Research becomes personal, grounded in the researchers' own cultural framework. The theoretical lenses the teacher educators/researchers use fit their lives, their experiences, their classrooms, as the authors' positionality is centered.

Just as Pansori offered a culturally grounded lens to reflect on the students' experiences, the research methodologies that these researchers use are also grounded on their lives as teacher educators. Much of the research reported here is what Musanti calls a "self-study approach." Sometimes it involves a lesson or class/course case. But other times it goes beyond a single event, reflecting on a life of experience, as do Hadjioannou or Khote in their chapters. These studies use research methodology to collect data that is internal to the case, rather than external methodologies that are distant from the source. The research subjects are richly described, for the researchers are intimately connected to them. There is no need for additional interviews, for the researchers know their participants. The researchers base their findings on class artifacts such as slide decks and handouts, instructor notes, assignments. Other times, they use language portraits or what Ceballos-Zapata and Kim call "narrative knowledge." But their reflections are deep and knowledgeable, for they are intimately connected to the students who produce these.

Multimodality is a central part of this research process. Pontier audio-records the discussion in his course, a special topic course on translanguaging. And he and Tian extend course data with graphic organizers, pictures, memes, tweetable quotes, all produced during the course. But beyond this micro-classroom data, the researchers also rely on meso-level data, such as the language and messages that surround their own lives – billboards, tv and radio shows, and language in food stores, churches, parks. Finally, they also consider regulations of the state of Florida at the macro level. The researchers in this book can bring all these levels of data together because they are positioned to understand the classroom and its sociopolitical ecology deeply.

This book shows how translanguaging transforms not only pedagogical practices, but also research itself. Because translanguaging centers the internal languaging of bilingual students, rather than externally imposed definitions of A language and bilingualism as TWO languages, the boundaries between traditional formal categories of data become fuzzy. Meaning of the data is made not about the students, but *with* the students and their teachers in intimate connection. Just as translanguaging pedagogical practices require that the emphasis be on what emergent bilingual students *do* with language, research on translanguaging focuses on how the students and their teachers do language in ways that promote social and cognitive justice. Translanguaging research requires an artistry that does not rely on external criteria that prevents us from seeing the view from the other side of what decolonial scholar Boaventura de Sousa Santos calls "the abyssal line," from the side that has been rendered invisible and powerless by institutions and especially school. Instead, translanguaging research goes deeply inwardly, attempting to capture the vision of the rich languaging experiences of bilingual students. The re-seeing that this book provides is made possible by focusing the pedagogical and research lens on the bilingual students and their teachers themselves. By showing readers what are the consequences of a translanguaging pedagogical approach, this book opens spaces for re-seeing teaching and academic research as a fruitful endeavor that liberates rather than controls and constricts. The effect for the reader is one of letting go of assumptions about language, bilingualism, bilingual students, teachers of bilingual students, and academic research in ways that deepen understandings.

Ofelia García
New York City

# Contents

**Note from the series editor —— V**

**Preface —— VII**

Ofelia García
**Foreword: Re-Seeing translanguaging in teacher education and research —— IX**

Zhongfeng Tian and Nicole King
**Introduction —— 1**

Sandra I. Musanti
**Chapter 1**
**"A veces encuentro más palabras en español": Taking a stance towards translanguaging as a socially just pedagogy for bilingual teacher preparation —— 11**

Abraham Ceballos-Zapata and Sharon Kim
**Chapter 2**
**Listening to culturally grounded translingual dispositions in teacher education —— 35**

Kathryn I. Henderson, Christian Fallas-Escobar, and Kristen Lindahl
**Chapter 3**
**Learning from Latinx pre-service teachers' understandings of their linguistic repertoires —— 59**

Ryan W. Pontier and Zhongfeng Tian
**Chapter 4**
**"If you want to be taken seriously, you have to speak like a white person": TESOL graduate students' grappling with translanguaging-as-social justice stance —— 81**

Xenia Hadjioannou
**Chapter 5**
**Starting with the teachers: Pursuing paradigmatic shift through the development of teachers' translanguaging repertoires —— 103**

Wayne E. Wright, Trish Morita-Mullaney, Woongsik Choi, and Haiyan Li
**Chapter 6**
**Building bilingual teachers' translanguaging repertoires in a new immigrant destination state —— 123**

Nihal Khote
**Chapter 7**
**A teacher's perspective of translanguaging *corrientes*: Contextualizing power and control in the translanguaging stance —— 145**

Peter Sayer
**Afterword —— 167**

**Index —— 173**

Zhongfeng Tian and Nicole King

# Introduction

Developing translanguaging repertoires in critical teacher education

## 1 Introduction

This book is grounded in our understanding of teaching as a political act (Freire 2000). We as editors believe in the transformative power of *translanguaging* as both theory and pedagogy to help teachers reconceptualize how we think of languages and engage in the political act of critical teaching with social justice orientations. To us, translanguaging as theory interrogates the duality of bilingualism and challenges colonial and modernist-era structuralist ideologies of language standardization (Makoni and Pennycook 2007) by liberating language-minoritized speakers' multilingual performances and legitimizing all their linguistic varieties (García and Li Wei 2014). Translanguaging as theory is grounded in the dynamic, emergent, daily language practices of marginalized and minoritized multilingual speakers (Li Wei 2018) and the new ways of knowing, being, and expressing that become possible. Translanguaging as pedagogy articulates a critical stance to leverage students' cultural and linguistic funds of knowledge (Moll et al. 1992) for meaningful learning to disrupt language hierarchies and academic monolingualism and promote minoritized students' education and identities (García 2009). It holds the promise of "liberating the voices of language minoritized students" (García and Leiva 2014: 200) and "enabling a more socially just and equitable education for bilingual students" (García and Kleyn 2016: 17).

With its *critical heteroglossic* stance (Flores and Rosa 2015) in theoretical and pedagogical implications, we see translanguaging offers one pocket of hope to counteract monoglossic orientations in language-in-education policies in U.S. classrooms. Many extant studies have illuminated the great possibilities that translanguaging could afford teachers in supporting learners' academic success and socioemotional well-being (e.g., Back et al. 2020; Cenoz et al. 2022; Dovchin 2021; Fu et al. 2019; Tian and Link 2019; Tian et al. 2020). To follow through on this promise, this volume argues that it is important to develop teachers' *translanguaging repertoires* in teacher education so that we have more competent and caring (con cariño, e.g., Bartolomé

**Zhongfeng Tian,** Rutgers University–Newark
**Nicole King,** University of Rochester

https://doi.org/10.1515/9783110735604-001

2008) teachers who could enact culturally and linguistically sustaining practices (Paris and Alim 2014) to transform U.S. schooling in ways that advance a social justice agenda.

We in this volume conceptualize **translanguaging repertoires** as an overarching framing to refer to teachers' stance, design, and shifts (García et al. 2017) in which they not only embrace a language-as-asset/resource orientation with social justice praxis, but also are capable of implementing and shifting translanguaging in instruction and assessment strategically across different classroom contexts and with their multilingual students. We see developing teachers' translanguaging repertoires in teacher education as a continuous, complex process, involving joint efforts among different educational stakeholders – teacher educators, pre- and in-service teachers. It is through the process of action, reflection and evaluation "juntos/together" (García et al. 2017: xii) that all the parties come to question and to better understand what translanguaging as theory means and how translanguaging pedagogies can be put to use for the purposes of critical education within the contextual parameters, affordances, restrictions, and in collaboration with multilingual students.

Ofelia García (2009) first took up the term translanguaging to talk about the flexible, agentive, norm language practices of marginalized and minortized speakers – emergent bilingual learners – primarily in the PK-12 context. Many of the first studies on translanguaging practices focused on the agentive ways that emergent bilingual learners utilized all of their sense-making repertoires to express themselves, to connect to content understanding and learning, and to illuminate the complex and inventive ways that emergent bilinguals language and push back against monolingual norms (e.g., Axelrod and Cole 2018; Sayer 2013; Velasco and García 2014). With the "multilingual turn" (May 2014) and "social justice turn" (Ortega 2019), translanguaging began to make its way into teacher education so that educators could learn to support, to celebrate, and to leverage the linguistic and cultural assets that multilingual learners bring into the classroom and to engage in pedagogy for equity and social justice.

Once García and colleagues (2017) led the way in defining and detailing what translanguaging pedagogy could look like and achieve in classrooms with multilingual learners, researchers and teacher educators began to look at how translanguaging pedagogy could be taught (e.g., Deroo et al. 2020; Morales et al. 2020; Tian 2020) in a variety of teacher education contexts. These authors sought to clarify translanguaging pedagogy as a transformation from the monolingual structures and ideologies which have dominated education policies and practices. While these studies present a needed perspective on the role of translanguaging in education, few of them shed light on the development of translanguaging repertoires within the teachers of multilingual students, particularly multilingual teachers who have also experienced marginalization and racialization. This volume sheds light on the dynamic, complex, situated process of teachers developing translanguaging repertoires over time.

## 2 Our volume

We explore the emergent process of developing translanguaging repertoires among teacher educators and pre- and in-service teachers in different U.S. teacher education contexts in this volume. It consists of seven chapters delving into a variety of ways to scaffold the development of translanguaging repertoires with different qualitative methodologies adopted to unpack the opportunities, challenges, and future directions in (re)envisioning critical teacher education through studies which embrace the connection between research and teacher education.

First in Chapter 1, **Musanti** explores her efforts as a bilingual teacher educator, teaching bilingual teacher preparation courses in Spanish at a Hispanic-serving institution on the US-Mexico border, *la frontera*, to embrace a translanguaging stance with the bilingual teacher candidates in ways that leverage their bilingualism through a self study. Drawing from an awareness of how language ideologies are deeply situated in multifaceted and historical contexts (Kroskrity 2010), her critical approach to bilingual teacher education calls for bilingual teacher candidates to interrogate the tensions of language ideologies and how they manifest in pedagogy and in discourse. Specifically, her work with bilingual teacher candidates works to build ideological clarity and critical awareness of linguistic injustice in education (Alfaro 2018; Bartolomé 2004; García 2015; Holguín Mendoza 2018; Leeman 2018). For her, bilingual teacher candidates' translanguaging repertoires evolve over time with this grappling. As she views translanguaging pedagogy as a political act, she models her translanguaging stance with the bilingual teacher candidates through carefully orchestrated pedagogical moves and linguistic fluidity and inclusiveness. By focusing her data collection during one course, "The Bilingual Curriculum in the Content Areas," she is able to show how she uses *aproximaciones a la práctica* [approaches to practice] (Grossman 2018) to model bilingual teacher core practices. While she is able to shed light on the translanguaging moves she utilizes to support candidates, Musanti also noticed that the candidates expressed a continuum of views on bilingualism from a static, monolingual view to a more dynamic, flexible view. Thus, she calls for a more critical, contextually-based (Irizarry 2017) look across bilingual teacher education courses, programs, and approaches to social justice to illuminate bilingual teachers' lived experiences, beliefs about bilingualism, and the hegemonic positioning of English in classrooms.

In Chapter 2, **Ceballos-Zapata** and **Kim** explore the development of a culturally grounded translingual disposition, *Pansori* (Yi 2008) lens of understanding by Kim, a pre-service teacher, through co-constructed dialoguing and journaling in her practicum course with her professor, Ceballos-Zapata. They drew on Kim's transcultural way of knowing of *Pansori*, a Korean opera that requires singers to train in nature and to respond to the emotions of the audience, to connect to teaching bilingual learners. Across the semester, they developed a situated understanding of the *Pansori* lens and began to reapply this lens to narrative knowledging (Barkhuizen 2011) of bilingual and minoritized students that allowed them to re-see and re-hear (Seltzer 2019) the students. Through the collaborative sense-making and knowledging process, Ceballos-Zapata and Kim were able to illuminate the unique voices of the students at the practicum placement and the contextualized history, politics, and marginalization present in sites of struggle experienced by the students. They situate *Pansori* pedagogy within translanguaging repertoires (stance, design, and shifts), as it allows for flexible language use in the performance of student identities, connection to instructional design, and is responsive to the classroom *corriente*. Their use of and framing through *Pansori* also resists efforts from the dominant culture to discount marginalized ways of knowing by translingual, transcultural educators.

In Chapter 3, **Henderson, Fallas-Escobar,** and **Lindahl** illuminate how Latinx pre-service teachers depicted their understanding of their linguistic repertoires through language portraits. They view a translanguaging stance as essential to translanguaging pedagogy and a part of the knowledge co-construction that occurs in classrooms; further, they understand this stance as part of a teaching mindset in which students, families, and communities are knowledge holders and classrooms are spaces to work towards social justice. Within this stance, they view the communities they engage with as sites of knowledge creation, not simply contexts of study (Avineri and Martinez 2021). Henderson and colleagues are particularly interested in the ways pre-service teachers understand how language is socially constructed and how pre-service teachers conceptualize and draw upon their linguistic repertoires in ways that disinvent and disrupt deficit perspectives. By exploring 80 language portraits they identified how the pre-service teachers configured their understanding of languages and the interconnections of language, body, emotion, and identity. After providing visual examples of the coding themes which emerged, they take a close look at three cases to show the unique, Latinx linguistic portraits and identities that came to light. While the pre-service teachers' portraits demonstrated the chaos, complexity, and heterogeneity of their language repertoires, Henderson and colleagues found that the pre-service teachers did not, as a whole, take up the identity as bilinguals even as they disrupted normative, monolingual language labels. Thus, they call for more work on classroom spaces that celebrate and name bilingual identities and bilingual ways of knowing.

In Chapter 4, **Pontier** and **Tian** investigate how graduate level TESOL students (a mixed group of pre- and in-service teachers) at a Southeastern university developed a translanguaging-as-social justice stance in a course on bilingualism framed not only from a translanguaging perspective but also through a social justice lens. In so doing, they illuminated tensions around translanguaging and other pedagogies associated with heritage language learning (e.g., Showstack 2015). They view translanguaging as a critical, dynamic heteroglossic perspective that transforms relationships, requires space for co-constructed learning, and values all language practices. They draw upon Peña-Pincheira and De Costa's (2021) ecological framework for leveraging teacher agency for social justice and Pantić's (2015) components of social justice to analyze a representative class conversation that took place during the third classroom session on translanguaging as theory. Findings indicated three principal tensions of the students' translanguaging-as-social justice stance: language expectations at home and at school, separationist and dynamic understandings of bilingualism, and translanguaging as theory and as pedagogy. Further, Pontier and Tian noticed competing influences at the micro-, meso-, and macro-levels that mediated students competency of a translanguaging-as-social justice stance. Even with these tensions, students were able to take up their translanguaging-as-social justice stances in a variety of ways, including naming oppression, pushing back, and forming a collective. Finally, they call for success in small steps in TESOL teacher education to engage in collaborative dialogues that frame translanguaging as transgressive and language policies that embrace heteroglossic ideologies and push back against existing power structures of and in language (e.g., Delpit and Kilgour Dowdy 2002).

In Chapter 5, **Hadjioannou** explores various efforts to develop in-service teachers' translanguaging repertoires based on her multi-year work as a teacher educator at a U.S. university. She sees translanguaging pedagogy as fundamentally justice-oriented, representing a paradigmatic shift from the traditional approaches informed by monolingual ideologies. Therefore, it is very important to create experiences in graduate level coursework that compel in-service teachers to conduct critical examinations of normalized practices in their professional contexts built around the notion of reseeing (Goodman 1996): re-seeing bilingualism and "English Learners," as well as one's own teaching and instructional contexts. To achieve these, Hadjioannou presents multiple concrete examples such as inviting teachers to analyze data from natural language interactions of experienced bilinguals to understand how bilinguals actually "do" bilingualism, asking teachers to interview and observe one of their emergent bilingual students with the purpose of developing a robust learner profile and a better understanding of their bilingual lives, and encouraging teachers to perform a mini ethnographic case study of their own schools and the experiences of bilingual students from minoritized communities within them. These initiatives were identified as promising in supporting in-service teachers' conception of more socially just alternatives and their curricular re-envisionments. However, Hadjioannou also noticed that shifts toward translanguaging-informed teaching can be frustrated by systemic resistance as well as by deeply rooted monolingual ideologies that may undercut teachers' best intentions.

In Chapter 6, **Wright**, **Morita-Mullaney**, **Choi**, and **Li** present a case study of their first cohort of in-service bilingual education teachers who completed Purdue University's English Language Learner (ELL) teacher licensure program and new Dual Language Bilingual Education (DLBE) Graduate Certificate Program. This teacher training program aimed to develop bilingual teachers' translanguaging repertoires (García and Li Wei 2014) and shift their language ideologies (Kroskrity 2004) to ensure the success of their students. Through analyzing teacher interviews and teacher coursework, Wright and his colleagues found that all teachers developed a more positive translanguaging stance and increased their translanguaging designs and shifts in their classrooms, moving away from monoglossic views of bilingualism. However, the in-service teachers expressed frustration and concerns that their district-prescribed model, curriculum and separate language instruction times/classrooms leave little room for bridging lessons and other forms of translanguaging. Furthermore, translanguaging instances were observed more frequently during Spanish times to benefit English-dominant students. Therefore, Wright and his team concluded that more work is needed to help teachers develop the critical consciousness and agency needed to create a more socially just classroom space for their ELL students.

Lastly in Chapter 7, **Khote** traces the development of his own translanguaging stance as a former in-service teacher based on his 13 years of teaching Mexican and Central American immigrant English learners (ELs) in a sheltered 9th grade ESOL language arts class in a school district in rural North Georgia, U.S. He argues that fostering a translanguaging classroom is most directly connected to the teacher's translanguaging stance, as it is within that stance that teachers exert authority in micro-interactional decisions to validate, or not, students' use of non-dominant languages. Accordingly, Khote in this chapter specifically examined the embedded relations of power and control in teacher-student interactions, i.e., translanguaging dialogs in Spanish and English in his classroom, adopting Bernstein's (1990) conception of classification and framing rules. Findings reveal that micro shifts in translanguaging *corriente* within a stance comprised waves of strong classification and framing followed by weak classification and framing to set up the groundwork for the translanguaging moment. Overall, this study provides new insights into micro/local dimensions of the translanguaging stance and on the discursive ecology of the classroom. Khote cautions future teacher candidates about simplistic views that characterize translanguaging pedagogy as a panacea and emphasizes that the key to a successful translanguaging stance is negotiating extant power relations in productive ways in each spatial, multimodal or linguistic instant and context.

Overall, these studies – representing teacher education initiatives taking place in various regions of the U.S. (including Texas, Florida, Michigan, Indiana, Pennsylvania, and Georgia) – showcase the promises of different educational stakeholders (teacher educators, and pre- and in-service teachers) working together in a praxis cycle to develop translanguaging repertoires in response to the multilingual, multicultural, and multiracial realities of U.S. classrooms. This volume offers a "constant skepticism" and a "restive problematization" (Pennycook 2001: 10) of language and power in U.S. teacher education and school spaces. By emphasizing the liberating purpose of translanguaging, we believe that this volume will be a timely contribution to the field of critical applied linguistics and move U.S. TESOL and bilingual teacher preparation one step closer toward critical language teacher education (Hawkins and Norton 2009) with an explicit social justice agenda to open up more humanizing spaces where students' cultural, linguistic repertoires are valued and sustained (Paris 2012), and teachers' active agency (Palmer 2018) are fostered and developed.

In some ways, the chapter authors are responding to the manifesto from García and colleagues (García et al. 2021) that asked teachers and teacher educators to critically interrogate the impact of named, bound languages on racialized multilinguals and to reject the dichotomization of language in favor of framing racialized multilinguals as agentive, creative architects of language (Flores 2020) who draw upon all of their linguistic, cultural, and racial ways of knowing to create knowledge and understanding. The chapter authors present some of the rippling effects of García and colleagues (García et al. 2021) in their grappling with developing their own translanguaging repertoires and supporting pre- and in-service teachers through their emerging mindset of criticality and translanguaging and suggest next steps for language educators and researchers.

## 3 Final remarks

In response to the "multilingual turn" (May 2014) and "social justice turn" (Ortega 2019) in language (in) education, this volume brings together a group of scholars from different U.S. contexts offering critical, justice-oriented perspectives on theorizing, integrating, and implementing translanguaging in teacher education. Given the varieties of qualitative research presented in each chapter (varying by methodologies, participant size, research focus, participant focus, and duration of study), this volume sheds light on the dynamic, complex process of developing translanguaging repertoires among teacher educators, pre- and in-service teachers. We hope that this volume will prove to be a valuable resource for students, teachers, teacher educators, and researchers who are striving to become or aiming to prepare culturally and linguistically competent and caring teachers with anti-oppressive orientations in the field of TESOL, bilingual, dual language, and world language education. We invite readers to engage with each chapter and learn alongside the authors to reimagine a more socially just future for our language-minoritized students.

## References

Alfaro, Cristina. 2018. The sociopolitical struggle and promise of bilingual teacher education: Past, present, and future. *Bilingual Research Journal* 41(4). 413–427.

Avineri, Netta & Danny C. Martinez. 2021. Applied linguists cultivating relationships for justice: An aspirational call to action. *Applied Linguistics* 42(6). 1043–1054.

Axelrod, Ysaaca & Mikel W. Cole. 2018. 'The pumpkins are coming . . . vienen las calabazas . . . that sounds funny': Translanguaging practices of young emergent bilinguals. *Journal of Early Childhood Literacy* 18(1). 129–153.

Back, Michele, Mihyun Han & Shih-Chieh (Angela) Weng. 2020. Emotional scaffolding for emergent multilingual learners through translanguaging: Case stories. *Language and Education* 34 (5). 387–406.

Barkhuizen, Gary. 2011. Narrative knowledging in TESOL. *TESOL Quarterly* 45(3). 391–414.

Bartolomé, Lilia I. 2004. Critical pedagogy and teacher education: Radicalizing prospective teachers. *Teacher Education Quarterly* 31(1). 97–122.

Bartolomé, Lilia I. 2008. Authentic cariño and respect in minority education: The political and ideological dimensions of love. *International Journal of Critical Pedagogy* 1(1). 1–17.

Bernstein, Basil. 1990. *Class, codes and control. vol. 4. The structuring of pedagogic discourse*. London: Routledge.

Cenoz, Jasone, Alaitz Santos & Durk Gorter. 2022. Pedagogical translanguaging and teachers' perceptions of anxiety. *International Journal of Bilingual Education and Bilingualism* 0(0). 1–13. doi: 10.1080/13670050.2021.2021387

Delpit, Lisa & Joanne Kilgour Dowdy (eds.). 2002. *The Skin that we Speak: Thoughts on Language and Culture in the Classroom*. New York: The New Press.

Deroo, Matthew R., Christina M. Ponzio & Peter I. De Costa. 2020. Reenvisioning second language teacher education through translanguaging praxis. In Zhongfeng Tian, Laila Aghai, Peter Sayer & Jamie L. Schissel (eds.), *Envisioning TESOL Through a Translanguaging Lens: Global Perspectives*, 111–134. Cham: Springer International Publishing.

Dovchin, Sender. 2021. Translanguaging, emotionality, and English as a second language immigrants: Mongolian background women in Australia. *TESOL Quarterly* 55(3). 839–864.

Flores, Nelson. 2020. From academic language to language architecture: Challenging raciolinguistic ideologies in research and practice. *Theory into Practice* 59(1). 22–31.
Flores, Nelson & Jonathan Rosa. 2015. Undoing appropriateness: Raciolinguistic ideologies and language diversity in education. *Harvard Education Review* 85(2). 149–171.
Freire, Paulo. 2000. *Pedagogy of the oppressed (30th anniversary edition)*. New York: Continuum.
Fu, Danling, Xenia Hadjioannou & Xiaodi Zhou. 2019. *Translanguaging for Emergent Bilinguals: Inclusive Teaching in the Linguistically Diverse Classroom*. New York: Teachers College Press.
García, Ofelia. 2009. *Bilingual Education in the 21st century: A Global Perspective*. Malden: Blackwell.
García, Ofelia. 2015. Critical multilingual language awareness and teacher education. In Jasone Cenoz, Durk Gorter & Stephen May (eds.), *Language Awareness and Multilingualism*, 1–17. (Encyclopedia of Language and Education 6). Switzerland: Springer International Publishing.
García, Ofelia, Nelson Flores, Kate Seltzer, Li Wei, Ricardo Otheguy & Jonathan Rosa. 2021. Rejecting abyssal thinking in the language and education of racialized bilinguals: A manifesto. *Critical Inquiry in Language Studies* 18(3). 203–228.
García, Ofelia & Tatyana Kleyn (eds.). 2016. *Translanguaging with Multilingual Students: Learning from Classroom Moments*. New York: Routledge.
García, Ofelia & Camila Leiva. 2014. Theorizing and enacting translanguaging for social justice. In Adrian Blackledge & Angela Creese (eds.), *Heteroglossia as Practice and Pedagogy*, 199–216. New York: Springer.
García, Ofelia & Li Wei. 2014. *Translanguaging: Language, Bilingualism and Education*. Basingstoke: Palgrave Macmillan.
García, Ofelia, Susana Ibarra Johnson & Kate Seltzer. 2017. *The translanguaging classroom: Leveraging student bilingualism for learning*. Philadelphia: Caslon.
Goodman, Yetta M. 1996. Revaluing readers while readers revalue themselves: Retrospective miscue analysis. *The Reading Teacher* 49(8). 600–609.
Grossman, Pamela (ed.). 2018. *Teaching core practices in teacher education*. Cambridge: Harvard Education Press.
Hawkins, Margaret & Bonny Norton. 2009. Critical language teacher education. In Anne Burns & Jack C. Richards (eds.), *Cambridge Guide to Second Language Teacher Education*, 30–39. New York: Cambridge University Press.
Holguín Mendoza, Claudia. 2018. Critical language awareness (CLA) for Spanish heritage language programs: Implementing a complete curriculum. *International Multilingual Research Journal* 12(2). 65–79.
Irizarry, Jason G. 2017. "For us, by us": A vision for culturally sustaining pedagogies forwarded by Latinx youth. In Django Paris & H. Samy Alim (eds.), *Culturally Sustaining Pedagogies*, 83–98. New York: Teachers College Press.
Kroskrity, Paul V. 2004. Language ideologies. In Alessandro Duranti (ed.), *A Companion to Linguistic Anthropology*, 496–517. Malden: Blackwell.
Kroskrity, Paul V. 2010. Language ideologies – evolving perspectives. In Jürgen Jaspers (ed.), *Language Use and Society. Handbook of Pragmatics Highlights*, 192–211. Amsterdam: John Benjamins Publishing Company.
Leeman, Jennifer. 2018. Critical language awareness and Spanish as a heritage language: Challenging the linguistic subordination of U.S. Latinxs. In Kim Potowski (ed.), *Handbook of Spanish as a Minority/Heritage Language*, 345–358. New York: Routledge.
Li Wei. 2018. Translanguaging as a practical theory of language. *Applied Linguistics* 39(1). 9–30.
Makoni, Sinfree & Alastair Pennycook (eds.). 2007. *Disinventing and Reconstituting Languages*. Clevedon: Multilingual Matters.

May, Stephen (ed.). 2014. *The Multilingual Turn: Implications for SLA, TESOL, and Bilingual Education*. London: Routledge.
Moll, Luis, Cathy Amanti, Deborah Neff & Norma Gonzalez. 1992. Funds of knowledge for teaching: Using a qualitative approach to connect homes and classrooms. *Theory into Practice* 31(2). 132–141.
Morales, Julio & Jamie L. Schissel. 2020. Pedagogical sismo: Translanguaging approaches for English language instruction and assessment in Oaxaca, Mexico. In Zhongfeng Tian, Laila Aghai, Peter Sayer & Jamie L. Schissel (eds.), *Envisioning TESOL Through a Translanguaging Lens: Global Perspectives*, 161–183. Cham: Springer International Publishing.
Ortega, Lourdes. 2019. SLA and the study of equitable multilingualism. *The Modern Language Journal* 103 (S1). 23–38.
Palmer, Deborah. 2018. Introduction to the special issue: Teacher agency and "pedagogies of hope" for bilingual learners (in a brave new world). *International Multilingual Research Journal* 12(3). 143–144.
Pantić, Nataša. 2015. A model for study of teacher agency for social justice. *Teachers and Teaching: Theory and Practice* 21(6). 759–778.
Paris, Django. 2012. Culturally sustaining pedagogy: A needed change in stance, terminology, and practice. *Educational Researcher* 41(3). 93–97.
Paris, Django & H. Samy Alim. 2014. What are we seeking to sustain through culturally sustaining pedagogy? A loving critique forward. *Harvard Educational Review* 84(1). 85–100.
Peña-Pincheira, Romina & Peter I. De Costa. 2021. Language teacher agency for educational justice-oriented work: An ecological model. *TESOL Journal* 12(2). 1–13. https://doi.org/10.1002/tesj.561.
Pennycook, Alastair. 2001. *Critical Applied Linguistics: A Critical Introduction*. London: Routledge.
Sayer, Peter. 2013. Translanguaging, TexMex, and bilingual pedagogy: Emergent bilinguals learning through the vernacular. *TESOL Quarterly* 47(1). 63–88.
Seltzer, Kate. 2019. Reconceptualizing "home" and "school" language: Taking a critical translingual approach in the English classroom. *TESOL Quarterly* 53(4). 986–1007.
Showstack, Rachel E. (2015). Institutional representations of 'Spanish' and 'Spanglish': Managing competing discourses in heritage language instruction. *Language and Intercultural Communication* 15(3). 341–361.
Tian, Zhongfeng. 2020. Faculty first: Promoting translanguaging in TESOL teacher education. In Sunny Man Chu Lau & Saskia Van Viegen (eds.), *Plurilingual Pedagogies: Critical and Creative Endeavors for Equitable Language in Education*, 215–236. Cham: Springer International Publishing.
Tian, Zhongfeng & Holly Link (eds.). 2019. Positive Synergies: Translanguaging and Critical Theories in Education. [Special issue]. *Translation and Translanguaging in Multilingual Contexts* 5(1).
Tian, Zhongfeng, Laila Aghai, Peter Sayer & Jamie L. Schissel (eds.). 2020. *Envisioning TESOL Through a Translanguaging Lens: Global Perspectives*. Cham: Springer International Publishing.
Velasco, P. & Ofelia García. 2014. Translanguaging and the writing of bilingual learners. *Bilingual Research Journal* 37(1). 6–23.
Yi, Yong-sik. 2008. *Pansori*. Seoul, Korea: The National Center for Korean Traditional Performing Arts.

Sandra I. Musanti
# Chapter 1
# "A veces encuentro más palabras en español": Taking a stance towards translanguaging as a socially just pedagogy for bilingual teacher preparation

**Abstract:** Informed by recent explorations on translanguaging practices in higher education and teacher education, this self-case study explores how a bilingual teacher educator, teaching bilingual teacher preparation courses in Spanish at a Hispanic-serving institution on the US-Mexico border embraces a translanguaging stance to leverage teacher candidates' bilingualism while preparing them to produce and use academic and professional forms of Spanish discourse for teaching. Findings illustrate how a bilingual teacher educator purposefully embeds translanguaging moves to leverage bilingual teacher candidates' bilingualism to develop a linguistically inclusive bilingual teacher candidates' repertoire of practice. In addition, the study shows how candidates' evolving understanding of linguistic inclusiveness situates them in a continuum from a monolingual to a more dynamic vision of bilingualism and language use in the classroom. Implications of a translanguaging practice-based approach for a socially just pedagogy in bilingual teacher preparation are identified.

## 1 Introduction

I teach and live in *la frontera*, a borderland region between Mexico and the US running along the Rio Grande River that is the juncture of histories, cultures, languages, identities, and power struggles (Anzaldúa 2012). This culturally and linguistically rich context creates ideal conditions to build new understandings about language difference in teacher education pedagogies that challenge traditional and dominant values and beliefs about language, teaching, and learning. Since my arrival in 2011, the transnational, transcultural and bilingual roots of the region and my students have pushed me to critically question my Latinx identity and my stance as a bilingual teacher educator. I am originally from Argentina

---

**Sandra I. Musanti,** University of Texas Rio Grande Valley

https://doi.org/10.1515/9783110735604-002

where I grew up in a monolingual Spanish speaking/teaching context. Spanish was the language of instruction and the language of learning and knowledge construction. Nonetheless, the hegemonic presence of English was part of my upbringing in multiple ways filtering through music, movies, and famous TV shows. One way that stands out was my mother's push to learn English as a foreign language instead of Italian which is part of my heritage – all my great grandparents immigrated from different regions in Italy. She, like many parents in the borderland region of the Rio Grande Valley, believed that English was the key to many opportunities.

After graduating from college in Argentina, I became a teacher educator guided by the belief in the power of teachers who can truly see students for who they are, and who can understand and embrace what students bring to the classroom as resources for learning. As the product of K-18 public education, my schooling background and personal and professional experiences reaffirmed my conviction that quality education is a human right. It was not until after graduating from college in Argentina that I dived into the world of bilingual education during a year-long experience living and researching in Barcelona and experiencing the wonders of bilingualism and bilingual education in Catalan and Spanish. Several years later life took me to New Mexico, where I completed my graduate education and immersed myself in the world of dual language education, and I became passionate about how to better prepare bilingual teachers. My journey as a bilingual teacher educator in the US involved acknowledging the implications and meaning of being a South American White Latinx woman in academia. In the process, I renegotiated my ascribed identity as an English learner, rejecting this label product of an hegemonic monolingual paradigm and embracing myself as a sequential bilingual reflecting my ideological shift towards an heteroglossic and dynamic view of bilingualism. Becoming bilingual in Spanish and English was a dreamed accomplishment for me, but for years I perceived myself as ill-equipped, measuring my language proficiency through a monolingual standard, and an imposed sense of correctness, believing that "my English" was not up to par to that of a native. It took me years to be able to challenge this misperception and the language ideology underscoring it, a common experience to many teachers and teachers-to-be who are still gauging their bilingualism and that of their students as the sum of two native speakers.

As teacher educators, we need to conceptualize our work as socially and historically situated and negotiated among students, institution, and community (Hamilton, Hutchinson and Pinnegar 2020). Since my arrival in 2011, I wondered about the linguistic creativity and the fluidity of the language practices in this borderland region. When I asked my students to describe their bilingualism, one teacher candidate almost in an apologetic tone explained that "a veces encuentro más palabras en español" [sometimes I find more words in Spanish] her home language. While bilingualism and biliteracy in English and Spanish are marketable and valuable assets both within and outside the university setting, we, as educators and citizens of *la frontera*, continue to encounter views about language that privilege a standard variety of both English and Spanish (Sayer 2013; Sutterby, Ayala and Murillo 2005).

To contribute to a critical approach to bilingual teacher education, I envisioned this chapter as another opportunity to revisit my journey as a bilingual teacher educator, my struggles and accomplishments embracing a dynamic and holistic understanding of bilingualism, and what I have learned from my bilingual teacher candidates about identifying and counteracting contradicting language ideologies in my own practice. Drawing from the field of linguistic anthropology and sociolinguistics, understanding how language ideologies are rooted on wider sociocultural, political, and economic contexts (Kroskrity 2010) and are enacted in educational practices is at the core of preparing teachers with the ideological clarity to be critically aware of linguistic injustice in education (Alfaro 2018; Bartolomé 2004, García 2015; Holguín Mendoza 2018; Leeman 2018).

As bilingual teacher educators we need to deepen our commitment to promote linguistic equity embracing a fluid and dynamic understanding of language and questioning the static representation of language boundaries (García and Li Wei 2014; Leeman 2018). Critical language awareness pedagogies and translanguaging pedagogies call for an advocacy lens in the preparation of bilingual education teachers (Dávila and Bunar 2020; Holguín Mendoza 2018; Leeman 2018). If our commitment is to equity and social justice, advocacy needs to be at the core of a bilingual teacher educator instructional approach "to support teachers as they strive to advocate for their students, develop their students' multilinguistic repertoires and optimize their academic achievement" (Dávila and Bunar 2020: 17). We need an unwavering commitment to preparing bilingual teachers who can advocate for their students' cultural and linguistic identity, fostering the development of translanguaging repertoires through modeling and enacting pedagogies that embrace the diverse and fluid cultural and linguistic practices of students and their community, engaging their "critical understandings of language and language learning to avoid reinforcing hegemonic ideologies, policies, and practices" (Dávila and Bunar 2020: 17). As teacher educators we need to ensure that teacher candidates deepen their ideological clarity and are able "to examine the political and cultural role that counter-hegemonic resistance can serve to contest and transform the exclusionary, harmful, and fundamentally undemocratic values and beliefs that inform dominant educational practices in the United States (Bartolomé 2004: 98). From this perspective, the importance of engaging in self-inquiry goes beyond a narrow and individualistic vision of teaching and learning to critically position our pedagogical approach as socially constructed, and ideologically charged. In this chapter I shared findings from a self-study I designed to take a closer look into my practice as bilingual teacher educator (Hamilton, Hutchinson and Pinnegar 2020). This study responds to my conviction that today more than ever, it is critical to dive into the practice of teacher educators to better understand how to reframe teacher preparation to enact linguistically and culturally sustaining pedagogies (Paris 2012) moving away from monolingual ideologies and cultural hegemony towards developing what García (2015) identified as critical multilingual awareness (CMLA) in teacher education. Teacher education across contexts should target developing linguistic tolerance, a critical understanding of the language suppression that occurs through the normalization of monolingual ideologies, and "the understanding that language is socially created, and thus, socially changeable to give voice and educate all students equitably" (García 2015: 6).

As my autobiographical introduction shows, I position myself as a Latinx bilingual teacher educator, teaching bilingual teacher preparation courses in Spanish at a Hispanic-serving institution on the US-Mexico border. In my practice, I embrace a translanguaging stance to leverage teacher candidates' bilingualism (García 2017) and to expand their linguistic repertoire while preparing them to produce and use academic and professional forms of Spanish discourse for teaching (Aquino-Sterling 2016).

Gutiérrez and Rogoff (2003: 22) defined teachers' linguistic and cultural repertoires of practice "in terms of their familiarity with engaging in particular practices on the basis of what is known about their own and their community's history." In pursuing this study, a central goal was to explore bilingual teacher candidates' (BTCs) evolving translanguaging repertoire focusing on how they grappled with language use and their understanding of linguistically inclusive practices in planning and reflecting on and about instruction for bilingual learners. From a self-study perspective, this goal was critical to understand the implications of my practice to advance a socially just pedagogy for bilingual teacher preparation. Accordingly, the research questions guiding the study were: How does a teacher educator grapple with linguistic inclusiveness while designing and implementing instruction in Spanish in the context of preparing bilingual teacher candidates (BTCs)? How did BTCs use their translanguaging repertoire in planning instruction for bilingual learners? How did BTCs' understandings of linguistically inclusive practices in the classroom shift (or not) after completing the course?

Drawing on the work of Grossman (2018), I identify translanguaging core practices in bilingual teacher preparation to develop bilingual teacher candidates' translanguaging repertoires as integrated by resources and skills to disrupt monolingual discourses and practices while advocating for linguistic diversity. I provide an example of the enactment of my translanguaging stance describing the pedagogical moves of a linguistically fluid instructional approach. Lastly, I explore ways in which my attempt at modeling linguistic inclusive practices reflects on BTCs' translanguaging repertoire and how they understand the use of language in their bilingual instructional design. I conclude highlighting the implications of a translanguaging practice-based approach for a socially just pedagogy in bilingual teacher preparation.

## 2 Preparing bilingual teachers in the borderlands

The transnational and translingual community of the Rio Grande Valley is located along the US-Mexico border extending for many miles. The university reports that 90.5% of the student body identifies as Hispanic or Latinx. Most of our students are low-income (81%), and 59% are first-generation students. In addition, 65% of our student population identify as bilingual, speaking Spanish and English. Most importantly, this university prepares most of the bilingual education teachers in the region. In previous studies, I have documented how most bilingual teacher candidates in our program received their education in the United States mostly through early exit programs that focus on transitioning students to English only instruction while some have experienced most or part of their schooling in Mexico (Musanti 2014; Rodríguez and Musanti 2017). Clearly, an asset-based perspective is needed to capitalize on the linguistic and cultural practices of this bilingual and bicultural community.

A translanguaging pedagogy has been defined as a political act that advances social justice challenging the artificial boundaries between languages and the monoglossic view of bilingual education still prevalent in bilingual teacher preparation (Flores 2014; García and Leiva 2014). Moving away from the traditional and dichotomic view of bilingualism that results in a language-compartmentalized approach to instruction calls to embrace a translanguaging stance (García 2017) and a purposeful and strategic planning of translanguaging spaces to position bilingual students' rich linguistic repertoire as an asset and a resource (García and Kleyn 2016).

Grounded on the work on culturally sustaining pedagogy (Paris 2012), and critical multilingual awareness (García 2015), I argue that preparing bilingual teachers in *la frontera* requires to identify, design, and implement core translanguaging practices where teacher candidates critically engage with language issues while planning and analyzing instructional practice intended to provide equal opportunities for learning (Musanti, Cavazos and Rodríguez 2020). This is particularly important given that studies addressing the pedagogical implications of integrating translanguaging practices in teacher education are still scant, particularly regarding teacher candidates' perceptions of linguistically inclusive pedagogies (García and Li Wei 2014).

Recent research on bilingual teacher preparation highlights the importance of advocating for a dynamic view of bilingualism grounding program and course design in raciolinguistic frameworks, culturally sustaining pedagogies, critical language awareness, and translanguaging (Collins, Sanchez and Espana 2019; Flores and Aneja 2017; Holguín Mendoza 2018; Musanti and Rodríguez 2017; Zúñiga 2019). In addition, research has pointed out the criticality to explore how bilingual teacher educators' pedagogical responses are shaped by institutional and program discourses that continue to legitimate English as the language of science and learning devaluing students' multilingual repertoires (Mazak and Caroll 2017). Holguín Mendoza (2018: 76) documented a Spanish Heritage Language curriculum that promoted the "ability to identify and to analyze language ideologies anchored in exclusionary or elitist discourses and social practices" where "classroom becomes the laboratory in which these ideologies, discourses, and practices can and are encouraged to surface." Marshall (2020) explored instructors' perceptions of preservice teachers use of language. The study showed how tensions related to translanguaging practices when the expected product or assignment was monolingual affected instructors' understandings of their students' translanguaging practices, played a key role in framing instructors' own pedagogical responses to the linguistic diversity in their classes. Research has also identified opportunities and challenges of integrating a translanguaging pedagogy in teacher preparation. Barros et al. (2020:13) discuss the resistance teacher candidates encounter when confronting language hierarchies and monolingual language ideologies. They argue that translanguaging approaches open "opportunities to enhance their ability to instrumentally engage with difference beyond what standard language ideologies predicate about 'appropriateness' in classroom discourse, especially as the focus shifts from 'correct' language to communicative competence and greater sociolinguistic awareness."

As Guerrero and Guerrero (2017) and Aquino-Sterling (2016) have pointed out, one of our main responsibilities and goals as bilingual teacher educators is to support BTCs' development of academic and pedagogical Spanish competencies. From a translanguaging standpoint, providing opportunities for our BTCs to further develop and enrich their linguistic repertoire by increasing their Spanish literacy competency is a social justice issue besides a required skill to effectively teach bilingual students. From a teacher educator standpoint, accomplishing this confronts us and our BTCs with the lack of opportunities they have been afforded to use and expand their bilingual assets throughout their schooling experience. The demands imposed on bilingual teacher preparation programs and BTCs are significantly superior to candidates in monolingual preparation tracks. Guerrero and Guerrero

(2017: 16) explained "Moreover, the expectation is that the bilingual pre-service teacher should be able to master general content, pedagogical knowledge, and bilingual education content, as well as appropriate academic Spanish, within the same amount of time as monolingual-English candidates master only general content and pedagogical knowledge." More recently, Zuñiga (2019) explored how she models a dynamic and linguistically inclusive approach to teaching while supporting the development of preservice teachers' pedagogical Spanish language competencies through the careful design of assignments aimed at unpacking hegemonic ideologies and uncovering the linguistic diversity of border communities. Her experience designing and implementing the course entailed a personal exploration of her own language and literacy practices, crucial to her professional identity and development. More studies on bilingual teacher educators' practices could shed light on how instructors' translanguaging stance and BTC's language use and diversity understandings converge to create optimal teaching and learning spaces that leverage students and instructors' linguistic repertoires.

## 3 A bilingual teacher educator self-study approach

I use a self-study approach to teacher education practices (Hamilton, Hutchinson and Pinnegar 2020; Loughran 2007; Peercy 2014) grounded in recent explorations of translanguaging practices in higher education (Canagarajah 2013; Mazak and Herbas-Donoso 2015) and bilingual and ESL teacher education (Musanti and Rodríguez 2017; Musanti and Cavazos 2018; Tian 2020; Zuñiga 2019). I embrace self-study in teacher education as a generative way to explore my practice, to understand the impact of my instructional design, to identify tensions and contradictions in what I do and what my students learn, and as a catalyst for innovation (Hamilton, Hutchinson and Pinnegar 2020; Loughran 2007; Peercy 2014). I believe my practice has evolved as a result of opening spaces for critically looking at how my translanguaging pedagogical stance is apparent and enacted – or not –, in the way I design instruction, and in the linguistically fluid pedagogical moves that I typically include in my teaching. Insights and implications have been documented in previous publications (i.e., Musanti and Rodríguez, 2017; Musanti and Cavazos 2018; Rodríguez, Musanti and Cavazos 2021). In this chapter, I am exploring one of the courses I regularly teach in our bilingual education teacher certification program entitled "The Bilingual Curriculum in the Content Areas." The course focuses on teaching language through content and planning in bilingual classroom settings. This course is one of the last courses of the bilingual education course sequence taught in Spanish that includes Foundations of Bilingual Education and ESL, The Development of Bilingualism, Early Biliteracy, and Language Arts in the Bilingual Classroom. BTCs are expected to take this course during the third semester in the program. In addition, in this course BTCs are expected to design instruction in Spanish and English in different content areas considering the cultural and linguistic needs and characteristics of diverse bilingual learners. While most readings, assignments, and learning tasks are in Spanish, I take time at the beginning of the semester to discuss my translanguaging stance and its implications for teaching and engage in conversations on their experiences using language for teaching and learning. This class involved 17 preservice teachers, all female, bilingual Latinx students. The following quote illustrates how most of my students describe their use of English and Spanish: "*Mi idioma mayoritario es el español. Lo uso para comunicarme en casa y con mis amigos. El inglés lo uso en el trabajo y en la escuela*" [ My main language is Spanish. I use it at home and with friends. I use English at work and at school]. Spanish is identified as the primary language used with family (N = 14) and friends (N = 9). Some BTCs reported to also use English with some family members (N = 4). English was identified as the language used at work and at the university. Only four students indicated Spanish as a language used for learning and eleven students indicated they use mostly English, even though at least four of the classes they take during the last two semesters in the program are taught in Spanish.

In this chapter, I am focusing on data collected during one semester, including class artifacts (e.g., slide decks, handouts), instructor's notes, completed assignments, and students' reflections. In addition, for the purposes of this study, I collected a questionnaire on BTCs perceptions of bilingualism, bilingual education and the role of culture and language in teaching and learning that I administered at the beginning and at the end of the semester. Questions were open ended and questions in the pre-post questionnaire were the same to make comparison possible (See Appendix). The questions were provided in Spanish and in English in between brackets. The instructions indicated to answer in the language of preference. Sixteen students responded to the pre-questionnaire and 15 responded the post-questionnaire. Only two students chose to answer in English in each round. Questionnaires were not graded but BTCs received credit for completing both.

The course included practice-based inspired activities entitled *aproximaciones a la práctica* [approximations to practice] (Grossman 2018). I design these activities to model core practices such as activating background knowledge, writing language objectives, using graphic organizers, integrating cognates, and scaffolding writing with sentence frames. These activities provide opportunities for students to practice strategies in contained settings, either with peers acting as students or using simulation scenarios. Following an adaptation of the learning cycle proposed by Teaching Works (n/d), these group activities typically include an iterative cycle of approximation to linguistic inclusive practice with four moments (See Figure 1). Initially, I introduce or model the activity or strategy, then BTCs in groups design and plan an activity applying key concepts. This is followed by a moment of rehearsal when each group member takes turns to enact or demonstrate the activity. During and after the rehearsal BTCs receive feedback from peers and instructor. Peers are instructed to focus their feedback on strengths and suggestions for improvement, especially how the activity leverages students' linguistic repertoire. Receiving feedback during rehearsal is a critical component as it gives each group the opportunity to reflect, revise, and adjust the activity before the next member of the team gets a chance to practice. For peers, providing feedback serves as an opportunity to critically look back at how their own lesson or activity leverages language for learning.

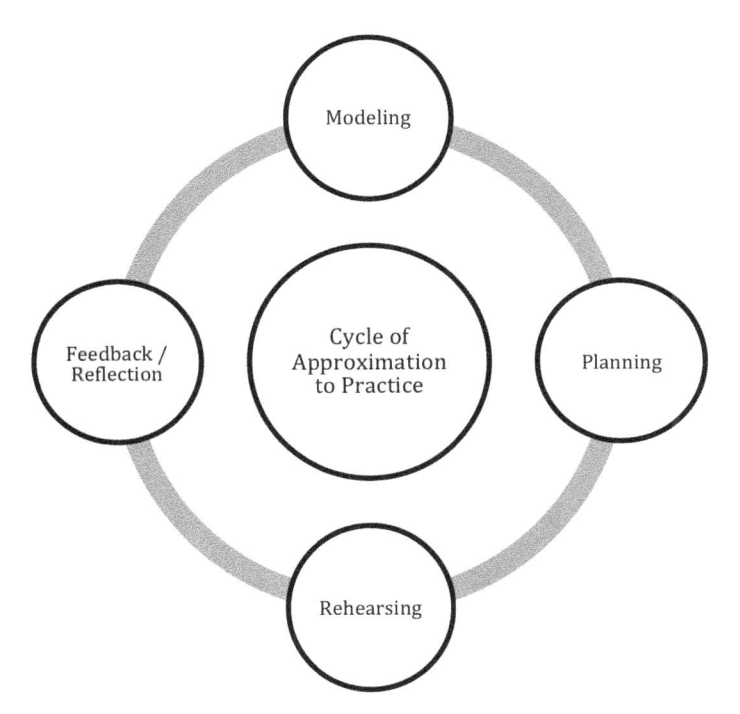

**Figure 1:** Cycle of Approximation to Practice.

In this chapter, I am centering the analysis on one approximation to practice that involved using a TeachLivE™ Mixed Reality Simulation (MRS) scenario I designed for students to collaborate in small groups planning and delivering an interdisciplinary activity to activate background knowledge. TeachLivE is a mixed-reality classroom simulator environment where candidates can interact with avatar students to practice the different skillset needed for teaching (Dieker et al. 2014). The MRS scenario I designed introduces a lesson that integrates Spanish Language Arts and Social Studies using *"Cajas de Cartón"* (Jiménez 2000) as the supporting text. Specifically, the MRS Spanish written scenario asks BTCs to plan how to engage students in a conversation to activate prior knowledge, introduce key vocabulary in Spanish and prepare students for the first activity that is to create an outline of a short autobiographical story. Instead of planning a typical lesson, I asked BTCs to create a script of how they imagine the interaction between teacher and students, focusing on what teacher and students do and how they use language. For this activity, BTCs drew upon previous approximations to practice such as video analysis where they are asked to watch a lesson delivery, identify the lesson objectives, describe activities and teacher-student interactions (i.e., type of grouping, use of questioning, etc.). After rehearsing the activity in the context of the mixed reality classroom, BTCs wrote a reflection drawing from their personal experience and the feedback received from peers and myself. For this study, I analyze the activity script each group designed and the individual reflections after completing the simulation.

The first cycle of analysis involved using in vivo coding of questionnaires and reflective assignments to keep the data rooted in BTCs own words (Saldaña 2013), codes such as *"cómo aprenden* how they learn]; *de dónde vienen* [where they come from]; *no hablan inglés* [they don't speak English], *más de un idioma* [more than one language], *hay que tener respeto* [respect is needed], *los lenguajes se deben usar por igual* [languages must be used equally] emerged. A second cycle involved descriptive coding to summarize basic topics emerging from the data (knowledge of students, planning, scaffolding language use, teaching approach, responding to students' needs, acknowledging culture, addressing language, language use) and analytical codes grounded on the theoretical framework (metalinguistic awareness, deficit view of bilingual learners, asset view of bilingual learner, translanguaging, critical understanding of diversity) (Saldaña 2013). While organizing coded data into larger categorical themes (see examples in Table 1), the iterative analysis process allowed me to stay close to the data while gaining some distance in terms of time lapse since I taught the course to avoid bias derived from what I perceived as meeting – or not – course expectations.

In what follows, first, I describe how a teacher educator teaching in Spanish to prepare bilingual teacher candidates grappled with the integration of linguistic inclusiveness and embedding intentional translanguaging moves to support BTCs translanguaging repertoire development. Second, I analyze the outcomes of an activity designed to foster critical bilingual awareness and to integrate opportunities for teacher candidates to explore issues that intersect culture, language, and

**Table 1:** Themes, Codes, and Data Examples.

| Themes | Pre-questionnaire | Post-questionnaire |
|---|---|---|
| Understanding emergent bilingual students | **Code: Knowledge of students**<br>Every student is different (learning rhythm and styles)<br>*No hablan inglés y necesitan ayuda* [They don't speak English and need help]<br>*No todos tienen el mismo nivel de educación* [Not all students have the same educational level]<br>*Ver cuál es el lenguaje dominante* [identify dominant language]<br>*Si son ESL o si no saben español* | **Code: Knowledge of students**<br>*Identificar el nivel de competencia de lenguaje de los estudiantes bilingües*<br>*Tener en cuenta el nivel de inglés, que aprenden diferente y la cultura*<br>*Conexión – Tener en cuenta el nivel de los estudiantes*<br>Take into account different levels and needs of each student. Get to know each student.<br>*El nivel en cada idioma –*<br>*Nivel de español e inglés* |
| Building understanding of teaching in a bilingual classroom | **Code: Teaching approach / language use / asset**<br>*Usar ambos lenguajes*<br>*Siempre mantener los dos idiomas presentes*<br>*Poder practicar los dos idiomas*<br>**Code: Teaching approach / language use / deficit**<br>*No combinar dos idiomas*<br>*Usando los dos lenguajes pero no en "modo Spanglish"* | **Code: Planning/ Addressing language**<br>*Usar objetivos de lenguaje . . .*<br>*Integración de enseñanza de la lengua y el contenido / vocabulario / diferentes estrategias*<br>*ELPS – TEKS – nivel de proficiencia*<br>*Integración de la enseñanza de la lengua y el contenido* |
| Evolving understandings of language use and linguistic inclusiveness | **Code: Acknowledging culture**<br>*La cultura y los valores de los niños*<br>*Cultura y la lengua y conocimiento previo del estudiante*<br>**Code: language use/ Translanguaging**<br>*Se deberían usar ambos lenguajes y traducirles las palabras que tengan más difíciles* | **Code: Teaching approach/ Scaffolding language use**<br>*Introducir la lección en ambos idiomas, de forma comprensible*<br>Make them verbally demonstrate their English language speaking ability. Use background knowledge, graphic organizers scaffolding with native language<br>**Code: Teaching approach/ metalinguistic awareness**<br>*Uso de cognados usar bridging* |

**Table 1** (continued)

| Themes | Pre-questionnaire | Post-questionnaire |
|---|---|---|
| | | **Code: language use/ translanguaging**<br>*En una aula bilingüe se debe usar el translenguaje, el uso de una lengua para enseñar la segunda lengua.* |
| Grappling with a more critical understanding of diversity | **Code: Diversity / Addressing culture**<br>Hay muchos niños que vienen de diferentes países porque en una aula, habrá estudiantes de diferentes culturas y regiones No todos vienen de la misma cultura. Sin embargo, en la región que vivimos no hay tanta diversidad cultural pero es bueno poder aprender sobre la cultura. | **Code: Diversity / Addressing culture / critical understanding of diversity**<br>how to live and work in a society where every individual is unique. Diversity improves critical thinking skills, builds empathy and encourages students to think differently<br>Los estudiantes podrán entender que en el mundo hay diversidad cultural.<br>Porque no debemos excluir a ningún estudiante por tener diferentes creencias<br>Si tenemos estudiantes que se clasifican como latinos pero pueden venir de diferentes lugares latinoamericanos |

social justice in the classroom. Third, I discuss evidence on BTCs' understandings of linguistic inclusiveness. Finally, I present implications for a socially just pedagogy in bilingual teacher preparation.

# 4 Modeling linguistic inclusiveness through intentional translanguaging moves

It is difficult to acknowledge that my practice has been permeated by a monoglossic ideology. Like many of us in the field of bilingual education, I have taught about the need to keep language separated and I have advocated for the negative effects of translation in bilingual education. My teaching then contributed to legitimize only standard forms of either Spanish or English rendering students' language use and the variation of Spanish spoken in the region incorrect or inappropriate when using vocabulary variations such as *haiga* instead of *hay* [there is], or asking them to avoid using colloquial forms or expressions such as *muy padre* commonly used to describe something that is appreciated or good. I still remember during my first year teaching my attempts to neutralize my own Argentinean variation of Spanish to make sure I modeled the use of standard forms of Spanish. In hindsight, this was not one of my proudest moments but maybe a necessary one. It was in that effort to neutralize my way of speaking Spanish (e.g., using the pronoun *"tu"* [you] instead of *"vos"*) and my students' way to speaking Spanish that I confronted my bias, the imposition of colonized ways of speaking and the rendering of our linguistic and cultural roots as erasable and unwanted.

In my work and research, I had defined language as a resource and as a right (Ruiz 1984), but it was the coming across the work of García (2017) on languaging and translanguaging, the conceptualization of an integrated linguistic repertoire, and the call for a socially just approach in bilingual education (García and Leiva 2014), that helped me to resignify my linguistic struggle, and that of my students in terms of a pedagogical approach. My practice shifted to incorporate intentional translanguaging moves to create spaces that legitimize and leverage how BTCs engage in learning through languaging, a "process of making meaning and shaping knowledge and experience through language" (Swain 2006: 98). When explaining concepts, I make explicit connections to BTCs' English repertoire, asking them to contribute with specific terms, and analyzing similarities and differences in language use. For instance, we discuss the concept of literacy in English and *literacidad, lectoescritura,* and *alfabetización* in Spanish (Lopez-Bonilla and Fragoso 2013). We look at the nuanced meaning of each term, its origin and use with the goal to amplify BTCs' linguistic repertoire in both languages. Another intentional translanguaging move is to ask BTCs to think of a similar approach to work with words with students, adding a metalinguistic level of analysis to our inquiry on words. Another translanguaging pedagogical move through which I purposefully ask my students to shuttle through languages is using (and reflecting on) translation. Some course content requires that BTCs read texts in English, such as the Texas English Language Proficiency Standards, a key planning resource for Texas teachers. We read the document in English, but we intentionally discuss it in Spanish. When we encounter terms or ways of saying that require some translation effort, we discuss the role of translation in the classroom, the skillfulness that it requires to interpret meaning navigating across languages in their daily life like when language brokering for family members. I also explain my pedagogical decision-making process for using translation strategically in this course to build on their biliteracy skills making apparent the connections between my translanguaging stance and my instructional design. I believe that it is through building my own repertoire of translanguaging moves (i.e. strategic use of translation to support meaning making, shuttling between texts in Spanish and English; designing activities that model how to leverage students' linguistic repertoire), being explicit about my pedagogical intent, and being critically reflective about the impact of languaging in the classroom that I can contribute to develop a linguistically inclusive bilingual teacher candidates' repertoire of practice.

# 5 Building bilingual teacher candidates' translanguaging repertoire

A goal of the course under analysis is for BTCs to "create authentic and purposeful learning activities, experiences, and assessments in all content areas that promote bilingual learners' development of concepts and skills in Spanish and English" (Fall 2019 course syllabus). The MRS approximation to practice was designed for BTCs to dive into teaching disciplinary content in Spanish, specifically immigration in the US and an autobiographical story such as "Cajas de Cartón" by Francisco Jimenéz (2000) that describes the life of Panchito, a migrant child and his family. The activity intentionally situated BTCs to think about immigration through an interdisciplinary connection with the Spanish version of Panchito's story, originally published in English as *The Circuit*. With this content in mind, for the rehearsal, BTCs planned a short activity to activate background knowledge, a core practice to design effective instruction. The assignment created a space to build language awareness as BTCs explored the language describing migrant workers identifying key vocabulary.

This activity illustrates elements of critical bilingual awareness (García 2015) and the importance of extending translanguaging pedagogies to integrate opportunities for teacher candidates to grapple with issues that intersect culture, language, and social justice in the classroom. BTCs worked in groups to co-construct a shared understanding of a social studies theme to be taught in Spanish, as a way to counteract the common approach -at least in the region- to teach social studies in English. BTCs had to reflect on the connections between the story and immigration creating a script to reflect those ideas in Spanish, adding pedagogical Spanish features to their bilingual repertoire. One of the groups constructed the script around the concept of *mudanza* [moving] and the concept of *bracero* [laborer], skillfully connecting it with the word *brazo* [arm] and the type of work the migrant workers do.

Teacher: *¿Por qué se habrá mudado a los Estados Unidos?* [Why did they move to the United States?]

Students: *Porque ya no había trabajo entonces fueron a buscar.* [Because there was no more work, they went looking for it]

Teacher: *¿Por qué otra razón creen [que] se mudan personas a los Estados Unidos?* [For what other reason do you think people are moving to the United States?]

Students: *Para estar junto a su familia. Para estudiar inglés* [to be with their families, to study English]

Teacher: *¡Muy bien! ¿Alguien me puede decir como se les llama a los trabajadores qué trabajan en el campo?* [Very good, can someone tell me how workers are called when working in the field?]

Students: *Es una palabra que se parece a brazo.* [It is a word that looks like "brazo"]

Teacher: *Si, miren en el primer párrafo. ¿Qué parte de este párrafo les dice que es un bracero?* [Yes, look at the first paragraph. What part of this paragraph tells you is a laborer?]

Students: *Pizcador, vino a trabajar.* [picker, came to work.]

Teacher: *¡Muy bien! Acuérdense, la palabra braceros tiene la palabra brazos. Los braceros hacen trabajo usando sus brazos.* [Very well! Remember, the word "braceros" has the word "brazos". Laborers who work using their arms.]

In another example the group imagines a dialogue on the meaning of the word *capataz* [foreman]. In the scene, the teacher shows students a picture of the baby in the movie "Boss Baby" asking students to explain the meaning of the word "boss", then connecting to the word *capataz*, and identifying a synonym in Spanish in the word *jefe* [boss]. Teaching new vocabulary while activating background knowledge challenged them to think about meaningful ways to connect what they assumed was new knowledge with students' understandings. In reflecting about their MRS lesson and rehearsal, BTCs gained awareness related to ways in which students could transact meaning grappling with content and language. For instance, Viviana in her reflective paper explained how the questions they asked students supported higher order thinking skills *"porque la conexión no se encuentra dentro del texto y requiere que los alumnos analicen que conexión puede existir entre el vocabulario cosecha, braceros e inmigración"* [because the connection is not found within the text and requires students to analyze what connection may exist between the vocabulary harvest, braceros, and immigration]. Diana shares how she believes many students could identify with the main character's feelings given that for many the experiences are similar, *"al igual que los niños que vemos a diario en el puente o los que luchan por las leyes que los protegen tales como DACA"* [just like the children we see every day on the bridge or those who fight for the laws that protect them such as DACA]. It is not just about how they use language, it is about understanding the patterns of oppression and the experiences of marginalization of their students, critically engaging in designing instruction that taps into and honors the socio cultural and linguistic background and experiences of students and their communities. In this regard, a translanguaging pedagogy commits to a socially just approach "as an important voice-giving mechanism and as a tool for learning, creativity, and criticality" (García 2015: 7) essential to fight linguistic and cultural oppression and to restore bilingual teachers' sense of agency.

# 6 Bilingual teacher candidates' evolving understandings of linguistic inclusiveness

There is no doubt that we need to rethink teacher preparation from a cultural and linguistic asset-based perspective (Bustos Flores, Sheets, and Clark 2011; Irizarry 2011; Paris 2012; Valenzuela 2016), and that this vision and its implementation is "highly contextual, meaning that there is no one-size-fits-all cookie cutter model that can be implemented in any setting" (Irizarry 2017: 94). Moreover, we cannot assume that beliefs are static or uniform across the Latinx population, while commonalities exist BTC's understandings are shaped by their lived experience. The pre and post questionnaire I implemented in this course was meant to deepen my understanding of BTCs' perceptions of the role and use of language when teaching in bilingual contexts. Responses to the pre-questionnaire situated across a continuum from privileging a monolingual and static conceptualization of bilingualism to a more dynamic vision of bilingualism and language use in the classroom that embodies students' cultural identity. The notion that bilingual learners *"necesitan ayuda"* [need help] because *"ellos no saben inglés"* [they don't know English] or they have different proficiency level in each language is still very present in BTCs' responses. Also prevalent is the belief that teaching languages should not be mixed or used together, mirroring the social rejection to localized linguistic practices illustrated in defining language fluidity as *"maña"* or bad habit that *"con el tiempo se me quito . . . ya que mi papá me decía o hablas inglés o hablas español"* [with time it went away because my father used to tell me you either speak English or you speak Spanish]. However, these beliefs appeared intertangled with the understanding that both languages are needed in the classroom and should be used *"igualmente"* meaning in the same way or same amount of time, with an emphasis in teaching students the vocabulary they do not know.

BTCs' translanguaging repertoire is an expression of their embodiment of linguistic inclusiveness and their repositioning as bilingual individuals. The pre-questionnaire showed that they see bilingualism as an asset and the capacity to effectively use two languages. For instance, a BTC wrote that being bilingual is the "*habilidad de poder hablar, entender y practicar dos idiomas*" [ability to talk, understand and practice two languages]. The post-questionnaire showed a movement towards a more critical understanding of bilingualism from a linguistic inclusive perspective. For instance, a BTC challenged the dominant perception of bilingualism as a problem or a deficit: "*significa ser mejor que los demás. Por muchos años yo pensé que saber español era una debilidad. . . . Para mí el ser bilingüe es una verdadera bendición*" [means being better than everyone else. For many years I thought that to speak Spanish was a weakness . . . For me being bilingual is a true blessing]. Another BTC reflected on the transnational roots of her bilingual identity: "It means having two different countries in my blood and being able to share the love of two backgrounds. It means being able to celebrate differences and similarities of the two counties I hold dear to my heart." It could be argued that BTCs gained in ideological clarity as they questioned their belief system about being bilingual acknowledging the unfairness of how bilingualism is perceived in the dominant society (Bartolomé 2004).

The responses in the post questionnaire did not show a significant shift in the students' positioning in relation to language in the continuum but a more nuanced capacity to conceptualize the use of language and a deeper awareness of factors impacting bilingual students. For instance, a BTC grappled with contradictory discourses while demonstrating pedagogical understanding of core practices, explaining that it is important to plan "different activities that allows them to use both languages, by grouping them strategically, allowing some scaffolding with the native language, or using sentence frames to give students practice with academic language, but mostly accomplishing the goal to help students learn a second language quickly, while preserving the native language and cultural heritage." Another BTC reflected on the importance of embracing linguistic inclusiveness in the bilingual classroom:

> *En una (sic) aula bilingüe se debe usar el translenguaje, el uso de una lengua para enseñar la segunda lengua. La maestra debe usar cognados, ilustraciones, organizadores gráficos, y el uso de las dos lenguas en varias maneras para la comprensión*" [In the bilingual classroom, we must use translanguaging, the use of a language to teach a second language. The teacher needs to use cognates, images, graphic organizers, and both languages in different ways for comprehension.

This BTC showed awareness of core practices to support bilingual learners and acknowledged the importance of using both languages when teaching. However, she framed translanguaging from a monolingual understanding of the bilingual learner that maintains the hegemonic presence of English positioning them as second language learners. To prepare culturally and linguistically competent BTCs (Bustos Flores, Sheets, and Clark 2011), calls for a next step in the pedagogical approach at the course level and a collective action at the program level, deepening our efforts to identify ways to build on BTCs' translanguaging repertoires while gaining critical awareness of the implications of how they define bilingualism and language use in the classroom.

## 7 Implications for a socially just pedagogy in bilingual teacher preparation

In reflecting on the experience rehearsing the activity planned for the MRS assignment, a BTC felt more confident because the lesson was in Spanish given that *"a veces encuentro más palabras en español"* [sometimes I find more words in Spanish], another BTC shared her feelings of inadequacy during the rehearsal because "Se me olvidó como traducir las palabras en español" (sic) [I forgot how to translate the words to Spanish] referring to her difficulties retrieving certain academic terms. I believe assignments such as the one described here foster critical bilingual awareness (García 2015; Holguín Mendoza 2018; Leeman 2018) where BTCs imagine teaching scenarios drawing from and incorporating their knowledge of the subject matter, pedagogy, and language while leveraging their knowledge about students' cultural background and bilingualism. While working in groups investigating the topic, reading the text, and creating the script, BTCs leveraged and amplified their bilingual repertoire and engaged in metalinguistic reflections on key vocabulary searching for ways to establish linguistic connections. Moreover, while writing and rehearsing the teaching script in Spanish they grappled with how language is used in the classroom and uncovered the complexity of teaching realizing that *"Los estudiantes en la simulación como los estudiantes en la vida real te contestarán lo que ellos sientan en ese momento sin uno poder saber que"* [The students in the simulation as the students in real life will answer you what they feel at that moment without one being able to know what]. A translanguaging pedagogical approach should go beyond planning activities where teacher candidates engage in using both languages, intentionally creating spaces to privilege Spanish as the language for learning and knowledge construction. The assignment was developed and implemented in Spanish, content and text were transacted in Spanish, BTCs imagine instruction happening in Spanish where English could be integrated as a resource for learning, and discussions and reflections about the assignment were carried out predominately in Spanish. During this process, BTCs and me were constantly drawing from our integrated bilingual repertoire.

In looking back at the MRS assignment, I can see its potential to go deeper in the possibilities to explore the prevailing deficit views of immigrant students that permeated some of the scripts with statements like *"Muchos de ellos no tienen educación, no saben leer ni escribir. Siempre han estado expuestos al trabajo desde muy pequeños"* [Many of them have no education, they cannot read or write. They have always been exposed to work from a very young age]. I am committed to further my *concientización* (Bustos, Sheets and Clark 2011: 4), my awareness as a teacher educator to be able to act against oppressive ideologies and to design instruction that challenges BTCs to critically examine their assumptions while thinking critically about their own experiences and beliefs, and the socio historical constraints shaping bilingual education.

A socially just pedagogical approach needs to consider both Latinx BTCs' lived experience with language and constructed through language while leveraging their bilingualism as a resource for learning. Such an approach requires to intentionally design instruction for BTCs to grow more critically aware of the hegemonic presence of English in the bilingual education discourse, to question linguistic and cultural oppression explore, and to plan and rehearse practices that enable them to counteract monoglossic pedagogies.

To conclude, I argue that we are in need for a translanguaging practice-based approach in bilingual teacher preparation that contributes to advance social justice and equity in education. Such an approach entails to embrace a translanguaging mindset mirrored in clear principles for program and course design, anchored in the notion that BTCs' translanguaging practices are an expression of biliteracy competence as well as a medium to develop those competencies. We need programs that intentionally and strategically "nurture the translanguaging capacities of students and to develop standardized varieties of one and the other language as used in school" (García 2015: 8). This entails a focus on modeling linguistically inclusive practices to leverage bilingual teacher candidates' linguistic repertoire, developing metalinguistic awareness through opportunities to reflect on how they use languages to convey meaning, what linguistic features they are adding to grow their linguistic repertoire, and how to design instruction that fosters students' metalinguistic understandings. Ultimately, we need programs that create spaces for *concientización* of linguistic diversity, and critical reflection on the enactment of a translanguaging mindset –the possibility to plan for and/or engage in actions to support linguistic diversity and translanguaging in teaching and learning (Musanti, Cavazos, and Rodriguez 2020).

Ultimately, this teacher educator self-study contributes to portray the complexity of engaging in transformative models of bilingual teacher preparation attempting to respond to the multilingual turn and its role in language learning pedagogies (García 2015; Flores and Aneja 2017). In what relates to Latinx higher education contexts, the study highlights the criticality of purposefully design approximations to practice as spaces for BTCs to safely grapple with the implications of leveraging cultural and linguistic repertoires for equitable instruction. As teacher educators, it is important we aspire to inspire Latinx bilingual teacher educators to engage in critical reflections on holistic linguistic pedagogies in bilingual education for social justice.

# Appendix

## Pre and post questionnaire

1. *Explique como usa el idioma español e inglés en su vida diaria.* [Explain how you use both languages in your daily life: home, school, work, etc.]
2. *¿Qué significa ser bilingüe para usted?* [What does it mean to be bilingual for you?]
3. *Por favor, explique por qué quiere ser un/a maestro/a bilingüe.* [Please, explain why you want to become a bilingual teacher?]
4. *Al enseñar en un aula bilingüe, ¿qué es lo que tendrá en cuenta?* [What will you consider when teaching in a bilingual classroom?]
5. *¿Cómo se deben usar los lenguajes en un aula bilingüe para asegurarse que los niños aprendan lo que se espera para el grado?* [How should languages be used in a bilingual classroom to make sure students learn at grade level?]
6. *¿Cómo puede integrar la cultura de sus alumnos para tener en cuenta la diversidad en su clase? Por favor, explique y de un ejemplo.* [How do you integrate culture to address the diversity in your classroom? Please, explain and provide an example]
7. *¿Por qué usted piensa que es importante tener en cuenta la diversidad cultural en el aula?* [Why do you think is important to consider the cultural diversity in the classroom?]
8. *¿Cómo maestra bilingüe qué es lo que usted considera esencial conocer sobre sus alumnos para poder enseñarles en forma adecuada?* [As a bilingual teacher what do you consider essential to know about your students to be an effective teacher?]

# References

Alfaro, Cristina. 2018. The sociopolitical struggle and promise of bilingual teacher education: Past, present, and future. *Bilingual Research Journal* 41(4). 413–427.
Anzaldúa, Gloria. 2012. *Borderlands. La Frontera. The New Mestiza*. San Francisco: Aunt Lute Books.
Aquino-Sterling, Christian R. 2016. Responding to the call: Developing and assessing pedagogical Spanish competencies in bilingual teacher education. *Bilingual Research Journal* 39(1). 50–68.
Barros, Sandro; Lisa M. Domke, Carrie Symons & Christina Ponzio. 2020. Challenging monolingual ways of looking at multilingualism: Insights for curriculum development in teacher preparation. *Journal of Language, Identity & Education*. 1–16. DOI: 10.1080/15348458.2020.1753196
Bartolomé, Lilia I. 2004. Critical pedagogy and teacher education: Radicalizing prospective teachers. *Teacher Education Quarterly* 31(1). 97–122.
Bustos Flores, Belinda, Rosa Sheets & Ellen Clark (eds.). 2011. *Teacher Preparation for Bilingual Student Populations: Educar para Transformer*. New York: Routledge.
Canagarajah, Suresh (ed.). 2013. *Literacy as Translingual Practice: Between Communities and Classrooms*. New York: Routledge.
Collins, Brian A, Maite Sanchez & Carla Espana. 2019. Sustaining and developing teachers' dynamic bilingualism in a re-designed bilingual teacher preparation program. *International Journal of Bilingual Education and Bilingualism*. 1–17.
Dávila, Liv T. & Nihad Bunar. 2020. Translanguaging through an advocacy lens: The roles of multilingual classroom assistants in Sweden. *European Journal of Applied Linguistics* 8(1). 107–126. https://doi.org/10.1515/eujal-2019-0012.
Dieker, Lisa A., Jacqueline Rodriguez, Benjamin Lingnugaris-Kraft, Michale Hynes & Charles E. Hughes. 2014. The future of simulated environments in teacher education: Current potential and future possibilities. *Teacher Education and Special Education* 37(1). 21–33. doi: 10.1177/0888406413512683
Flores, Nelson. 2014. "Let's not forget that translanguaging is a political act." The Educational Linguist. https://educationallinguist.wordpress.com/2014/07/19/lets-not-forget-that-translanguaging-is-a-political-act/ (last modified 19 July 2014).
Flores, Nelson & Geeta Aneja. 2017. "Why needs hiding?" Translingual (re)orientations in TESOL teacher education. *Research in the Teaching of English* 51(4). 441–463.
García, Ofelia. 2015. Critical multilingual language awareness and teacher education. In Jasone Cenoz, Durk Gorter & Stephen May (eds.), *Language Awareness and Multilingualism*, 1–17. (Encyclopedia of Language and Education 6). Switzerland: Springer International Publishing.
García, Ofelia. 2017. Translanguaging in schools: Subiendo y bajando, bajando y subiendo as afterword. *Journal of Language, Identity & Education* 16(4). 256–263.
García, Ofelia & Tatiana Kleyn. 2016. *Translanguaging with Multilingual Students: Learning from Classroom Moments*. New York: Routledge.
García, Ofelia, & Camila Leiva. 2014. Theorizing and enacting translanguaging for social justice. In Adrian Blackledge & Angela Creese (eds.), *Heteroglossia as Practice and Pedagogy*, 199–216. Switzerland: Springer International Publishing.
García, Ofelia & Li Wei. 2014. *Translanguaging: Language, Bilingualism and Education*. New York: Palgrave Macmillan.
Grossman, Pamela. (ed.). 2018. *Teaching Core Practices in Teacher Education*. Cambridge: Harvard Education Press.

Guerrero, Michael D. & Maria Consuelo Guerrero. 2017. Competing discourses of academic Spanish in the Texas-Mexico borderlands. *Bilingual Research Journal* 40(1). 5–19. https://doi.org/10.1080/15235882.2016.1273150.

Gutiérrez, Kris D. & Barbara Rogoff. 2003. Cultural ways of learning: Individual traits or repertoire of practice. *Educational Researcher* 32(5). 19–25.

Hamilton, Mary Lynn, Derek A. Hutchinson & Stefinee Pinnegar. 2020. Quality, trustworthiness, and S-STTEP research. In Julian Kitchen, Amanda Berry, Shawn Michael Bullock, Alicia R. Crowe, Monica Taylor, Hafdís Guðjónsdóttir & Lynn Thomas (eds.), *International Handbook of Self-Study of Teaching and Teacher Education Practices*, 299–338. (Springer International Handbooks of Education). Netherlands: Springer.

Holguín Mendoza, Claudia. 2018. Critical language awareness (CLA) for Spanish heritage language programs: Implementing a complete curriculum. *International Multilingual Research Journal* 12(2). 65–79.

Irizarry, Jason G. 2011. En la lucha: The struggles and triumphs of Latino/a preservice teachers. *Teachers College Record* 113(12). 2804–2835.

Irizarry, Jason, G. 2017. "For us, by us": A vision for culturally sustaining pedagogies forwarded by Latinx youth. In Django Paris & H. Samy Alim (eds). *Culturally Sustaining Pedagogie*s, 83–98. New York: Teachers College Press.

Jiménez, Francisco. 2000. *Cajas de Cartón: Relatos de la Vida Peregrina de un Niño Campesino*. Boston: Houghton Mifflin.

Kroskrity, Paul V. 2010. Language ideologies – evolving perspectives. In Jürgen Jaspers (ed.), *Language Use and Society. Handbook of Pragmatics Highlights*, 192–211. Amsterdam: John Benjamins Publishing Company.

Leeman, Jennifer. 2018. Critical language awareness and Spanish as a heritage language: Challenging the linguistic subordination of U.S. Latinxs. In Kim Potowski (ed.), *Handbook of Spanish as a Minority/Heritage Language*, 345–358. New York: Routledge.

Lopez-Bonilla, Guadalupe & Carmen Fragoso. 2013. Debates actuales en torno a los conceptos "alfabetización", "cultura escrita" y "literacidad". In Alma Carrasco Altamirano & Guadalupe López-Bonilla (eds.), *Lenguaje y educación. Temas de investigación educativa en México*, 21–45. Mexico: Fundación SM.

Loughran, John. 2007. Researching teacher education practices: Responding to the challenges, demands, and expectations of self-study. *Journal of Teacher Education* 58(1). 12–20.

Marshall, Steve. 2020. Understanding plurilingualism and developing pedagogy: Teaching in linguistically diverse classes across the disciplines at a Canadian university. *Language, culture, and curriculum* 33(2). 142–156.

Mazak, Catherine M. & Kevin S. Caroll. 2017. *Translanguaging in Higher Education. Beyond Monolingual Ideologies*. Bristol: Multilingual Matters.

Mazak, Catherine. M. & Claudia Herbas-Donoso. 2015. Translanguaging practices at a bilingual university: A case study of a science classroom. *International Journal of Bilingual Education and Bilingualism* 18(6). 698–714.

Musanti, Sandra I. 2014. *"Porque sé los dos idiomas."* Biliteracy beliefs and bilingual preservice teacher identity. In Yvonne Freeman & David Freeman (eds.), *Research on Preparing Preservice Teachers to Work Effectively with Emergent Bilinguals*, 59–87. Bingley: Emerald.

Musanti, Sandra I. & Alyssa G. Cavazos. 2018. "Siento que siempre tengo que regresar al inglés." Embracing a translanguaging stance in a Hispanic higher education institution. *EuroAmerican Journal of Applied Linguistics and Languages* 5(2). 44–61.

Musanti, Sandra I., Alyssa G. Cavazos & Alma D. Rodríguez. 2020. Embracing a translanguaging stance and redefining teacher preparation practices in a Hispanic-serving institution. In Janine M. Schall, Patricia Alvarez McHatton & Eugenio Longoria Sáenz (eds.), *Teacher Education at Hispanic-Serving Institutions: Exploring Identity, Practice, and Culture*, 66–87. New York/London: Routledge.

Musanti, Sandra I. & Alma D. Rodríguez. 2017. Translanguaging in bilingual teacher preparation: Exploring pre-service bilingual teachers' academic writing. *Bilingual Research Journal* 40(1). 38–54.

Paris, Django. 2012. Culturally sustaining pedagogy: A needed change in stance, terminology, and practice. *Educational Researcher* 41(3). 93–97.

Peercy, Megan M. 2014. Challenges in enacting core practices in language teacher education: A self-study. *Studying Teacher Education* 10(2). 146–162.

Rodríguez, Alma D. & Sandra I. Musanti. 2017. Pre-service bilingual teachers and their Spanish academic language proficiency as neasured by the BTLPT: Perceptions and performance. *Journal of Bilingual Education Research & Instruction* 19(1). 1–25.

Rodríguez, Alma, Sandra I. Musanti, & Alyssa G. Cavazos. 2021. Translanguaging in higher education in the US: Leveraging students' bilingualism. *Critical Inquiry in Language Studies*. 18(4). 353–373.

Ruíz, Richard. 1984. Orientations in language planning. *NABE: The Journal for the National Association for Bilingual Education* 8(2). 15–34.

Saldaña, Johnny. 2013. *The Coding Manual for Qualitative Researchers*. Los Angeles: SAGE Publications Inc.

Sayer, Peter. 2013. Translanguaging, TexMex, and bilingual pedagogy: Emergent bilinguals learning through the vernacular. *TESOL Quarter* 47(1). 63–88

Sutterby, John A., Javiar Ayala & Sandra Murillo. 2005. El sendero torcido al español [The Twisted Path to Spanish]: The development of bilingual teachers' Spanish-language proficiency. *Bilingual Research Journal* 29(2). 435–501.

Swain, Merrill. 2006. Languaging, agency and collaboration in advanced second language learning. In Heidi Byrnes (ed.), *Advanced Language Learning: The Contributions of Halliday and Vygotsky*, 95–108. London: Continuum.

Tian, Zhongfeng. 2020. Faculty first: Promoting translanguaging in TESOL teacher education. In Sunny Man Chu Lau & Saskia Van Viegen (eds.), *Plurilingual Pedagogies: Critical and Creative Endeavors for Equitable Language in Education*, 215–236. Switzerland: Springer International Publishing.

Valenzuela, Angela (ed.). 2016. *Growing Critically Conscious Teachers: A Social Justice Curriculum for Educators of Latino/a Youth*. New York: Teachers College Press.

Zúñiga, Christian E. 2019. Supporting "pedagogical" Spanish language competencies: Bilingual teacher education en la frontera. *Teacher Education Quarterly* 46(3). 79–98.

Abraham Ceballos-Zapata and Sharon Kim
# Chapter 2
# Listening to culturally grounded translingual dispositions in teacher education

**Abstract:** In this paper, we analyze the stories of two students Aaron and Jasmine through a theoretical lens of *Pansori*, a Korean musical genre, that guided our research experiences as co-researchers in the context of U.S. teacher education. Through narrative knowleding as our methodology and *Pansori* as lens, we as Mexican and Korean nationals were able to negotiate diverse linguistic resources for situated construction of meaning. Using *Pansori* as lenses, our research enacted an iterative process of journaling, narrative analysis, and critical discussions. Data analysis consisted of a process of "articulation of self-awareness" (Trahar 2009) that led to re-seeing narratives of students. Our translanguaging design created a *corriente* between teacher education spaces in the university and pre-service classroom practice. This research process allowed us to re-see and re-hear students (Seltzer 2019) as unique sounds leveraging our own translingual dispositions in culturally grounded ways. This work provides a way forward for educators to honor their culturally grounded translingual dispositions.

## Introduction

This research project emerged from the need to center our own experiences as international educators and to honor our fluid language practices in English speaking institutions. In our early interactions we realized that our experiences as minority language educators in a majority language context made us aware of our own foreignness in our professional environments. Such realization fueled our search for a pathway in teacher education to include our translingual practices. It inspired us to construct knowledge with solidarity.

To guide you, our reader, through this chapter, we want to introduce several actors. A teacher educator, Abraham, started a research project with a pre-service teacher, Sharon, in the context of an introductory course to Bilingual and ESL

**Abraham Ceballos-Zapata,** Calvin University
**Sharon Kim,** Hope Academy

https://doi.org/10.1515/9783110735604-003

education and placement. We then started meeting to discuss Sharon's notes and reflections and to unpack her experiences in her school placement. Week by week, Sharon brought several narratives she had written based on her experience. Through the methodology of narrative knowledging (Barkhuizen 2011), we chose to focus our conversation on two students in Sharon's classroom. To maintain their real names anonymous, we will refer to them as Aaron and Jasmine. Finally, the pedagogical principles embedded in a Korean musical genre known as *Pansori* became the lens through which both Sharon and Abraham analyzed the stories of Aaron and Jasmine.

This project is a work of solidarity. Together, we found ways to use cultural heritage as resources to strengthen our understanding of translingual dispositions. In doing so, we explored a pathway for prospective teachers from diverse backgrounds to use their own culturally grounded tools to negotiate meaning when they are learning to teach through their clinical experiences. After years of reflection and interacting with research, we named such pathways as culturally grounded translingual dispositions. A pathway that would allow us to have conversations from the vantage point of our cultural backgrounds. A culturally grounded translingual disposition materialized when we started exploring *Pansori*, a Korean musical genre and tradition.

*Pansori* functioned as a meaning-making tool for us that allowed us to analyze and reconstruct the stories of two students, Aaron and Jasmine. When Sharon was enrolled in the practicum course, much of her daily coursework consisted of writing reflections and analyzing our experiences by answering specific prompts. As Sharon reflected on her practicum experiences with Abraham, she explained to him that often she had to write her thoughts and feelings in Korean first, and then translate those thoughts into English. Since it took Sharon much longer to write reflections and submit her homework, she explained that she found it somewhat frustrating to continuously translate ideas back and forth. After hearing this, Abraham explained that the majority of coursework and stories that are told in higher education, come from an English dominant speaking population and suggested that for the reflections, Sharon could use Korean words or specific multicultural knowledge and culture to explain her thoughts. At that time, Sharon had heard Kpop singers incorporating traditional *Pansori* cries within their songs, and decided to research more about *Pansori*.

*Pansori*, also known as the Korean-style Opera, is etymologically derived from two parts. The first root word, *pan*, refers to both a place where events occur informally as well as a place for public entertainment. The second root word *sori* means 'sound' or 'song'. The compound word *Pansori* can be interpreted as a song performed at a place where people gather for entertainment (Kang 2016: 16). The singers, known as *sorikkun*, seek to express this vocal art with a unique voice. Furthermore, a *Pansori* performance centers on one singer depicting various characters through variation in vocals. The pace of music varies according to the character's emotions or the mood of the audience. *Pansori* shares some common aspects with the Western opera; they both involve performing in front of an audience using music, drums, and movement. However, unlike opera that consists of many performers, *Pansori* only consists of two performers, a singer storyteller and a drummer who accompanies with beats and melodies (Kang 2016: 3–4).

The closer we examined the singers, or the *sorikkun's* life, artistry, and training process, the more we noticed the striking similarities with learning to teach. Young trainees of the art, led by a *Pansori* master, undergo a phase in which they devote themselves to mastering the essential *Pansori* techniques and skills. The induction process, however, does not culminate with mastering technique. Trainees continue their preparation by spending time surrounded by nature where they learn how to hear its sounds, to discern them, and then, to become their own unique sound. It was such a process of finding their unique voices in the multiplicity of natural sounds that resonated with Sharon's experiences learning to teach.

By using *Pansori* as a meaning-making tool, Sharon was able to enact a translingual disposition that was specifically grounded in cultural knowledge. A focus on translingual dispositions in the classroom has the potential to decenter and resist dominant deficit perspectives that are too often imposed on racially and linguistically minoritized students (Seltzer 2019). By using *Pansori* pedagogies as lenses, Sharon was empowered to seek the expression of her unique voice in the contexts of her experiences learning to teach. In the following section, we will explain how *Pansori* became our lenses that later helped make meaning out of the stories of two students in Sharon's classroom.

# 1 Theorizing *Pansori* as culturally grounded translingual dispositions and as lenses

In this section we will describe *Pansori* in connection to culturally grounded translingual dispositions. To do that, we will define the notion of translingual disposition. Then we will explain how cultural knowledge is crucial in the enactment of translingual dispositions. After building upon this idea, we will then propose the concept of culturally grounded translingual disposition. Then as an example of a cultural translingual dispositions, we will describe the role of *Pansori* as pedagogy and how it served as lenses in helping us interpret our experiences.

## 1.1 Defining translingual dispositions

According to Canagarajah (2013: 1) the term translingual includes "all acts of communication and literacy as involving a shuttling between and a negotiation of diverse linguistic resources for situated construction of meaning". This general openness towards language and the diverse forms of language, can allow English speakers to move beyond the rigid structure of standard or correct English, and instead view language differences as a resource for meaning making (Lee and Jenks 2016; Zheng 2017). For teachers, this can bring an awareness that languages are "always in contact and complement each other in communication (Canagarajah, 2013: 4)". It is important to point out that simply having a multicultural or multilingual background does not guarantee enacting translingual dispositions. Even though the term "disposition" is used, it is not an automatic process (Zheng 2017). Translingual dispositions can be socially acquired through reflection, embodied practices and experiences, and they are to be cultivated and developed (Lee and Canagarajah 2019).

Lee and Canagarajah (2019: 354) include three key elements of translingual dispositions, namely, language awareness, social values, and learning strategies. The first element, language awareness, plays the role of language ideology that challenges norms, and prioritizes the voice of the speaker. In our own research, we looked for ways to include our own cultural knowledge. We asked questions that would allow us to evaluate whether those narratives were centering the experiences of speakers. The second element of a translingual disposition are social values. They refer to the openness to coexisting with others. We used an asset-based approach to teaching and research that allowed us to avoid blaming students. The narratives in this study, created an space to coexist with students because they decentered our focus from their behavior and directed our attention to contextual and societal factors impacting students' lives. The last element, learning strategies, refers to how teachers are proficiently inclined as lifelong learners and engaged with various language differences and social diversity. We believe that the *Pansori* pedagogy has allowed us to build a framework in which we can vocalize our own experiences, and can continuously be cultivated and developed further.

## 1.2 The role of cultural knowledge in the development of culturally grounded translingual dispositions

Cultural knowledge plays an important role in the enactment of a translingual disposition. Recent literature on translingual dispositions has been unpacking how cultural knowledge is crucial to meaning-making practices of bilingual learners. In a study of translingual dispositions of bilingual international students, Wang (2017: 60) explains that "translingual dispositions encompass . . . cultural knowledge as resources for learning, and meta-vocabulary to describe, theorize, and strategize translingual practices". In our study, we explored how Sharon's cultural knowledge stemming from her identity as a Korean scholar was crucial to developing the meta-vocabulary to theorize her experiences learning to teach. When we started working together, Abraham had been theorizing about his experiences as a TESOL educator with several of his colleagues. One of the benefits of such collaboration was learning how to enact the meaning making practice of naming experiences. As international scholars, we believed that we had a wealth of knowledge but in order to theorize them we needed to discursively articulate them. Wang (2017: 61) argues that "the development of translingual dispositions is central to negotiating meaning across hybrid ways of knowing, communicating, and performing identities." In this study, Sharon's identity as an international student from Korea explicitly hybridized her ways of knowing, and represented her translingual disposition.

We also believe that cultural knowledge is integral to teachers' identities. Zheng (2017: 32) defines a translingual teacher as "someone who is able to embrace and integrate his/her multiple linguistic identities as he/she becomes a teacher. In other words, a translingual teacher is different from a bilingual teacher in that his/her multiple linguistic identities are integrated, instead of separated, in ways that create a synergy." Zheng (2017) argues that to develop a translingual-identity-as-pedagogy is necessary to provide explicit support to instructors.

Building on the notions of translingual disposition, hybrid ways of knowing, and translingual identities, we propose the term Culturally Grounded Translingual Disposition (CGTD) as "the negotiation of diverse linguistic resources for situated construction of meaning explicitly *guided by cultural understandings of the world*". Learning to teach involves a complex process of negotiation and construction of meaning, and such negotiation and construction of meaning guided by a cultural understanding of the world became evident when we articulated *Pansori* as lenses.

We acknowledge that words and meanings are not produced in a vacuum. We align with the notion that a critical translingual approach recognizes the power dynamics of language that occurs in those spaces (Zapata 2020). By proposing the notion of culturally grounded translingual dispositions, we foreground the speaker's cultural background as spaces for situated construction of meaning.

## 1.3 The relationship between *Pansori* and culturally grounded translingual disposition

As stated above, our working definition of a culturally grounded translingual disposition is the "negotiation of diverse linguistic resources for situated construction of meaning explicitly *guided by cultural understandings of the world*". Seeing *Pansori* as a pedagogy that could be situated in our experiences within teacher education, empowered us to honor aspects of our experiences that were hard to name, categorize, and communicate. It helped us explore meanings as international scholars that otherwise we would not have been able to capture.

When Abraham learned that *Pansori* singers perform narratives with a unique voice, he started encouraging Sharon to seek in the telling and retelling her own unique voice and that of her students. Furthermore, in the way that *Pansori* singers bring their characters and the audience into conversation, together we started to draw meaning not only from our conversations, but also by listening attentively to Aaron and Jasmine stories. Both *Pansori* and our experiences in teacher education drew from narratives as a meaning-making practice for situated construction of meaning. In this research study, *Pansori* became the lens through which we viewed the stories of Aaron and Jasmine (see Figure 1). In the process of listening to the stories, it served as a framework to ask questions, to attune the sensibilities to students' unique voices, and to elicit unique responses to various situations encountered. Each story is an effort towards becoming a *sorikkun* master. By writing them, we hope the stories told will continue to reverberate with more audiences.

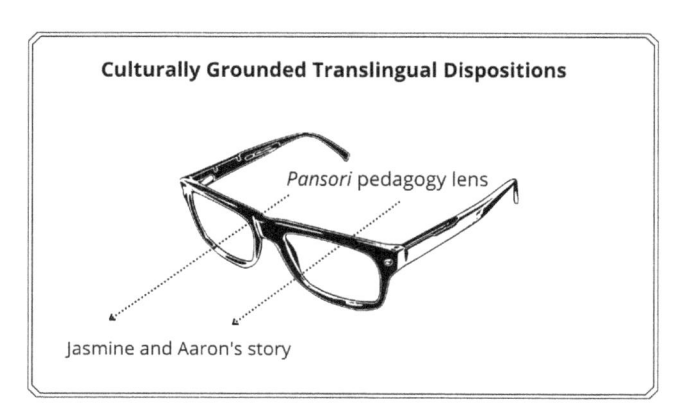

**Figure 1:** Pansori as lenses.

The narratives presented in this study demonstrates how translingual dispositions culturally grounded in the notion of *Pansori* became a site for situated meaning-making processes between a pre-service teacher and professor.

## 1.4 Situating how *Pansori* is used in this study

In this study, Sharon's understanding of the notion of *Pansori* as a meaning making tool in her classroom, opened new possibilities to re-see students. During the study, we constantly asked the question, what does it mean to read and think through Sharon's journals through the lenses of a *Pansori* pedagogy? Each time we read her journals and the stories in it, new perspectives on the students started to emerge. In our initial conversations reflecting about Aaron,[1] we highlighted his struggles. Sharon eventually would come to explore Aaron as a unique voice in her classroom guided by *Pansori* masters' idea that students are unique sounds. In Jasmine's story, a seemingly uneventful occurrence in the classroom led us to talk about inequalities in U.S. classrooms. Jasmine voice became a pathway to listening to the voice of grief in the face of linguistic injustice.

Each narrative is told with expressiveness. In our conversations, it became crucial to read and tell those stories in unique ways. Sharon recalls not only a sequence of events but narrates them with a lyricism that resembles a *Pansori* trainee looking for her own voice in the multitude of sounds of her classroom.

# 2 Developing and enacting culturally grounded dispositions

In 2018, as a pre-service teacher, Sharon took a student internship course along with an English as a Second Language (ESL) course taught by Abraham who was teaching in the Education and Spanish department. The participants of this study were students and teachers who Sharon had observed throughout her practicum in a second grade classroom within a low-income public school located in Grand Rapids, Michigan. Historically, Grand Rapids has a large group of Dutch and German immigrants who are located in the western region of Michigan, and according to the American Community Survey Census Bureau, the racial composition consists of 65% White, 10% Black, and 5% other races in the city. Sharon's school

---

[1] All names included in this chapter, outside of the authors', are pseudonyms.

placement was located on the south side of town where there was a large Hispanic population. In a survey done by the National Center for Education Statistics (Institute of Education Sciences), the school's minority student enrollment at the time of the study was 97%, and 85% of the student population were children of Hispanic immigrants; and about 97% of the students were considered to be economically disadvantaged.

While Sharon was observing, the students did not participate or volunteer to be involved in activities, but rather they would do their normal routine activities that the teacher taught within the classroom and she would take notes on the interactions between them. The teacher was an elderly, white female teacher, who was not bilingual, and had taught at the school for over two decades. In the classroom, there were 27 students within the grade level – 22 of them had a Hispanic background, 4 of them were African American and there was one white student. 14 of the students were designated as English Language Learners (ELL), and 4 of them had special needs. Four of the students had been in the country for less than a year, and struggled with understanding the teacher's directions because of the language barrier. Due to the varying needs of the students, classroom management seemed to be a constant focus in the classroom.

After coming back from the internship placement everyday, Sharon would write reflections where she noted the events, feelings, and conversations that she could recall. Throughout the week, Abraham would provide feedback and comments on a collaborative document, and biweekly we would discuss the feedback he had provided or collaboratively examine new perspectives that unfolded during our discussions. When Sharon retold her experiences, Abraham listened to the stories, provided questions for reflection, and shared his own personal experiences. The discussions were based on narrative inquiry, where we gathered stories and analyzed the written, oral, and visual narratives, and we could hear different narratives that led to profound and sometimes different understandings (Trahar 2009). Together, as narrative researchers, we would "elicit, co-construct, interpret, and in the retelling, represent participant's accounts of lived and imagined personal experiences" (Barkhuizen 2011: 393). This process can be referred to as inquiry based on collaborative sense making and narrative knowledging.

Narrative knowledging occurs when researchers understand that meaning changes over time and attempts to make sense of an experience by continuously interpreting and reinterpreting their narratives. Through this process, we were able to understand the experience more deeply, and may interpret their data differently each time (Barkhuizen 2011). As we interpreted our data together, through narrative knowledging, our translingual disposition orientation helped us approach new ideas, opinions, and topics that spontaneously emerged, with fluidity and respect. Ultimately, all the different conversations, whether they were texts, emojis, images, phone calls, or video conferences, we believe that it helped us shape each other to form new understandings.

One example of narrative knowledge that occurred was when Sharon wrote about an African American student, Jasmine, who was frustrated because of her disheveled hair. In our preliminary discussions, Sharon had mostly depicted her as an upset girl who continued to look for someone who would help her tidy up her hair. She was not able to find or explain anything beyond her temporal emotions and disruptiveness. However, in our discussions, Abraham brought into the discussion the idea of African American hair as a site of struggle and often embrace their natural hair is an act of resistance. Through this type of learning and knowledge construction, Sharon was able to expand her understanding and empathy towards Jasmine. Furthermore, the story about Jasmine and her hair lit up a spark in our conversations and we reflected on the history, politics, and marginalization of students. This kind of collaborative sensemaking led us to discussing how we can make sense of an experience using our cultural knowledge and background, such as *Pansori*. Narrative knowledging was important in these conversations as we recognized our implicit biases, and explored pathways in which minority students can draw from their cultural knowledge as spaces for meaning making.

A central element of *Pansori* is that the artist, over an extended period, discerns the sounds of their surroundings which is in turn performed with music, singing and dancing. This form of storytelling is onomatopoeic. We also realized early on that if we wanted to think about *Pansori* as a pedagogy we did not necessarily need to perform stories with music, rather it was the musicality and sensibility of the *Pansori* artist that could be part of the process of narrative inquiry. The stories presented seek to reflect the surroundings as well as the voice of the storyteller, just as teachers adapt their teaching to the corriente (García, Johnson, and Seltzer 2017) of the classroom.

Translingual practice is a broad meaning-making process engaged in by language users who go beyond the confines of one language and perform their hybrid identities. Instead of focusing on categories of performance and behavior, started to pay attention to other layers of meaning in Sharon's memos and journals. We then analyzed them, avoiding binary classifications of students and realized that there were more nuances to what Sharon had first interpreted. We focused on different aspects of the stories, considered Sharon's discourse and paid attention to other moments, spaces, and silences in order to apply the *Pansori* lens. Even though Sharon and Abraham interpreted and reflected on the narrative data together to "shift understandings as they know, re-know, and un-know the reported experiences (Barkhuizen 2011)" in order to provide a better narrative of *Pansori* and share the process of reflective activity, we will proceed to share the analysis of the learning experiences in first person written and narrated by Sharon.

## 2.1 Listening to stories from the field: Aaron's story

It was another normal day in the second grade classroom, as I (Sharon) went to observe Mrs. Building's classroom. Today, the class was reading the book, *The Bad Seed* (John 2017), and while the teacher was doing a read aloud, I was scribbling down notes as I observed. Most of the memos pointed towards struggling students who were confused or not following the teacher's instructions. One student in particular, Aaron, was another Spanish-speaking English Language Learner in Mrs. Building's second grade classroom who had just immigrated from Ecuador to the United States a year ago and was one of the four students who received support from the school's reading specialist. Since he was frequently pulled out during teacher instruction and also had difficulty understanding English, I had subconsciously labeled him as a struggler or a student who was falling through the cracks. But after coming back from the practicum, Abraham and I reflected upon and discussed the comments that I had written towards Aaron. In this discussion, Abraham asked how we could highlight the students' – including Aaron's – linguistic and cultural resources, while emphasizing the student's identities, and avoiding deficit based analyses. Through the iterative process of re-seeing that happened through collaborative sensemaking, a different picture emerged. Seltzer (2019) describes this process as re-seeing students through a translingual approach. I present below the story of Aaron:

When I first saw Aaron, he smiled shyly. His big, brown eyes sparkled, and his plump round cheeks moved up, showing a big toothless smile. His two front-teeth were missing which made a slight lisp while he talked, but Aaron was quite proud of the fact that they were growing. Most of his friends had lost their incisor teeth and so sometimes Aaron compared his teeth with his friends, wondering why his were growing so slowly. Aaron's missing front teeth made it hard for him to chew and eat food sometimes. He would complain about this. He simply loved food and would tap his pudgy stomach with his hands during Language Arts class, which was right before lunch, and continued to tap his fingers on the table to express his hunger. Like his slow-growing teeth, he walked slowly and dragged his feet everywhere.

Aaron loved drawing. He would draw on his lined white notebook, and after jiggling his pencil in the air, he would get to work. Rather than writing in words to explain his thoughts, he would place himself in his own world of Spiderman, turtles, trains, and jungles. This is how he expressed himself through pictures. When he started drawing, he was concentrated, focused, and entertained. His blue container of colored pencils and Scholastic pens never had a chance to rest, as he always took them out of his table and relentlessly drew shapes and characters that moved inside his head.

The teacher said that Aaron was one of the low-reading level students and that he had a particularly hard time "concentrating when he's hungry," and that he was still "writing at a Kindergarten/First Grade level." I believed her, and in order to improve his writing skills, I would take Aaron and a handful of other low-level students to practice writing and spelling. The five of us, six including me, would trot to the art room across the hall, and Aaron would carry the thin white board markers and mini dry erase boards. We would sit on the carpet and practice simple phonics. I thought to myself, 'They're low-level students, so we should practice the basics.' In the beginning, I had the students practice their spelling quiz vocabulary words. Mostly the words were simple Consonant-Vowel-Consonant words like bat, cat, mop. Sometimes, I threw in some more difficult words like kite, dad, and black and Aaron would write down cit, bab, and drac. Quickly, I realized that Aaron and the other students still struggled with differentiating alphabet sounds, especially b and d, and so I would retrace my steps so that they could practice words with b in them like bad, bob, bee, and then move onto words with d like dim, dot, dip. The process was repetitive and quite frankly, boring. The excitement of writing on whiteboard markers soon wore off, just like how children abandon their brand-new fidget spinners after a couple weeks. In my defense, I had never learned how to teach writing or spelling, and at that time I thought that it was important for Aaron to practice spelling out things by himself first, and then I could model how to write the correct answer later.

One day, for Language Arts period, Mrs. Building called the students to sit down on the carpet in front of the classroom. "We're going to read the book, The Bad Seed," she told them. The students, including Aaron, sat next to each other side by side on the bright, colorful carpet and looked up towards Mrs. Building, as she started reading the story book. "I'm a bad seed." Mrs. Building read aloud. "A baaaaaaaaaaaaaaad seed." Immediately, Aaron started giggling, and his eyes were glued onto the book. Mrs. Building continued, "I'm late to everything . . . ." And she paused for a little bit to show the illustrations of the book to everyone. "I never wash my hands. Or my feet . . . I lie about pointless stuff . . . . I cut in line. Every time." As I continuously watched Aaron, I could see his face light up with delight and glee as Mrs. Building turned the pages over and showed the book around to her second graders.

After Mrs. Building finished the book, when the children had quieted down from laughing, and the students had returned to their seats to do their individual reading, Aaron quietly skipped to the front of the classroom and tapped on Mrs. Building's leg as she was erasing the white-board. He pointed to the Bad Seed book that was awkwardly leaning against the wall, and he asked if he could see the book one more time. Mrs. Building nodded, and Aaron smiled, his shy, but sparkling smile. He stood there, in front of the classroom on the carpet, next to

Mrs. Building, facing his peers, as he flipped through the pictures of the book. After skimming through, he closed the book and looked satisfied, as if he had just finished eating his favorite lunch of hot dogs and French fries. He was happy.

Aaron skipped to the class drawer to take out a white sheet of paper, and dashed back to his table to take out a pencil from his blue container. He jiggled his pencil in the air again and seemed to brainstorm what his picture would look like, similar to how adults write outlines and rough drafts before writing out an essay. Then he got to work. The white paper began to fill up with lines, squares, and sketches. He drew the bad seed, and then another, and two more, until the page was filled with drawings of the bad seed. I asked Aaron, "What did you draw inside the boxes?" and he responded with "it's the bad seed story! Here . . . he cut in line. He's real baaaad. And here . . . he lying." Once he was done with his illustration, he skipped his way to Mrs. Building and presented it to her. When the teacher asked what it was, Aaron said "it's a present for you! About the bad seed. 1st graders can see when they come to 2nd grade." He smiled his shy, toothless smile and dashed away, like a boy scampering away after giving daisies to the girl he likes.

Sharon's story is one told with attention to detail towards Aaron's surroundings and a drastic shift of perspective compared to the initial observations. For instance, Aaron was described beyond his academic duties and behavior within the classroom, and was seen holistically, starting from his favorite food to the way he engaged in writing. Through our interactions, we were able to interpret stories differently and came to appreciate Aaron's ways of expression and the high level of comprehension he showed after reading the story. This aspect of attuning our senses to our surroundings, is one the core elements of *Pansori* storytelling and proved to be fundamental as we interpreted the stories using a *Pansori* framework.

## 2.2 Situated meaning-making through Aaron's story

Using the *Pansori* framework as our theory of narrative, we listened to Aaron's story, analyzed it, and became attuned to Aaron's unique voice that he was singing. Through the *Pansori* lens framework that we enacted, we learned that there were two parts of the training of a *Pansori* master – the first was to copy the master's voice, and afterwards was being let go to seek their own unique voices. The singers generally begin very young as a child and are trained from the master who is usually a family member or neighbor. In this stage, Yi and Kim explain that "they learn the basic techniques of interpretation and performance" (2008: 78), and the novice practices in a way that is extremely similar to the style of their teacher. They are essentially, attempting to imitate the master's sound and movements.

This is where *The Bad Seed* story presents us with a unique character, Aaron, who is labeled as one of the low-reading level students. Aaron goes through the process of repetition of consonants and syllables. In this case, our character and student-teacher, Sharon, fulfilled her duties and described in the narrative that the process was dull, and made very little progress. The student-teacher recognized the importance of working with Aaron on his reading struggles.

Once the initial training is finished under the tutelage of a master singer, then the *sorikkun* can move on to the next part of their training. The next important step in becoming a master is that of *dokkong* (독공) where the student strengthens the sounds they have learned by isolating themselves, physically and emotionally. The trainee would seek out an empty cave on top of a mountain, or next to a waterfall and practice in a secluded environment. Through this practice, they perfect their art and create a unique voice of their own that is different from the master's and other *sorikkun* (Willoughby 2000). This creates a personalized voice – a sound that is distinctly unique.

Aaron was inclined to draw and sketch out his thoughts. At first, it was not evident to Sharon that Aaron's inclination for drawing and sketching could show his comprehension of the lessons. Constantly drawing and sketching was Aaron's own "cave" where he was perfecting his art and crafting his unique voice. Out of those lines, squares, triangles, and spirals emerged a drawing that reflected Aaron's understanding of the reading. When Abraham observed the picture (see Figure 2) he could see plot details, story sequences, and emotions that he captured from the story when he was glued to the book. It was a carefully crafted message.

After the process of collaborative sense making, Sharon began to see that a *Pansori* pedagogy would, in place of differentiated instruction, *let students go* to perfect their own unique voice.

## 2.3 Listening to stories from the field: Jasmine's story

We consider our process of learning to narrate through the *Pansori* lens as ongoing. Soon after we reflected about Aaron, there was another incident that happened at the elementary school that Abraham and I discussed in great lengths. Only four of the students in Mrs. Building's classroom were African American, but Jasmine was the only black girl in the class. When Sharon first started observing the black students, all four of them were perceived as rude by Mrs. Building. Perry-Campbell (2020) explains that black students are usually perceived as 3D – disruptive, defiant, and disrespectful by the teacher. Sharon was able to account

**Figure 2:** Aaron's drawing of the bad seed.

for the same 3D aspects in Jasmine's story as well. Often during instructional time, Mrs. Building would reprimand the student's behavior or attempt to control how loud or often they talked. Jasmine's story taught us to look beyond instructional processes of the classroom and reflect on the cultural biases we have towards students who do not share the same cultural backgrounds as us. It also challenged us to connect to another element of *Pansori: Han* (한). This notion highlights the collective grieving of a community, particularly of those who have suffered through severe trauma and brutality, such as slavery, encampment, or colonization. Similar to Aaron's story, below is another narrative that we have retold and actively reconstructed as a sense-making activity:

    One Thursday morning, Jasmine started pouting and not paying attention to the teacher. 'Typical,' I thought to myself, and stopped paying attention to her. Mrs. Building was in the middle of explaining the difference between nouns and pronouns. Jasmine asked, "Ain't my hair weird? Can't you tie it up again?" Mrs.

Building walked to Jasmine and scanned her hair, and she said "It looks fine Jasmine, don't fiddle with your hair during class".

Jasmine sulked and faced her head towards the table, but then she looked around and caught me staring at her hair. She sheepishly raised her hand again while looking at me and asked "Miss, can yah tie my hair up again?" I looked at Jasmine hesitantly and told her, "I can try, I guess". So I stood behind her and examined what the problem was. A braid strand had come undone, so my mission was to braid her hair, then tie it up in a knot, and then put the bead back into place. For me, this was the equivalent of playing the HaeGeum, a Korean fiddle with two silk strings and a bow. I knew in theory that you had to tighten the strings, and pull the bow along the strings to play, but not how to make a beautiful sound. Similarly, I knew the theory behind braiding hair, but had never done it in practice. I attempted to braid her hair, but it was so tightly coiled that it was impossible for me to part the hair strands. I told Jasmine, "I'm sorry, I don't think I can do it. And like Mrs. Building said, you shouldn't play with your hair during class," and I left her to continue her work. I sometimes wonder if I was maybe unconsciously punishing her previous bad behavior by not trying any further, I'm not sure. But I had left Jasmine by herself, knowing that she would pout and sulk with her head bowing on top of the table. I assume she probably felt uncared for, abandoned, and ignored, because two of the teachers in the classroom didn't care about something that was extremely important for her.

Jasmine's pouting continued until it was time to go outside for recess. The bell rang, and Jasmine wore her jacket and walked outside of the school building. In the corner of her eye she saw the school's vice principal strolling around the classrooms, so she ran to the vice principal. Mrs. VP, who is also African American, looked at Jasmine's obviously grouchy face. She walked towards her, and bent her knees. When she was almost eye-level with Jasmine, she asked gently "Why are you in a bad mood, honey?" The miserable little girl explained that her braids got undone and that she was sad because it made her look ugly. Mrs. VP listened to her carefully, and very empathetically. She nodded her head whenever Jasmine finished her sentence, and wiped away the child's tears. In the hallway, there were 5th grade boys running around with basketballs, teachers chatting to one another, shoes tapping, doors squeaking, and tiny Kindergarteners crying, but at that moment, to Jasmine, all that she could hear was Mrs. VP's soft and soothing voice, and the comforting words of "it'll be okay". With a warm smile, Mrs. VP talked about how she also spent hours and hours trying to make her hair look nice in the morning, and that she also feels bad when her naturally curly Afro hair doesn't look like how she wants it to. "Come here," Mrs. VP said as she motioned Jasmine to come closer, and opened up her arms to give Jasmine a big hug. Mrs. VP stood up, "turn around and let's see if I can fix your hair," and with a quick magical touch, she had braided the bead back on the hair.

The short meeting with Mrs. VP and Jasmine was a normal life encounter, but it was also something uniquely special soaked within the same old thing, like a great song, like a fluffy Christmas sweater, or a cold tangerine on a hot day. It was just a normal day, but something bigger happened to Jasmine, and to me as well.

As the story is introduced, it becomes evident that Jasmine did not feel understood or heard when both Mrs. Building and Sharon did not recognize her frustrations. Jasmine's unique voice was in disharmony with her surroundings. This could have been because neither of them had a strong supportive relationship with Jasmine nor did they understand the significance of hair in black culture, but it took a kindred spirit, Mrs. VP, who acknowledged Jasmine's emotions and shared her own story of experiencing the same difficulties for Jasmine's unique voice to be protected. There was a connection, or a call and response, between Mrs. VP where *chuimsae* took place between the two. In contrast, Sharon had journaled about Jasmine's actions in terms of disruptive behavior. For example, in one section of the journal Jasmine's cry is described as "pouting unnecessarily". The collaborative sense-making discussions prevented us from perceiving Jasmine's behavior as disrespectful, defiant, and disruptive and to challenge "perceived stereotypes, implicit bias, color blindness, and lack of cultural competency" (Perry-Campbell 2020: 6).

## 2.4 Situated meaning making of Jasmine's story

Similar to Aaron's story, we again used the *Pansori* lens framework for Jasmine's story to reevaluate and become attuned to the unique voice that Jasmine had to offer. Yi and Kim (2008) explain that in *Pansori*, the text cannot merely be emotionlessly recited, particularly because there are variations of rhythm and beats that are improvised to express the character's tension or relaxation. In order to fully comprehend this rhythm, the *sorikkun* needs to experience, feel, and then express it as if it were the performer's own life story they were relating. The *sorikkun* or the master singer internalizes the story's deeper meaning and explains the trials and joys of the character through music. If the *Pansori* singer can truly and effectively communicate the character's feelings, and construct a dramatic effect, then the audience will respond to the performance and actively participate. The audience would make exclamations like *Eolsigu! Jalhanda!* which can be translated as Yippee! Good job! This *chuimsae* (추임새), or call and response participation of the audience, connects the story to the musicians and audience (Wie 2020).

Upon closely examining the events, Jasmine's story opened a conversation regarding how schools, companies, and jobs require straight hair from black students and employees, where they are forced to adhere to white beauty standards, or they risk being deemed unprofessional. Furthermore, along with depicting black culture negatively, often African American Vernacular English (AAVE) is viewed as linguistically and intellectually inferior to what White Mainstream English students speak. Smitherman (2006: 6) argues that this "standard English" which is usually spoken by the white, male, and upper middle-class, is accepted as the standard because it derives from the dominant race, class, and gender in U.S. society. This linguistic racism is experienced by most African Americans in school, which leads to black students who train themselves to see their language, identity and culture "through a white gaze that negates their value, sense of self, and worth" (Baker-Bell 2020: 25). Through these discussions, Sharon realized that she was not able to give back adequate *chuimsae* to Jasmine, and also could not fully relate or understand the context and background of what Jasmine was experiencing.

As we discussed about these racial inequalities that occur in schools and in society, we also recognized that this came in the context of the painful struggles of African Americans and the history of American slavery. By connecting this to a *Pansori* pedagogy we acknowledged the importance of expressing emotions of grief and frustration in the face of injustice.

*Pansori* played an important healing function in Korea. *Pansori* is known as the "sound of Han" (Willoughby 2000) and these musical stories express the character's feelings of sorrow, resentment, anger, and suffering that is collectively shared among the Korean people. Through traditional songs or performances, Koreans expressed their shared experiences of suffering that they felt together as a country – during the Japanese occupation, enslavement, war, oppression, and the division of the country. Though each *Pansori* tells a different story, they share similar themes of struggle, tragedy, and hardship that the *sorikkum* performs. Although a difficult notion to translate, *han* rage is an inherent part of being Korean and is often defined as accumulated and unresolved resentment or anger against injustice. The term *han* originates from two different Chinese characters conveying pity and regret, and one denotes the mind and the other the state of limitation. It has been recognized that *han*, similar to trauma, suffers from its delayed manifestation which results in its transgenerational quality (Wie 2020). People say that some die because of *han*, what doctors refer to as *Hwabyong* (화병), or anger illness (Boman 2020). However, despite the sense of bitterness, the *sorikkun* also makes sure to include a sense of hope and a communal sense of resilience towards the end of the performance.

As we dug deeper into the concept of *Pansori* to express deep sadness of oppression and injustice, we also discussed how jazz and the blues were developed under similar circumstances. The work songs that the slaves would sing, would help them keep their pace as they worked in the fields, and "expressed a yearning for a better life . . . named the slave owner's deceit and hypocrisy . . . and emphasized the slave's hope for freedom and the future" (Crosby 2014). Like *Pansori*, the work songs brought up deep feelings of distress for people who did not have a voice, and this later turned into a jazz movement that expressed black people's emotional reaction to oppression. As the journalist Volle suggests "an entire genre of American music arguably coalesced around the notion [of *han*]: the Blues, sung by African-Americans in the Deep South" (2015).

Considering Jasmine's story through a *Pansori* lens, the grief in the face of injustice experienced by African Americans reverberated in that pouting and frustration. Our conversations helped us recognize that hairstyle was not just an isolated experience or issue that was unique to Jasmine but needed to be understood under a wider context of systemic racism. We also recognized the necessity of an Antiracist Black Language Pedagogy (Baker-Bell 2020) that gives space to students for examining how language, race, white supremacy, and anti-blackness intersect with each other. One way to do this is for teachers to embrace a critical translingual approach that is centered around transformative language learning – studies that center around learning the literary traditions of minoritized communities and challenge epistemological racism. Teachers can also counter monolingual norms in classrooms by providing multimodal texts written by culturally and linguistically diverse writers where their understandings about language, identity, and power are articulated (de los Ríos, Seltzer, and Molina 2021). By designing curriculum and instruction that are related to observing power, privilege, and diversity, teachers can assist with dismantling linguistic racism.

Through the culturally grounded translingual framework, such as the *sorikun's chuimsae*, or the overwhelming sense of *Han*, we were engaging in critical conversations that advocated towards linguistic and racial justice. Through these discussions with Abraham, Sharon was able to shift her perspective of Jasmine; Jasmine's tears of frustration were perceived differently – Jasmine was singing out her emotions to Mrs. VP, and like Ella Fitzgerald, or the countless *sorikkun*, expressing her deep frustrations and sorrow through beautiful and powerful music.

## 3 Implications for translanguaging

Sharon's enactment of a culturally grounded translingual disposition (CGTD) created spaces for translanguaging pedagogy. According to García and Kleifgen (2018: 61), the starting point of translanguaging is "not the named languages of nation-states, but the linguistic system of words, sounds, constructions, and so forth that make bilinguals speakers' vibrant linguistic repertoires continuously shaped by social interactions". Without dismissing named teacher education frameworks such as those provided by the National Council of Teachers of English (NCTE) and Michigan ESL standards, our pedagogical approach of CGTD shows that, we as teachers informed by cultural ways of knowing can attune to students' needs and be attentive to the students' linguistic repertoires. By using *Pansori* as a frame of reference and meaning-making tool, we were able to re-see and rethink the stories portrayed in Sharon's journals which in turn enabled us to articulate our cultural ways of knowing in the context of our intellectual endeavors.

As García, Johnson, and Seltzer (2017) explain, out of the three strands of the translanguaging classroom, a translanguaging stance operates with the firm belief that teachers need to leverage the entire linguistic repertoire of students. We believe that we were able to enact this through the process of collaborative meaning-making of our *Pansori* stories, as we reflected and rethought our way of what language teaching was, and also searched for our own voice as a teacher and teacher educator allowing our cultural backgrounds to be a source of meaning.

Another important element of translanguaging is its design (García, Johnson, and Seltzer 2017). The design intentionally connects the student's home language practices to the school setting, so that teachers can ensure that students are not marginalized by the school practices. Our *Pansori* pedagogy gave us the opportunity to re-see our surroundings and listen intently to students' multilingual discourses, so that we can detect school practices that further marginalize students. For example, in Aaron's assessment of the *Bad Seed*, we recognized the need to provide assessments that differentiate between the general linguistic performances from their language specific performances. In initial discussions, Aaron was portrayed as a child who could not differentiate between *b* and *d*, who was not capable of writing at the normal second-grade level, and was at an even lower reading-level. However, after using the *Pansori* lenses, Aaron emerged as a highly attentive, and inquisitive minded student who fully enjoyed stories and could demonstrate his nuanced understandings. This evidence emerged once Aaron was able to create his own project and from a translanguaging perspective, we were able to see Aaron's full repertoire of capabilities and ways to make meaning.

Through our conversations we also observed that a translanguaging shift had occurred, though it didn't happen abruptly. It was the result of our efforts to keep meaning-making and learning at the center of our focus, and to go with the flow of the *corriente* (García and Seltzer 2016: 23) that was generated when we brought culturally translingual dispositions to the table. The more we explored our ways of knowing, the wider and stronger that *corriente* became. Using culturally meaningful metaphors to interpret new experiences allowed us to break through new ideas even during moments of communication breakdown.

# 4 Implications for teacher education

Student teachers from diverse cultural backgrounds (i.e. international, heritage, minority cultures, etc.) can make contributions to our knowledge base for teacher education. This project aims at exploring a pathway to create dialogue between students' knowledge and the knowledge base of teacher educators. In this case, Sharon's conceptualization of *Pansori* was a familiar space that provided concepts and constructs that facilitated the process of meaning making in her practicum site.

This research project illustrated a roadmap of how such dialogue between different epistemological vantage points may happen. In such dialogue, both Sharon and Abraham negotiated educational meanings. For instance, when Sharon explained the process of preparing *Pansori* masters, Abraham identified similarities with learning to teach that resonated with his experience in the US. At the same time, Abraham's understanding in learning to teach was expanded by considering key ideas such as listening intently and allowing students' unique voices to flourish.

Such dialogue has the potential to open up multiple venues of meaning making even for students who might feel they have to hide their own cultural assets in their clinical practice learning to teach. In 1903, the African American civil rights activist, W.E.B. Du Bois in *The Souls of Black Folk*, introduces the concept of double consciousness as the struggle that African Americans face to remain true to black culture, while at the same time attempting to conform to the dominant white society. Often, students from diverse cultural backgrounds develop a similar double consciousness to fit the culture and language in which they are developing their profession, and switch back and forth. Our research demonstrated a way forward for disrupting such a divided mind and modeled a way to inform learning to teach. We observed that by learning to listen intently for the uniqueness of students' voices, teachers may find new spaces for meaning making. The process of connecting

*Pansori* to learning to teach, exemplifies ways that prospective teachers from diverse and minority backgrounds can use culturally grounded tools to negotiate meaning in practice and placements. Processes of articulation, open up welcoming intellectual spaces in which students can bring their own cultural understandings.

# 5 Conclusion

This research project started in 2018 with Abraham and Sharon discussing the reflections that Sharon had written during the practicum of her sophomore year in college. By 2022, Sharon had graduated college, worked as an ESL and Title I teacher, and faced the challenges of the covid pandemic as a novice teacher. Throughout the five years of conversations we had together, we were able to recognize the biased attitudes as well as deficitarian perspectives of ourselves as educators. Together, we challenged these ingrained beliefs by navigating our linguistic and cultural identities as minority educators and building ideas regarding *Pansori* that created the backbone of culturally grounded translingual dispositions (CGTD). As Barkhuizen (2011: 393) put it: "In the process of constructing narratives, narrators make sense of their lived experience; they understand it, give it coherence, make connections, and unravel its complexity." Through understanding the notion of *Pansori* and using it as a meaning making tool, we opened new possibilities of empathizing and re-seeing students.

Chul Ho Kim, director general of the National Center for Korean Traditional Performing arts, cited in Yi and Kim (2008: 54), phrased his insights of *Pansori* that deeply resonated with us, ". . . the student must develop, on top of what the teacher has taught, his or her own artistry, which cannot be imitated by anyone else in the world. Each singer is like a container which will hold its own creative sound". A *Pansori* pedagogy allowed us to search for our voices, and that of the students we worked with.

Our intention in this study is not to prescribe a fit-all solution, and we certainly do not claim to have completely understood everything there is to know about our own unique voices. However, we believe that we discovered a path forward in that direction, and that our *Pansori* framework has provided a glimpse into how CGTD can foster cultural creativity, and model how to pursue justice within academia. We hope that our journey will help educators embark on their own unique journey of embracing their cultural identities, and mining their own culturally grounded translingual dispositions by connecting them to their pedagogies – particularly those educators whose positionality as foreigners might give them the illusion that one must simply adapt to the dominant culture.

# References

Baker-Bell, April. 2020. *Linguistic Justice: Black Language, Literacy, Identity, and Pedagogy*. New York: Routledge, Taylor & Francis Group.

Barkhuizen, Gary. 2011. Narrative knowledging in TESOL. *TESOL Quarterly* 45(3). 391–414.

Boman, Bjorn. 2020. From oldboy to burning: Han in South Korean films. *Culture & Psychology* 26(4). 919–932.

Canagarajah, A. Suresh. 2013. *Literacy as Translingual Practice. Between Communities and Classrooms*. [electronic resource]. New York: Routledge.

Crosby, Pamela. 2014. "Part of history, African-American spirituals still heal." The People of The United Methodist Church. https://www.umc.org/en/content/part-of-history-african-american-spirituals-still-heal.

de los Ríos, Cati V, Kate Seltzer & Arturo Molina. 2021. 'Juntos somos fuertes': Writing participatory corridos of solidarity through a critical translingual approach. *Applied Linguistics* 42(6). 1070–1082.

García, Ofelia, Susana Ibarra Johnson & Kate Seltzer. 2017. *The Translanguaging Classroom Leveraging Student Bilingualism for Learning*. Philadelphia: Caslon.

García, Ofelia & Joanne Kleifgen. 2018. *Educating Emergent Bilinguals; Policies, Programs and Practices for English Learners*. New York: Teachers College Press.

García, Ofelia & Kate Seltzer. 2016. The translanguaging current in language education. In Björn Kindenberg (ed.), *Flerspråkighet Som Resurs*, 19–30. (Multilingualism as a resource 31). Stockholm: Liber.

Institute of Education Sciences. (n.d.). Search for Public School Districts: Grand Rapids Public School. National Center for Education Statistics (NCES).

John, Jory. 2017. *The Bad Seed*. New York: HarperCollins.

Kang, Bomi. 2016. *Pansori*. Las Vegas: UNLV Theses, Dissertations, Professional Papers, and Capstones.

Lee, Eunjeong & Suresh Canagarajah. 2019. The connections between transcultural dispositions and translingual practices in academic writing. *Journal of Multicultural Discourses* 14(1). 14–28. https://doi.org/10.1080/17447143.2018.1501375.

Lee, Jerry Won & Christopher Jenks. 2016. Doing translingual dispositions. *College Communication and Composition* 86(2). 317–344.

Perry-Campbell, Janeen. 2020. *Black girls in 3D disruptive, defiant, and disrespectful: Case studies of culturally responsive and sustaining classroom management practices in an urban middle school*. Norfolk: Old Dominion University Dissertation.

Seltzer, Kate. 2019. Reconceptualizing "home" and "school" language: Taking a critical translingual approach in the English classroom. *TESOL Quarterly* 53(4). 986–1007.

Smitherman, G. 2006. *Word from the Mother: Language and African Americans*. New York: Routledge.

Trahar, Sheila. 2009. Beyond the story itself: Narrative inquiry and autoethnography in intercultural research in higher education. *Forum Qualitative Sozialforschung / Forum: Qualitative Social Research* 10(1). https://doi.org/10.17169/fqs-10.1.1218.

Volle, Adam. 2015. "Behind the myth: Is "Han" uniquely Korean?" https://gwangjunewsgic.com/arts-culture/korean-myths/behind-the-myth-is-han-uniquely-korean/ (last modified 02 April 2021).

Wang, Xiqiao. 2017. Developing translingual disposition through a writing theory cartoon assignment. *Journal of Basic Writing* 36(1). 56–86.

Wie, Jungyoon. 2020. *Han: Otherness and syncretism*. Ann Arbor: University of Michigan dissertation.

Willoughby, Heather. 2000. The sound of Han: P'ansori, timbre and a Korean ethos of pain and suffering. *Yearbook for Traditional Music* 32. 17–30.

Yi, Yongsik & Kyunghee Kim. 2008. Theory of Pansori. Chapter in *Pansori* (Ser. Korean musicology series, 2). *The National Center for Korean Traditional Performing Arts*.

Zapata, Angie. 2020. Cultivating a critical translingual landscape in the elementary language arts classroom. *Language Arts* 97(6). 384–389

Zheng, Xuan. 2017. Translingual identity as pedagogy: International teaching assistants of English in college composition classrooms. *The Modern Language Journal* 101(17). 29–44.

Kathryn I. Henderson, Christian Fallas-Escobar, and Kristen Lindahl
# Chapter 3
# Learning from Latinx pre-service teachers' understandings of their linguistic repertoires

**Abstract:** This chapter presents what we learned from Latinx pre-service teachers' (PSTs) understandings of their linguistic repertoires as depicted through language portraits. Drawing on the concept of the *translanguaging stance* or an educator's way of being that views students' families and communities as holders of knowledge and the classroom as a democratic space to work towards social justice, we demonstrate what we learned from Latinx PSTs language portraits (N = 80) with respect to the disinvention and reconfiguration of languages and the connections between language, the body, emotions, and linguistic identities. The findings we report in this chapter contribute to the burgeoning research on the use of translanguaging in higher education by demonstrating that (a) Latinx PSTs' bodily-emotional lived experience of language may lead them to disinvent named languages and reconstitute language practices in ways that reflect complex and nuanced translanguaging stances, and that (b) understanding translanguaging stance as an ever-changing and context-bound disposition that can shift through time and space has implications for teacher education.

## Introduction

This chapter presents a study based on the premise that preparing pre-service teachers (PSTs) to leverage learners' diverse language practices as a resource (translanguaging pedagogy) implies inviting them to embrace a *translanguaging stance*. We draw on García, Johnson, and Seltzer's (2017) definition of *translanguaging stance* as an educator's way of being that views students' families and communities as holders of information for the co-construction of knowledge and frames the classroom as a democratic space for collaborative work towards social justice. However, we expand this definition to include PSTs, since the successful implementation of a translanguaging pedagogy also depends on PST's dispositions to view their own and others' linguistic repertoires in expansive

**Kathryn I. Henderson, Christian Fallas-Escobar, Kristen Lindahl,** The University of Texas at San Antonio

https://doi.org/10.1515/9783110735604-004

ways. We surmise that fostering the development of a translanguaging stance necessitates that both PSTs and teacher educators first look inwards and develop an awareness of their own linguistic repertoires and the ways their lived experience of language impacts their language practices. Furthermore, teachers must be open and responsive to students' understandings of language and language practices. We argue that this introspection helps center a translanguaging stance in the PST preparation classroom.

In this chapter we focus on Latinx PSTs' (N = 80) reflections on their own language practices, their language learning history, and their emotional responses to different linguistic contexts via the creation of language portraits during their coursework (Coffey 2015). We chose to focus this chapter on the linguistic repertoires of Latinx PSTs because of the historical and institutional deficit framing of their dynamic language practices (May 2014). As demonstrated throughout this chapter, the students in our study identified linguistically in complex ways beyond the binary of monolingual/bilingual. The purpose of having PSTs engage in the creation of their own language portrait was to invoke their awareness of and perspectives towards the diversity and heterogeneity of their language repertoires, which we connect directly to a translanguaging stance. Our central guiding research questions were: (a) How do Latinx pre-service teachers make sense of their linguistic repertoires? and (b) How do Latinx pre-service teachers' explanations of their linguistic repertoires reflect or contribute to a translanguaging stance?

We present the findings divided into two sections: a summary of results across our 80 participants, and a selection of three portraits to provide insight into the ways Latinx pre-service teachers made sense of their linguistic repertoires. The findings we report in this chapter contribute to the burgeoning body of research on the use of translanguaging in higher education by demonstrating that (a) Latinx PSTs' portray their language practices in ways that reflect complex and nuanced translanguaging stances, and that (b) understanding translanguaging stance as an ever-changing and context-bound disposition that can shift through time and space has implications for teacher education.

# 1 Translanguaging in teacher preparation

In the context of teacher preparation, researchers have advocated for a translanguaging perspective. Musanti, Cavazos, and Rodríguez (2020) advocated for embracing a translanguaging stance in a border town university in Texas, calling for bilingual teacher education programs that prepare Latinx bilingual PSTs to work toward cultivating their translingual dispositions. As they argue, by tapping into these PSTs' entire linguistic repertoires, bilingual teacher educators can guide them to develop openness to linguistic diversity and the disposition to view their bilingual learners' language practices as assets. To do this, they explain, bilingual teacher educators should purposefully design linguistically dynamic learning spaces while also enacting translanguaging practices themselves, a position also expressed by Fallas-Escobar and Treviño (2021) in their study of two Latina PSTs' perceptions of language choice options in the teacher preparation classroom. Fallas-Escobar and Treviño argue that it is important that bilingual teacher educators be mindful of their language choices, since these may be interpreted by teacher candidates as de facto language policy and shape their future teaching practices.

As has been documented by other scholars, enacting translanguaging within teacher preparation is also central because it increases PSTs' confidence in their Spanish and their sense of advocacy for bilingual learners (Collins, Sánchez, and España 2019); a much-needed step forward in disrupting institutionally hegemonic monolingual notions of language and literacy (Murillo 2017). Still, more research is needed that centers the already complex and nuanced ideological stances to language diversity and dynamic bilingualism that PSTs may have already developed from their lived experiences using their linguistic resources across social and institutional spaces. We argue in this chapter that research that centers PSTs' rich community experiences, skills and knowledges can further expand our own translanguaging stances as teacher educators and help us imagine ways to counter ideologies of language as bounded, enumerable and separate systems (Makoni and Pennycook 2007) that still marginalize Latinx bilingual learners in US schools (Rosa 2019; Rosa and Flores 2017).

## 2 Translanguaging stance, linguistic repertoires, and disinventing languages

Following García, Johnson, and Seltzer (2017), we understand translanguaging pedagogy as teachers' attention to students' dynamic bilingualism and their intentional efforts to adjust their teaching and assessment practices to build upon what students can do with their linguistic repertoires. A translanguaging stance is a critical aspect of translanguaging pedagogy which is comprised of three collaborative *"juntos"* (joint) beliefs (: a) students bring linguistic and cultural practices from their homes and communities to school, which work *juntos* in student meaning making; b) students bring knowledge from their homes and communities that is valuable for instruction and curriculum; and c) classrooms are spaces for teachers and students to co-construct knowledge and actively work *juntos* for a more just society (García, Johnson, and Seltzer 2017). This framework proved useful, as it served as a reminder that we should see the communities we work with as sites of knowledge creation, rather than simply objects of study (Avineri and Martinez 2021). The framework simultaneously reminded us to be mindful of our own translanguaging stances as we examined the stances that our PSTs brought with them.

In an effort to embody a translanguaging stance ourselves while guiding our PSTs to further develop their own, we asked them to draw their linguistic repertoires as language portraits (described below in the methods section). As described by Busch (2017: 4), language portraits are tools for "gaining insight into everyday linguistic practices of bodily and emotional language experience, or of ideologically informed ideas about, of attitudes to, and of stance taking towards particular languages or modes of speaking". Busch's definition adds an additional lens by bringing our attention to the ways PSTs' bodily-emotional lived experience of language can shape their stance toward their own and others' linguistic repertoires. Indeed, we believe that a translanguaging stance is non-static and shifts with exposure to new PSTs, new experiences and language practices, and critical reflection. This aligns with the findings from Menken and Sánchez's (2019) study exploring how the implementation of translanguaging pedagogy led to shifts in educators' translanguaging stances. In this way, educators actively enhancing a translanguaging stance can be conceived of as engaging in what we term *forward stancing*. By transforming stance into a verb, we hope to underscore the dynamic and ever-changing nature of the stances we hold and the ways these are contingent upon the spaces we occupy, the individuals with whom we interact, and our bodily-emotional lived experiences of language (Busch 2017).

In this chapter, we are particularly concerned with the ways PSTs understand language as a practice that is socially constructed rather than a decontextualized object. This view on language is an integral component of critical language awareness (Alim 2010; García 2009, 2017; Martínez 2003), which we view as conceptually compatible with and a necessary part of developing and exercising a translanguaging stance. Makoni and Pennycook (2007) argue that critical awareness starts with acknowledging that named languages are inventions historically used as a device for colonial projects. Seltzer (2019), drawing on the work of Makoni and Pennycook, explains, "in acknowledging the "inventedness" of named languages, we can also "disinvent" related constructs that elevate certain language practices and speakers and marginalize others." Our data demonstrates that, contrary to beliefs we may hold as teacher educators, PSTs are not always entirely bound by circulating ideologies (Stroud and Kerfoot 2020). Instead, they often hold views that defy ideologies of language as bounded, separable, enumerable systems (García and Li Wei 2014; Makoni and Pennycook 2007). We share what we learned from these PSTs' language portraits and consider possible implications for teacher preparation to continue disrupting deficit linguistic perspectives.

## 3 Methodology

This multimodal qualitative study (Busch 2017; Coffey 2015) was guided by the research questions: (a) How do Latinx pre-service teachers make sense of their linguistic repertoires? (b) How do Latinx pre-service teachers' explanations of their linguistic repertoires reflect or contribute to a translanguaging stance?

### 3.1 Research context and participants

This study was conducted at a large public university in Southwest Texas, serving a large Hispanic student population (nearly 60%). Participants in our study included PSTs in different educational tracks (i.e. generalist, bilingual education, English as a second language) in two large ESL methods courses at this Hispanic serving institution. The larger study included PSTs who self-identified in multiple ways including white and African American. However, in this chapter we present data from PSTs who we broadly categorized as Latinx and identified with cultural or linguistic practices associated with the named language Spanish (N = 80). PSTs self-identified culturally and linguistically in many ways including as Mexican, Mexican-American, Tex-Mex, Guatemalan, Texas Hispanic, native Spanish speaker, Latina, Latinx, and Spanish heritage speaker. We focus on these PSTs to center the experiences of students of historically marginalized, minoritized, and/or stigmatized language practices. Furthermore, we chose the umbrella term Latinx to refer to our participants because it is a non-binary gender category and because one of our PSTs, Irene, explicitly connected Latinx with social justice, and we embrace this meaning.

### 3.2 Data collection and analysis

The data in this chapter come from a larger project exploring linguistically responsive instruction (Lucas and Villegas 2013) in teacher preparation (Lindahl, Fallas-Escobar, and Henderson 2021). As part of this pedagogical approach, students were asked to create a language portrait (Coffey 2015). During the weeks leading up to completing the language portrait students were introduced to the concept of linguistic repertoire (Busch 2017), translanguaging (García, Johnson, and Seltzer 2017), language as practice (Makoni and Pennycook 2007; Pennycook 2010) and critical perspectives on academic language (MacSwan 2020; Flores 2020) via direct instruction, course readings, and discussion.

The language portrait activity took place during a face-to-face class and students were asked to bring markers, colored pencils, crayons, or any other writing utensil to create their portrait. The professors also provided markers and crayons at the front of the classroom and students were encouraged to share. At the start of the lesson, students were asked to discuss with a partner, "What is language?" Following this interaction, the professors engaged in direct instruction on the perspective of language as practice (Pennycook 2010). Students were then asked to think, write, pair, and share their response to the nuanced question, "What language practices do you engage in across different spaces with different people." Following these interactions, the teacher introduced the language portrait activity. Students were asked to draw their linguistic repertoires (Coffey 2015) and to reflect on their own language practices and language learning history calling into mind the people, places, and emotions associated with different language practices. They were told to create a language repertoire portrait with a written explanation of the drawing and key to what the colors represent. The teacher modeled thinking about what to draw (i.e. I'm thinking about how I speak to my children in both English and Spanish and I want to represent that in my portrait) and how one could start the drawing. The teachers encouraged creativity and told students the language portrait could be anything they wanted including a symbol instead of a body. They shared their portrait with the class and submitting it at the end of class was optional.

The resulting data were analyzed multimodally and thematically to identify patterns across language portraits (Coffey 2015; Saldaña 2015). Multimodal analysis included consideration of facial and bodily expressions on PSTs' drawings (i.e. smiling face or position of arms), symbols (i.e. heart, brain, flag), and colors. Thematic analysis connected text (written discourse) to the multimodal analysis considering, for example, how emotions (i.e. sadness and anger) were represented in the portraits figuratively (i.e. sad face) and in writing (i.e. student wrote blue means sad). Another example is how PSTs depicted language identity symbolically (i.e. the heart is red and represents Spanish) and in writing (i.e. a student wrote "Spanish represents my whole heart because my family is from Mexico). The analytic process was inductive, collaborative, and iterative; researchers were open to diverse meanings present in the data during the coding process, discussed codes, and re-visited the data multiple times (Saldaña 2015).

During our first phase of coding (inductive coding), we read PSTs' language portraits and used in vivo, emotion, versus, and value coding to dissect data line by line. Our unit of analysis consisted of utterances (single words, phrases, sentences) or images embedded in PSTs' depictions, and which indexed PSTS' critical language awareness, emotional responses to their linguistic repertoires and language practices, and/or stances toward the heterogeneity of language. During our second phase of coding, initial codes (e.g., TexMex, Spanglish, slang, Mexico versus the US, school versus home, interlocutor, etc) were subject to axial coding for interrelatedness and formation of larger themes (e.g., nuanced understanding of place, context and interlocutor). At this stage, we drew on the concepts of translanguaging and linguistic repertoires, which in turn allowed us to identify the larger themes present across PSTs' language repertoires (e.g., disinventing and reconfiguring language). Once we felt our coding scheme was solid, we coded all language repertoires again (deductive coding). Our analysis was inevitably shaped by our cultural, linguistic and ethnoracial identities. All three authors identify as Spanish-English bilinguals, however Author 1 is an initially English dominant white speaker, Author 2 is an initially Spanish dominant Latino speaker and Author 3 is a heritage speaker of mixed ethnicity. Our diverse linguistic backgrounds were a strength for understanding and learning from our students' language portraits.

# 4 Learning across pre-service teachers' linguistic repertoires

The language portrait activity afforded a space for PSTs to consider and explore their language practices and identities through colors, symbols, metaphors and connections to the body. This section addresses two ways in which the activity made evident how our PSTs already exercised a heteroglossic, practice-oriented stance to their own and other linguistic repertoires: a) through disinventing languages; and b) by showing an awareness of the complex ways language, the body, emotions, and identity are intricately interconnected. Table 1 below shows a summary of the findings discussed in each section.

## 4.1 Disinventing and reconfiguring languages

Analysis of language portraits shed light on the various ways PSTs understood their linguistic repertoires, including their identification of linguistic variation and how language practices are socially constructed and context dependent.

**Table 1:** Findings Summary Table.

| Theme | Summary | Sub-themes |
|---|---|---|
| Disinventing and reconfiguring languages | PSTs depicted language and language variation in ways that disinvented and reconfigured languages and demonstrated how language practices are socially constructed and context dependent | – Language varieties as part of a student's language repertoire<br>– Awareness of how language changes by time, place, and interolucter<br>– Pushing language boundaries |
| Connecting language, body, and emotions | PSTs demonstrated the connection between language, the body, and emotion and how this connects to their identities and developing identities. | – Linguistic shame, insecurity, violence and discrimination<br>– Social justice orientation<br>– Embracing cultural and linguistic identity |

Across language portraits, students identified varieties of Spanishes and Englishes as part of their linguistic repertoire. Of the 80 participants 14 identified Spanglish, 11 identified Tex-Mex, 10 identified Mixed or both, and 8 identified slang as a language in their color key. Only 4 out of 80 participants used the label bilingual including lexemes like bilingualism and bilingual education in any part of the portrait. PSTs' identification of these language varieties – and reconceptualized linguistic practices (i.e. "Mixed") – as languages in and of themselves elevated their status and role alongside standardized and powerful named practices such as English and Spanish (Alim 2010; García 2009, 2017; Martínez 2003). In doing so, PSTs demonstrated their agency to reconfigure hegemonic language ideologies (Stroud and Kerfoot 2020) that frame Spanglish and TexMex as lesser forms of communication.

PSTs' knowledge of linguistic variation or dynamic bilingualism was present in depictions and descriptions of Spanishes and Englishes. For example, Paola's language portrait color key included both "Spanish" and "Spanish with my family in Mexico" and she wrote, "My Spanish is different when I speak to my family that still lives in Mexico." Similarly, Armando wrote, "in my family we speak Spanish and English and my dad's side of the family is very Tex-mex dialect while my mom's side is more Mexican dialect." Finally, Lorena identified "Spanish" and "mom's Spanish from Mexico City" as two separate colors in her key. Pamela included "Home Spanish" rather than Spanish in her portrait and explained:

> My mother and husband are from Mexico. Therefore, I speak more Spanish than English because I'm surrounded by it at home and when I go visit my parents. English is the language I most commonly speak amongst friends and my work environment. The Spanish I do

Chapter 3 Learning from Latinx pre-service teachers' understandings — **67**

speak is for the most part "street Spanish" just because it's a little informal and Tex-mexy. My academic Spanish has room for improvement.

Pamela's description recognizes variation in her language practices across place and space (home versus work) and across interlocutors (mother and husband versus friends). She identified two different varieties of Spanish (street Spanish and academic Spanish) and defined street Spanish as "informal" and "Tex-mexy." Her evaluation that her "academic Spanish has room for improvement" reflects the raciolinguistic ideology of languagelessness (Rosa 2016) embedded in the construct of "academic language" and the dichotomy between language practices acceptable and not acceptable at school for racialized students (Flores 2020).

Prevalent across the data was also PSTs' recognition of the way language shift is contingent upon interlocutors as well. Several participants identified a unique contextualized language practice connected to being a mom (i.e. "mom language" and "baby talk"; see Figure 1 "mommy"), to being pet owner (i.e. "dog talk" and "puppy talk"), and to engaging with a significant other including sibling, wife, boyfriend, grandparent, or friend (i.e. "love talk" and "family talk"). Still others identified the importance of the language we use with ourselves. Krystal attributed the color blue to "verbal self talk" and wrote, "our most important language is the way in which we speak to ourselves." Some participants also identified a connection between language practices and gender identification such as "girl talk."

**Figure 1:** Students' language keys.

As evident in Figure 1, PSTs also connected particular spaces or activities to particular language practices including math, church, and dentistry. Additional spaces and activities included music, sports, gaming, texting, social media (i.e. Tik Tok), and additional media outlets (i.e. TV and telenovelas). Some PSTs went beyond identifying linguistic varieties and demonstrated language awareness explicitly in their descriptions. For example, Veronica classified one of her languages in her color key as, "adaptation to language environment (English, Spanish, slang, etc.)." Similarly, Krystal wrote, "In each area I show up differently. Meaning my language varies between each one of the areas." Finally, Casia wrote, "My language practices change depending on where I am."

The multiple ways PSTs framed their language practices, highlighting the complexity of language practices, further point to their understanding of language as a set of context dependent practices, which is at the heart of a translanguaging stance. Several PSTs identified "languages" in their key that further pushed our own conceptualization of language and what language means to our PSTs (see Figure 2 for examples): guilt as language, ethnicity as language, language as uncertainty or insecurity, language as confusion. These labels disinvent and reconfigure the meanings of language and disrupt static understandings of language (Makoni and Pennycook 2007) and reflect the roles of purpose, context, and interlocutor (Grosjean 2008) in language use.

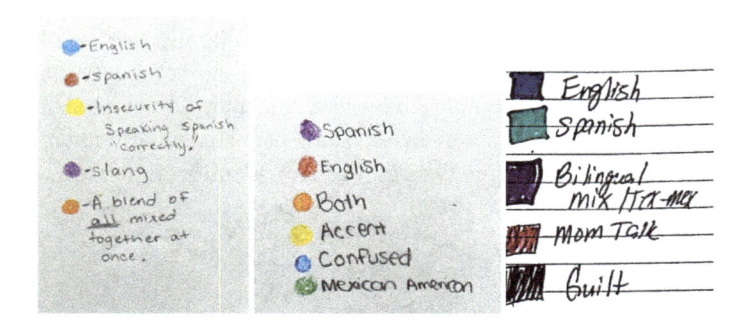

**Figure 2:** Language as insecurity, confusion, and guilt.

Indeed, three PSTs completed their language repertoires without using named languages (See Figure 3 below). Rather, they referred to different languages based solely on the activity or person. In Figure 3, Karina describes her language practices via her identities as "teacher", "friend", "work", "social justice", "chicana", "family", "dog mom" and "when no-one's looking". We wonder if PSTs, such as Karina, have solved the riddle of depicting and discussing languages without referring to named languages by referring instead to their multiple identities (Makoni and Pennycook 2007; Otheguy, García, and Reid 2015).

**Figure 3:** Portrait with no named language.

## 4.2 Connecting language, body, and emotions

Symbolically the language portrait afforded PSTs reflection spaces to consider the connection between language, the body, and emotion. Two particularly powerful symbols portrayed in most portraits were that of the heart and the brain. The metaphorical heart and brain allowed students to make direct connections between their language, the body, their identities, and their emotions (Busch 2017). For many students, the heart was drawn a color associated with a positive emotion including love and often associated with a specific person or people, frequently significant others and family members (see Figure 4). The brain was often a symbol to reflect on thoughts, thinking processes, or cognitive processing. Ariana (the second image in Figure 4) depicted Tex-Mex in her brain as the language that comes to her easier. These images graphically depict the importance of using home and community language practices as a resource in the classroom to reach students' hearts and brains (García, Johnson, and Seltzer 2017). This perspective was described by Maria who wrote, "The heart on my shirt represents my love for all humans and the ability to connect through kindness and love. I take pride in always trying to help others. I feel like kindness/love can be unspoken languages." When languages are

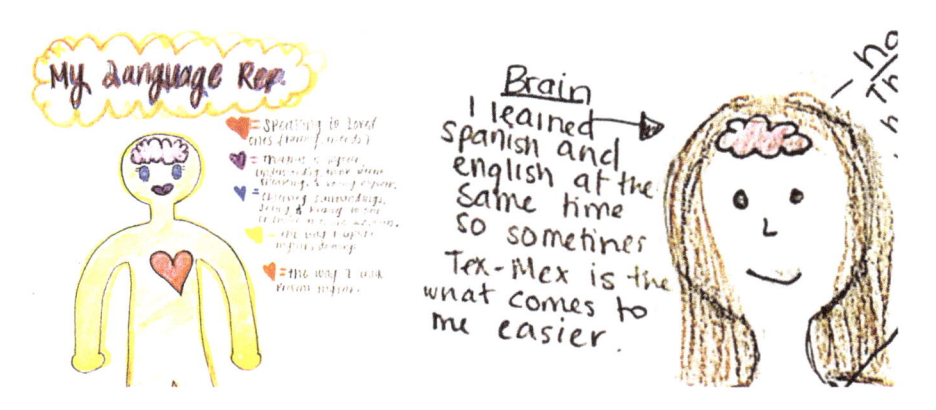

**Figure 4:** Heart and brain.

understood beyond bounded systems individuals can recognize the connection between language and the body including "unspoken languages."

Several PSTs depicted the heart as being split in connection to their linguistic and ethnic identities. As Gus described, "The reason for my heart being colored half blue and half green is because I grew up speaking Spanish then gained the knowledge of speaking English." Similarly, Fabiana drew her heart green (Spanish), blue (English), and red (mixed) and wrote, "My heart will always belong to Spanish, English, and, ultimately, will always be mixed." Mariana opted to draw not just her heart, but her entire body split with a line down the center and half of her body red and half of her body blue, which was observed in additional PSTs. Mariana explained the division, "This line represents the two completely different identities I feel like I have speaking English and Spanish. The people and situations in which I speak my two languages are very different, almost like I am a different person."

The process of drawing their linguistic repertoire evoked additional strong emotions. The language portrait was a space for PSTs to depict linguistic shame, linguistic insecurity, linguistic violence and discrimination (Ek, Sánchez, and Quijada Cerecer 2013; Tseng 2021). Adriana wrote, "the yellow represents my family not embracing their Spanish through systems of oppressions." Erica wrote, "The brown represents my fear of speaking Spanish at school in KY." Lisel identified the color yellow as representing "Insecurity of speaking Spanish "correctly"" (see Figure 2). In a similar way, Tania colored part of her brain blue representing Tex-Mex and wrote, "Tex-mex is located in my head because I constantly have to think about the "proper" way to say certain words in either English or Spanish." Lisel's and Tania's use of quotation marks around "correctly" and "proper" reflects their critical language awareness of ideologies of language standardization and the negative emotional impact for speakers of non-standard varieties and racialized students (Flores 2020; Leeman 2012; Tseng 2021).

Negative language experiences were depicted and described in other ways (see Figure 5) such as Enrique who chose to draw no mouth which he explained "symbolizes how I do not know what my Native language is, so I do not know how to speak my Native language," and Erica who drew a large blue frown on her face and wrote, "I decided the color blue for Spanish because both of my parents speak Spanish fluently but never taught, spoke, or engaged with me in Spanish. This makes me sad (the color blue) because I do not know how to speak, write, read, or respond in Spanish as a Latina woman." These experiences of strong shame and insecurity have been extensively documented in the literature (Ek, Sánchez, and Quijada Cerecer 2013; Leeman 2012; Tseng 2021), especially amongst heritage Spanish speakers who are constantly policed for Spanish proficiency in connection to their ethnic authenticity (Zentella 2014; Fallas-Escobar, Henderson, and Lindahl, 2022).

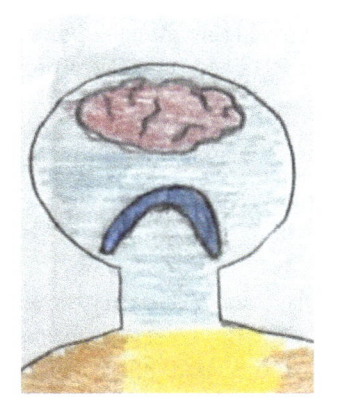

**Figure 5:** Negative emotions.

While several PSTs displayed a translanguaging stance through their awareness of processes of linguistic oppression, others demonstrated this awareness through their developing teacher and social justice identity. Eli drew the lips on her face pink and described this color in her key as representing, "cultural awareness, justice, and teaching things I'm passionate about." Irene drew the majority of her body in purple squiggly lines and identified purple in her key as "Latinx (social justice)." Furthermore, she colored her hands and feet in solid lavender explaining, "For my hands and feet I put a calming lavender because I want Teacher Irene to be safe. I want to walk into schools and use my hands and feet to change lives." Still other teachers demonstrated a translanguaging stance first by validating their own language practices and identities. For example, the way Octavia described her portrait represents a disruption of deficit views and ideologies of language standardization. She wrote, "My drawing represents myself as Mexican American. I speak English and Spanish. My first language is Spanish and I have an accent in English. I used to not like my accent but now I am very proud of it as part of my identity." Still, two additional PSTs, Ana and Blanca, identified their hands as the language of teaching recognizing the role of hands on learning for instruction. We will expand in the discussion on the power of these imagined teacher identities embodying a translanguaging stance.

# 5 Pre-service teacher language portrait cases

The rest of this chapter will present selected PSTs' language portraits for a complete look into the ways engaging in the process of language portraits evoked linguistic awareness and reflected Latinx PSTs' translanguaging stances before ending with a discussion of what we learned from our PSTs and implications for teacher preparation.

## 5.1 Lisa's language portrait: ". . . but I'm nowhere near fluent"

Lisa's work shown in Figure 6 illustrates the ways language portraits invite teacher candidates to examine and grapple with complexity, chaos, and heterogeneity in connection to their language practices. Her visual and verbal depictions show that although ideologies of language boundedness and ethnic authenticity (Chun 2011; Tseng 2021) still largely determine how she understands her linguistic repertoire, she makes connections that surface the bodily-emotional dimension of language (Busch 2017). First, we can see how Lisa frames language as a mental capacity by situating her English and Spanish in the brain and describing herself as thinking only in English. Expanding on this language-as-mental capacity ideology, Lisa also locates English on her arms and legs, evoking the bodily dimension of language: language as inscribed onto one's bodily dispositions. However, her disposition to use mostly/only English has brought about affective turmoil for Lisa: being Mexican herself, she is expected to be a Spanish speaker, which she hesitates to claim on the basis that she can understand and communicate in Spanish but is "nowhere near fluent."

As she reports, others' assumptions that she speaks Spanish due to her physical appearance trigger feelings of embarrassment and guilt (Mexican American

Chapter 3 Learning from Latinx pre-service teachers' understandings — 73

*(Figure: Lisa's language portrait — a hand-drawn figure of a person with a blue hat, purple shirt, yellow pants, and green shoes, surrounded by handwritten annotations.)*

Annotations on the drawing:
- "yeehaw" (pointing to hat)
- "I think only in english but a small part of my brain has spanish because I like spanish music"
- "mexican-american guilt" (purple)
- "english" (orange)
- "Spanish" (green)
- "Texan" (blue)
- "my shirt represents my appearance to others. People see me and often assume I speak Spanish. There's some embarrassment that comes w/ being mexican and not speaking spanish"
- "my shoes as Spanish show that I have some foundation to understand and communicate but I'm no where near fluent"

**Figure 6:** Lisa's language portrait.

guilt), which in turn are inscribed onto her body (see purple shirt in Figure 6). Lisa's portrait depicts her body as a site of contention connected to Mexicanness/ Spanish in ways that impose circulating notions (ideologies) of Spanish as a bounded system in connection to ethnic authenticity. Likewise, the way Lisa depicts how her body is interpreted by others suggests that for Lisa (as well as the other participants), the body often becomes an inescapable indexical element; one that becomes parsed by seeing others in ways that set in motion a number of expectations and assumptions.

The affective turmoil that these circulating notions (ideologies) cause her may have led her to highlight a perceived 'limited proficiency/capacity' in her Spanish, both visually in her depiction of the brain (receptive skills in Spanish), limited use of green, and also verbally in her disclaimer that she is "nowhere near fluent." These visual and narrative representations point to Lisa's orienting not only to speakers with whom she interacts (those who interpret her as being a Spanish speaker) but also to circulating figures of authority not immediately present: ideologies of language as a bounded system, bilingualism-as-double-monolingualism, and native speakerism. Also noteworthy is Lisa's invocation of place (Texas) as an important aspect of her lived experience of language. She does this by way of the blue Texan hat, the "yeehaw" lexical item, and the allocation of Texan as a distinctive feature of her linguistic repertoire. These three elements evoke the context of the American Southwest, while also serving as a reminder of the struggle for bilingualism/bilingual education and fight against the segregation of Mexican Americans within schools in the region (San Miguel 2013). Rather than becoming a backdrop, the notion of place in Lisa's language portrait points us to the need to situate her experiences within a particular socio-historical context (Rosa 2019).

## 5.2 Gilberto's language portrait: "School Spanish"

Gilberto's language portrait shown in Figure 7 defied rigid/traditional notions of language. While he referenced language practices traditionally thought of as languages (English and Spanish), he also included others often framed as lesser forms of communication: Spanglish (Ek, Sánchez, and Quijada Cerecer; Zentella 2014). The colors assigned to these language practices immediately draw attention to the Mexican flag Gilberto drew on the silhouette's face. Interestingly, while Mexico is commonly thought of as a Spanish speaking country, he assigned the color green to English and the color white to Spanglish, despite the circulating one language-one nation ideology (Auer 2005) that would connect English to the United States. Although Gilberto did not include explanatory text in his portrait, this color allocation may suggest that English and Spanglish could also be connected to Mexicans, particularly Mexican-Americans who grew up in the United States.

In addition, it is also important to draw attention to the fact that Spanglish (the color white) takes up most of the body of the silhouette, which indicates that it is a more common/frequent language practice for this participant. Spanglish, however, is depicted as covered by other, more conspicuous language practices not traditionally framed as languages: "bad puns" (red), "dog language" (brown), and "kid language" (purple). Underneath the silhouette's layers of outspokenness (light blue), bad puns, dog language, and kid language lie the language practices that take up most of his body: Spanglish. Further, although Gilberto had already included Spanish in his portrait, he also incorporated "school Spanish," which he assigned to the arm with which the silhouette seems to be defending himself. This could be interpreted to mean that school or academic Spanish is what he employs for work, especially considering that he assigned "gaming" (yellow) to his other arm, suggesting that one language practice is for work and the other for leisure.

Chapter 3 Learning from Latinx pre-service teachers' understandings — 75

**Figure 7:** Gilberto's language portrait.

## 5.3 Teresa's language portrait: "All of these make who I am"

Unlike most PSTs, Teresa chose a heart shape to represent her linguistic repertoire/language practices shown in Figure 8. However, just like many other PSTs, she also challenged traditional notions of language in the nation/state sense (e.g., English, Spanish). For instance, while Teresa mentioned English and Spanglish in her portrait (the latter of which she connected to Texas), she devoted the rest of her portrait to language practices that challenge how we think of language within and beyond the classroom. She used the biggest chunk of the heart where she depicted her repertoire for language in connection to activity: "love language" and "work language." She also employed a large section to depict language in connection to her role: "best friend language" and "teacher language." Further, she

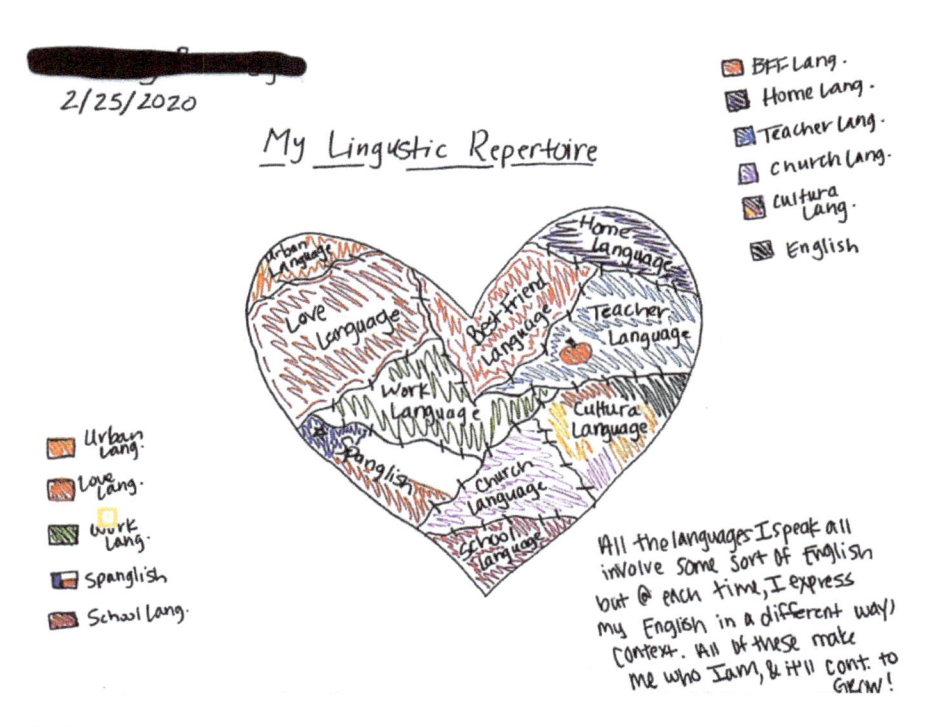

**Figure 8:** Teresa's language portrait.

depicted language practices in connection to space: "church language," "home language," "school language," and "urban language."

She stitched all of these language practices together using black thread, which in her code key represents English. She elaborates on this visual representation by saying, "All the languages I speak all involve some sort of English, but @ each time, I express my English in a different way, context." Here, Teresa powerfully draws attention to three points: (a) that for her there is not just one "sort of English," (b) that she is aware she uses English differently, and (c) that context (activity, interlocutor, and space) largely determines the ways she employs her linguistic resources. This visual metaphor of stitches is also observable in how she carved space for what she termed "cultura language," which she represented using a blend of colors. This blend of colors appears to suggest that this "cultura language" is the sum of her evolving repertoire. This is supported by her explanation on the lower right hand side that: "All of these make me who I am, and it'll cont. to grow!"

# 6 Discussion and implications

In this chapter, we view the language portrait as a space where complexity, chaos, and heterogeneity surfaces and it becomes a powerful tool for PSTs to make visible their translanguaging stance. This is the case because PSTs' visual and verbal depictions invite the rupturing of language boundedness and require that they strive to remain open and welcoming of complexity, chaos, and heterogeneity. That is, the language portrait makes visible that one's linguistic repertoire is "a heteroglossic realm of constraints and potentialities" (Busch 2017: 356), in that language practices that challenge ideologies of native speakerism, bilingualism-as-double-monolingualism, and language as bounded system, "can serve to construct belonging or difference" (Busch 2017: 342). PSTs' ability to connect their language repertoires to past experiences (biographical dimension of linguistic repertoires) and present socio-political conditions may shape their capacity to develop an expansive translanguaging stance.

As teacher educators, we have much to learn from the ways the Latinx PSTs identified and did not identify linguistically to inform our evolving translanguaging stance(s) (García, Johnson, and Seltzer 2017) or process of forward stancing. Students identified that they engaged in Spanglish, TexMex, mixed languages, and slang as well as communicated in different ways with particular people, in specific places, and during particular activities. By doing so, the PSTs disrupted traditional deficit views and ideologies of these "non-standardized" practices (Ek, Sánchez, and Quijada Cerecer 2013; Otheguy and Stern 2011). The language portraits also suggest that students have an understanding of language as practice and linguistic variation reflecting an important aspect of critical language awareness (Alim 2010; García 2009, 2017; Martínez 2003). Deeply engaging in the ways Latinx PSTs understood and framed their own language practices equipped us with a new degree of awareness regarding our PSTs' linguistic repertoires including the multifaceted ways these practices can be understood and re-named and disinvented (Makoni and Pennycook 2007). We learned that we can understand and define our linguistic repertoires by identifying our interlocutors (i.e. "language with mom") without naming a language. We learned that many of our Latinx PSTs identify as speakers of Spanglish, Tex-Mex and Mixed language, but that there are many other ways of identifying Spanishes including "mom Spanish; DF Spanish".

We also learned that the vast majority of PSTs did not identify as "bilingual" despite identifying bilingual language practices in their repertoires. Translanguaging pedagogy aims to normalize bilingualism and bilingual language practices and support bilingual identity development (García, Johnson, and Seltzer 2017). However, we are interested in the way this "bilingual" label is understood and generally not used in our community of PSTs. Our research suggests that identity work is figuratively (and literally in the portraits) at the heart of this issue. How can we encourage Latinx PSTs to adopt bilingual identities? Or, how do we celebrate and leverage different forms of dynamic bilingualism and name them in ways that resonate more with our communities? There are no simple answers. Creating spaces for students to develop bilingual identities is difficult work even in spaces that are designed for bilingualism (Palmer 2020). We have much work to do to create spaces that both celebrate and validate the linguistic identities of PSTs as well as provoke reflection on linguistic identities that are adopted and not adopted and why. We commit to ongoing reflection and consideration of these questions with ourselves, with our PSTs and in our communities to continue towards the creation of educational spaces that validate and celebrate diverse language practices.

PSTs' translanguaging stances were demonstrated in both their reflections on their linguistic histories and experiences, as well as imagined teacher identities. This active process of reflecting backwards and looking forward informing or challenging our understanding of and perspectives on diverse language practices we believe can shift our translanguaging stance and result in forward stancing. Gilberto's portrait depicts a physical defensive stance. Irene's portrait highlights her hands and feet – a forward moving physical stance – to represent social justice teaching. With these portraits in mind, we believe the body can powerfully represent, metaphorically and even literally, a translanguaging stance; our hearts representing our way of being that values our students' language practices, cultures, and identities for the co-construction of knowledge in a democratic classroom (García, Johnson, and Seltzer 2017), and our posture, arms, and feet moving and shifting our stances in nuanced ways that are responsive to our students and their diverse linguistic repertoires.

# References

Alim, Samy. 2010. Critical language awareness. In Nancy Hornberger & Sandra Lee McKay (eds.), *Sociolinguistics and Language Education*, 205–231. Clevendon: Multilingual Matters.
Auer, Peter. 2005. A postscript: Code-switching and social identity. *Journal of Pragmatics* 37(3). 403–410.
Avineri, Netta. & Danny C. Martinez. 2021. Applied linguists cultivating relationships for justice: An aspirational call to action. *Applied Linguistics* 42(6). 1043–1054.
Busch, Brigitta. 2017. Expanding the notion of the linguistic repertoire: On the concept of Spracherleben – the lived experience of language. *Applied Linguistics* 38(3). 340–358.
Chun, Elaine. 2011. Reading race beyond black and white. *Discourse & Society* 22(4). 403–421.

Coffey, Simon. 2015. Reframing teachers' language knowledge through metaphor analysis of language portraits. *The Modern Language Journal* 99(3). 500–514.
Collins, Brian. A., Maite (María Teresa) Sánchez & Carla España. 2019. Sustaining and developing teachers' dynamic bilingualism in a re-designed bilingual teacher preparation program. *International Journal of Bilingual Education and Bilingualism*. 1–17.
Ek, Lucila, Patricia Sánchez, & Patricia D. Quijada Cerecer. 2013. Linguistic violence, insecurity, and work: Language ideologies of Latina/o bilingual teacher candidates in Texas. *International Multilingual Research Journal* 7 (3). 197–219.
Fallas-Escobar, Christian, Kathryn I. Henderson & Kristen M. Lindahl. (2022). "I look Mexican, so they assume I speak Spanish": Latinx teacher candidates' grappling with raciolinguistic policing. *Modern Language Journal* 106(1). 196–215.
Fallas-Escobar, Christian & Alejandra Treviño. (2021). Two Latina bilingual teacher candidates' perceptions of language proficiency and language choice options: Ideological encounters with listening and speaking others. *Bilingual Research Journal* 44(1). 124–143.
Flores, Nelson. 2020. From academic language to language architecture: Challenging raciolinguistic ideologies in research and practice. *Theory into Practice* 59(1). 22–31.
García, Ofelia. 2009. *Bilingual Education in the 21st Century: A Global Perspective*. Malden: Wiley/Blackwell.
García, Ofelia. 2017. Critical multilingual awareness and teacher education. In Jasone Cenoz, Durk Gorter, & Stephen May (eds.), *Encyclopedia of Language and Education*, 3rd edn, 263–280. Cham: Springer International Publishing.
García, Ofelia, Susana Ibarra Johnson & Kate Seltzer. (2017). *The Translanguaging Classroom: Leveraging Student Bilingualism for Learning*. Philadelphia: Caslon.
García, Ofelia & Li Wei (2014). *Translanguaging: Language, Bilingualism and Education*. New York: Palgrave Macmillan.
Grosjean, François. 2008. *Studying Bilinguals*. Oxford: Oxford University Press.
Leeman, Jennifer. 2012. Investigating language ideologies in Spanish as a heritage language. In Sarah Beaudrie & Marta Fairclough (eds.), *Spanish as a Heritage in the US: State of the Science*, 43–59. Washington, DC: Georgetown University Press.
Lindahl, Kristen M., Christian Fallas-Escobar & Kathryn I. Henderson. (2021). Linguistically responsive pedagogy for bilingual teacher candidates: Shifting stances through language ideological dilemmas. *TESOL Quarterly* 55(4). 1190–1220.
Lucas, Tamara & Ana María Villegas. 2013. Preparing linguistically responsive teachers: Laying the foundation in preservice teacher education. *Theory Into Practice* 52(2). 98–109.
MacSwan, Jeff. 2020. Academic English as standard language ideology: A renewed research agenda for asset-based language education. *Language Teaching Research* 24(1). 28–36.
Makoni, Sinfree & Alastair Pennycook. 2007. *Disinventing and Reconstituting Languages*. Clevedon: Multilingual Matters.
Martínez, Glenn. A. 2003. Classroom based dialect awareness in heritage language instruction: A critical applied linguistic approach. *Heritage Language Journal* 1(1). 44–57.
May, Stephen. 2014. *The Multilingual Turn: Implications for SLA, TESOL and Bilingual Education*. London/New York: Routledge.
Menken, Kate & María Teresa Sánchez. 2019. Translanguaging in English-only schools: From pedagogy to stance in the disruption of monolingual policies and practices. *TESOL Quarterly* 53(3). 741–767.
Murillo, Luz A. 2017. "Aquí no hay pobrecitos": Decolonizing bilingual teacher education in the U.S.-Mexico borderlands. *Diaspora, Indigenous, and Minority Education* 11(4). 163–176.

Musanti, Sandra I., Alyssa G. Cavazos & Alma D. Rodríguez. 2020. Embracing a translanguaging stance and redefining teacher preparation practices in a Hispanic-Serving Institution. In Janine M. Schall, Patricia Alvarez Mchatton & Eugenio Longoria Sáenz (eds.), *Teacher Education at Hispanic-Serving Institutions: Exploring Identity, Practice, and Culture*, 69–87. New York/London: Routledge.

Otheguy, Ricardo, Ofelia García & Wallis Reid. 2015. Clarifying translanguaging anddeconstructing named languages: A perspective from linguistics. *Applied Linguistics Review* 6(3). 281–307.

Otheguy, Ricardo & Nancy Stern. 2011. On so-called Spanglish. *International Journal of Bilingualism* 15(1). 85–100.

Palmer, Deborah. 2020. "You're not a Spanish speaker!/We are all bilingual" The purple kids on being and becoming bilingual in a dual language kindergarten classroom. In Christian Faltis & Jeff MacSwan (eds.), *Code-Switching in the Classroom: A* Multilingual Perspective *on Language and Language practices*, 247–267. New York: Routledge.

Pennycook, Alastair. 2010. *Language as a Local Practice*. London/New York: Routledge.

Rosa, Jonathan. 2016. Standardization, racialization, languagelessness: Raciolinguisticideologies across communicative contexts. *Journal of Linguistic Anthropology* 26(2). 162–183.

Rosa, Jonathan. 2019. *Looking like a Language, Sounding Like a Race: Raciolinguistic Ideologies and the Learning of Latinidad*. New York: Oxford University Press.

Rosa, Jonathan & Nelson Flores. 2017. Unsettling race and language: Toward a raciolinguistic perspective. *Language in Society* 46(5). 621–647.

Saldaña, Johnny. 2015. *The Coding Manual for Qualitative Researchers*. London: Sage Publishing.

San Miguel, Guadalupe. 2013. *Chicana/o Struggles for Education: Activism in the Community*. Houston: Texas A&M University Press.

Seltzer, Kate. 2019. Reconceptualizing "home" and "school" language: Taking a critical translingual approach in the English classroom. *TESOL Quarterly* 53(4). 986–1007.

Stroud, Christopher & Caroline Kerfoot. 2020. Decolonising higher education: Multilingualism, linguistic citizenship & epistemic justice. *Working Papers in Urban* Language & Literacies 2(65). 1–21.

Tseng, Amelia. 2021. "Qué barbaridad, son latinos y deberían saber español primero": Language ideology, agency, and heritage language insecurity across immigrant generations. *Applied Linguistics* 42(1). 113–135.

Zentella, Ana Celia. 2014. TWB (Talking while Bilingual): Linguistic profiling of Latina/os, and other linguistic torquemadas. *Latino Studies* 12(4). 620–635.

Ryan W. Pontier and Zhongfeng Tian

# Chapter 4
# "If you want to be taken seriously, you have to speak like a white person": TESOL graduate students' grappling with translanguaging-as-social justice stance

**Abstract:** This study investigated a graduate level TESOL class's development of translanguaging-as-social justice stance–their grappling throughout the process of not only learning about bilingualism from a translanguaging perspective but also considering it as a form of social justice. The class focused specifically on translanguaging and consisted of nine multilingual, multicultural doctoral and masters-level students. Drawing on Peña-Pincheira and De Costa's (2021) ecological framework for leveraging teacher agency for social justice to analyze a representative class conversation, we found three overarching tensions that characterized students' translanguaging-as-social justice stance: (a) home v. school language expectations, (b) separationist v. flexible and dynamic understandings of bilingualism, and (c) translanguaging theory v. translanguaging pedagogy. Despite high levels of purpose and reflection, competing micro-, meso-, and macro-level influences contributed to students' varying levels of autonomy and competence. Across tensions, students showed development of their translanguage-as-social justice stances by (a) recognizing oppression, (b) combating feelings of powerlessness, (c) pushing back/transgressing, and (d) being part of a collective. To close the chapter, we provide key conclusions and implications for both research and practice.

## 1 Introduction

> Susie: Carolina was saying that she feels like it was hypocritical almost because you're supposed to translanguage and speak the way that you would feel more comfortable but then this is telling you, when you're dealing with certain aspects of society, to stick to the societal norms, for lack of a better way of putting it. And I told her that the way that I saw it was there's a time and a place for certain things or whatever, but I . . . So we were saying people translanguage and people speak differently because they're pulling from different languages

**Ryan W. Pontier,** Florida International University
**Zhongfeng Tian,** Rutgers University–Newark

https://doi.org/10.1515/9783110735604-005

they know, and they're not wrong, and it's ok, and we cannot tell them they're wrong. But we're telling them, "well, when you're with these people, this is how you have to talk." So, are we really doing them a favor? Where is this going? I don't think we're still holding them to the same place because you're still telling them [that] the better way is this [whatever is considered proper]. So, you're still saying their way is not good.

Carolina: I understand that, and thank you. However, I cannot get out of my thinking, 'how is this [i.e., translanguaging] social justice then' if you're still telling them [that they're not languaging properly]? I don't feel like they're . . . well, she said . . . a language that's more valued by certain people, the people in power. So you have a different value. One has more value than the other. So I don't think that social justice aspect of it because I think we're still telling them, "If you want to be heard, if you want them to consider you as a scholar . . ."

Ryan: I encourage you to think about that in terms of power. So, who gets to control what type of languaging we're told we're supposed to use–that it's better, proper, correct, academic?

Carolina: It's correct when you're with your friends and at your house, but at school, if you want to succeed, if you want to be somebody, **if you want to be taken seriously, you have to speak like a white person**.

In drawing on their own experiences as students and teachers in the preceding dialogue, Susie and Carolina, two bilingual Masters-level in-service middle school science and pre-service Spanish teachers, respectively, were debating whether and how translanguaging served as a form of social justice as they simultaneously grappled with competing messages of translanguaging-as-transgression and acquiescence to monolingual norms (Showstack 2015). In so doing, they identified major tensions that influenced their developing translanguaging-as-social justice stances, including individual interactions with power differentials, existing monolingual education policies, and societal beliefs about bilingualism. The interaction is a fitting microcosm for the multilingual, multicultural student discussions and learning that transpired in a graduate-level special topics TESOL course focused on translanguaging that Ryan taught in Summer 2019. It highlights the tensions that TESOL graduate students, some of whom are in-service teachers, experienced as they struggled through the process of not only learning about bilingualism from a translanguaging perspective but also considering it as a form of social justice. Throughout the course, students challenged the idea of translanguaging as a form of social justice. As such, we chose to investigate the following research question: What comprises TESOL graduate students' translanguaging-as-social justice stance?

We begin the chapter with our guiding perspectives and literature review, share the context of the focal class and our research methodology, present our findings, and finally situate what the students (and we, as researchers) shared and learned in our critical and evolving understanding of translanguaging as a transgressive practice and pedagogy.

## 1.1 Contextualizing translanguaging-as-social justice stance

Despite the multilingual nature of TESOL classrooms with students who could bring in rich cultural and linguistic resources, the field of TESOL has not yet fully moved away from the native-speakerism and monolingual bias in instruction and assessment (Ortega 2019). "Native speakers" are usually defined around white supremacist, imperialistic or colonial standards that favor white, middle or upper-class English speakers (Flores and Rosa 2015). Also, like heritage language teaching (Showstack 2015), traditional English teaching has been dominated by monolingual ideologies (Kroskrity 2000, 2004), enforcing students to ignore the metalinguistic affordances of their other languages and navigate English as a monolingual speaker according to valued, standardized notions of a national language while holding the native speaker as the idealized target model and positioning the teaching/learning goal as acquiring native-like proficiency (Prada and Turnbull 2018).

Translanguaging has introduced a marked theoretical and pedagogical shift to reimagine a multilingual TESOL that embraces teachers and learners' full linguistic repertoires (García and Li Wei 2014; Tian et al. 2020). As theory, translanguaging aims to combat the ideology of "native-speakerism" by problematizing the false dichotomy of "native vs. non-native," questioning structuralist ideologies of language standardization, and legitimizing language-minoritized speakers' multilingual performances and all their linguistic varieties. As pedagogy, translanguaging places students' emergent bilingualism at the center and strategically creates heteroglossic educational spaces for all learners to draw upon their entire cultural and linguistic repertoires as resources in meaning making and performing academic tasks (García 2009; García and Li Wei 2014). Therefore, for us, translanguaging represents a critical heteroglossic perspective (Flores and Rosa 2015) that has the potential to "transform relationships between students, teachers, and the curriculum" (Vogel and García 2017: 10) to necessitate a co-learning space (Li Wei 2013) where teachers and students learn from each other, and all language practices are equally valued, and ultimately to advance social justice to ensure that all students are educated deeply and justly (García, Seltzer, and Witt 2018).

Multilingualism, which includes translanguaging, embodies creativity and criticality through its tensions, conflicts, and differences in ideologies, policies, and practices (Li Wei and Martin 2009). As such, the process of developing translanguaging repertoires in teacher education can be simultaneously liberating and challenging (Robinson et al. 2019; Rodríguez, Musanti, and Cavazos 2021) and working toward and adopting this translanguaging-as-social justice stance is not the same for everyone. It is liberating in that it resonates well with bilingual students' own experiences. It is challenging because translanguaging as pedagogy may appear to be incompatible with societal language ideologies, theories that traditionally undergird TESOL teaching and learning, program policy, and even some personal experiences and beliefs. To view translanguaging as a form of social justice, then, may pose tensions for TESOL graduate students, which could include having to unlearn previous theory and practice and relearn according to translanguaging theory. As Anzaldua's (2015) theory of nepantla highlights, this transition is not immediate, is often painful, and requires active wrestling with new realities. For TESOL graduate students whose translanguaging-as-social justice stance is evolving, this encompasses the transition from viewing translanguaging merely as a scaffold to translanguaging as transgressive and transformative. In investigating teachers as agents of change in the promotion of social justice, Pantić (2015, as cited in Peña-Pincheira and De Costa 2021) provided four components to explain teachers' practices directed at the promotion of social justice, while also considering the role of micro, meso, and macro structural and cultural elements in shaping such justice:

- *Purpose*: how teachers conceive themselves as agents of change and engage and initiate such practices following a moral commitment.
- *Competence*: one's knowledge of rules and tactics to transform structures and cultures, as well as micro and macro awareness of how exclusion and disadvantage take place.
- *Autonomy*: the perceived sense of individual and collective relationship building, efficacy, and the perceived constraints and opportunities afforded by existing structures and cultures.
- *Reflexivity*: teachers' capacity for self-critical monitoring of their assumptions, actions, and decision making in their respective social contexts. (Peña-Pincheira and De Costa 2021: 3)

Originally developed to analyze one teacher's agency, we apply the framework to investigate translanguaging-as-social justice stance in a graduate-level TESOL teacher education program. Thus, we see TESOL graduate students' translanguaging-as-social justice stance influenced at the micro-level by immediate contexts of social activity such as engagement/interaction at classroom level, including conversation in the focal class; at the meso-level by the students' life, school, family, and community experiences; and at the macro-level by large-scale ideological structures such as belief systems, political, religious, cultural, and economic values of the U.S. context, and students' transnational experience/knowledge (see Figure 1). As such, we believe that TESOL graduate students' translanguaging-as-social justice stance is an intricately interwoven web of teacher purpose, competence, autonomy and reflexivity, and is influenced by micro-, meso-, and macro-level factors (Peña-Pincheira and De Costa 2021).

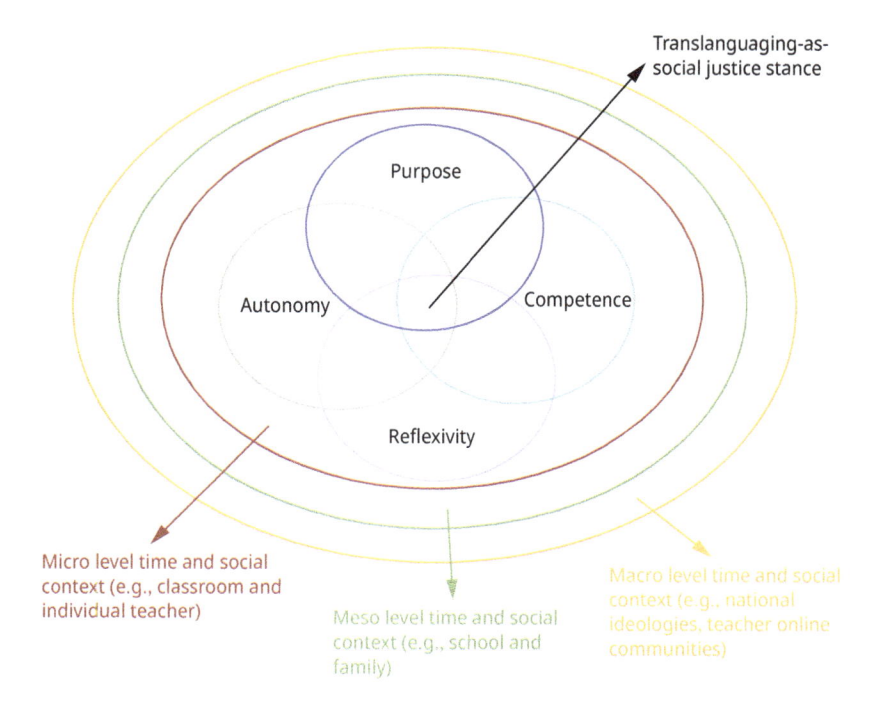

Chapter 4 "If you want to be taken seriously, you have to speak like a white person" — 85

**Figure 1:** Our conceptualization of "translanguaging-as-social justice stance" (adapted from Peña-Pincheira and De Costa 2021: 4).

# 2 Method

## 2.1 Study context

At the micro level (experiences in the focal class), this study drew on an audio-recorded TESOL graduate-level special topics course focused on translanguaging. The class was taught in Summer 2019 for six weeks, meeting two times per week for 3.5 hours at a public university in the Southeastern U.S. Classes were focused largely on the work of Ofelia García and colleagues.

The first part of the course explored translanguaging as theory via García and Li Wei (2014), and the second part explored translanguaging as practice and pedagogy in empirical studies with populations of different ages and different areas of study (e.g., PreK, general education, language education). In recognizing the social nature of learning in general and translanguaging specifically, Ryan, the first author, designed the course to be interactive. Class meetings were discussion-based, and Ryan both positioned and described himself to students as a facilitator. Students were asked to contribute to in-class discussions, co-lead discussions by preparing questions and/or activities in pairs, and complete out-of-class activities such as graphic organizers, pictures, memes, Tweet-able quotes, and an open-ended final project to show their growing understanding of translanguaging. As such, Ryan created space for students to engage not only with him, but also with each other, supporting individual and collective reflection.

The particular class meeting highlighted in this chapter was the third that focused on translanguaging as theory. The students had read chapters 1–4 of García and Li Wei (2014) and prepared a graphic organizer to show their developing understandings of theoretical underpinnings, affordances, and translanguaging strategies presented in chapter 4 (Translanguaging and Education). Throughout the conversation, as students recognized translanguaging as a form of transgression against traditional understandings and enactments of diverse and dynamic languaging practices, they also grappled with translanguaging as a form of social justice. As such, this class session served as a natural culmination of previous conversations around translanguaging, making salient the themes, perspectives, and struggles that students were identifying and experiencing.

At the meso level, such as experiences, expectations, and assumptions in the broader community, the surrounding community is multilingual and multicultural. Billboards, television and radio ads, and conversations in food stores, churches, and parks boast features of multiple named languages, but most notably Spanish and English. However, although community members decry the value of multilingualism, the expectations of the community are skewed toward monolingual performances and understandings of bi/multilingualism. For example, as a result of more macro level monolingual language ideologies, it is expected that you are a balanced bilingual to be considered bilingual. Similarly, although the focal university is one of the largest Hispanic-Serving Institutions in the U.S., students are expected to use standardized U.S. "academic" English.

At the macro level, including national expectations and ideologies, students were exposed to a monolingual mindset at the state and national levels. Although an "English as an official language" state, Florida's Department of Education has largely interpreted that to mean "English-only." Standardized assessments are only offered in English, English for Speakers of Other Languages (ESOL) programs far outnumber bilingual education programs despite Florida having the third highest population of English learners[1] in the country, students' linguistic and

---

1 Although we prefer strengths-based terms such as "emergent bilingual" or "multilingual learner," this is the term used by the Florida Department of Education.

academic performances are only recorded in English, and there is no bilingual education teacher certification option. Nationally, although xenophobia and racism have always been a part of U.S. history, regular explicit and insidious acts of hatred have been perpetrated on people of color, including bi/multilinguals, since the 2016 presidential election. In the federal government, this was seen with the erasure of languages other than English from the White House's webpage.

## 2.2 Participants

All nine students, a mix of Masters and doctoral levels, identified as multicultural and bi/multilingual, with their linguistic repertoires consisting of Spanish, Portuguese, Afrikaans, Arabic, Ukrainian, Russian, Turkish, French, and English. Countries of origin included Brazil, Ecuador, Peru, Cuba, Nicaragua, Egypt, Ukraine, South Africa, and the U.S. Some were currently teaching, but at different levels and in different programs, including adult ESL, K-12 general education, and university level modern language (See Table 1 for an individual student breakdown). Students came from a variety of socioeconomic backgrounds, with some only able to complete their program of study with the assistance of a scholarship and others paying full tuition.

**Table 1:** Student background information.

| Name[2] | Linguistic Repertoire | Teaching Experience | Program of Study |
|---|---|---|---|
| Carolina | Spanish, English | Pre-service K-12 | M.S. in TESOL |
| Susie | Spanish, English | In-service K-12 | M.S. in TESOL |
| Jorge | Spanish, English | Pre-service Adult ESL | M.S. in TESOL |
| Cassie | Afrikaans, English | Pre-service Higher Education | M.S. in TESOL |
| Mariah | Spanish, Turkish, English | In-service K-12 | M.S. in TESOL |
| Sam | Arabic, English | In-service Higher Ed (Modern Language) | Ph.D. |
| Ana | Portuguese, Spanish, English | Former K-12 | Ph.D. |
| Veron ca | Ukrainian, Russian, French, English | In-service Adult ESL | Ph.D. |
| Lauren | Spanish, English | Former Adult ESL | Ph.D. |

---

2 All student names are pseudonyms.

## 2.3 Researcher positionalities

Ryan identifies as a white bilingual male, speaks primarily Spanish with his two young daughters, and regularly translanguages with colleagues. On numerous occasions he has received praise for his use of Spanish while his former elementary school students were vilified for their developing bilingualism. This juxtaposition of experiences, among others, has led him to investigate teachers' language ideologies and instructional practices. He draws on his own translanguaging stance in his teaching and research, though his stance is evolving. For example, the focal class about translanguaging was taught mostly in English, even though the students were superdiverse in their linguistic, cultural, and socioeconomic backgrounds.

Zhongfeng, originally from China, identifies as a bilingual speaker of Mandarin and English with conversational fluency in Cantonese. His passion for translanguaging emerged from its close connection to his personal life as translanguaging legitimizes his lived experience and affirms his positive bilingual identity. Furthermore, translanguaging informs his teaching and research: he strives to provide bi/multilingual students with an equitable and inclusive learning environment in ESL and dual language immersion contexts, and prepare culturally and linguistically competent teachers with translanguaging-as-social justice orientations.

Ryan and Zhongfeng were introduced by a mutual colleague, who noted their shared interest in translanguaging. The two met via Zoom, discussed their research, and determined that they each had complementary experiences and perspectives that could enhance their work. Thus, they chose to explore the focal data and have been working together for almost two years at the time of writing.

## 2.4 Data collection and analysis

With IRB permission and all students' consent, classes were audio recorded and artifacts from out-of-class activities were collected. Both authors listened to the recordings, took notes of salient themes, met regularly to discuss their emergent findings, and with the support of a trained graduate student, transcribed verbatim each recording. We also included the course syllabus as a data point to support data triangulation. Through this initial deductive process, we identified social justice as a major theme, and chose one class session as a representative example of students' conversations and grappling.

We applied Peña-Pincheira and De Costa's (2021) framework to examine the theme of social justice in the class conversation. We found that the topics addressed the interrelationship of purpose, competence, autonomy, and reflexivity. That is, students discussed if and how they saw themselves as agents of change (purpose), what they knew about language rules and how to challenge structures and existing cultural norms (competence), and their perception of their ability to transform structures (autonomy), all of which engaged them in self-critical reflection around their assumptions, actions, and decision making (reflexivity). We recognize that a translanguaging-as-social justice stance is ongoing, leading us to examine and identify major tensions that arose throughout TESOL graduate students' discussions. In finding that these tensions were situated, we used an ecological perspective and mapped the tensions both within and across micro (self and classroom experiences), meso (community and assumptions), and macro (societal/national ideologies) levels of influence.

We used an iterative process of inductive and deductive analysis. The discursive nature of the conversation and the classification nature of our coding and analysis was difficult to reconcile. That is, conversations are naturally messier, going in a number of directions, whereas we have a tendency and an imposed requirement as researchers to maintain one focus at a time in our writing, like here in this chapter. Thus, at times, we struggled to code utterances as one layer of influence or another, especially when they addressed differing topics but were part of the same conversation. As such, our coding process included instances of intersectionality, or double-coding.

First, together, we read line-by-line through the transcript to engage in open coding, and we identified several tensions (e.g., agency v. structure, what is learned in class v. what is observed in schools, ideal v. realistic situations, fear of/embracing not understanding, unlearning/relearning, monolingual v. bilingual mindset) as students were working to see translanguaging as a form of social justice. We then applied Peña-Pincheira and De Costa's (2021) framework, as it proved useful in supporting our understanding of the emerging patterns in the data. Therefore, we analyzed the class conversations around the four components that Pantić (2015) identified as part of social justice (purpose, competence, autonomy, reflexivity), and then we examined the relationship(s) among those tensions, situating them using an ecological framework.

# 3 Ecological tensions in the development of TESOL students' translanguaging-as-social justice stance

Throughout their conversations, the students expressed desire to realize their purpose as agentive beings, but several struggled to overcome the tensions with which they grappled. They noted multiple messages and personal experiences reinforcing monolingualism at micro, meso, and macro levels. Specifically, their translanguaging-as-social justice stance was comprised of the following three interrelated tensions: (a) home v. school language expectations, (b) separationist v. flexible and dynamic understandings of bilingualism, and (c) translanguaging theory v. translanguaging pedagogy. To counter these interrelated tensions with multi-layered influences, students drew on reflexivity, purpose, competence, and autonomy to leverage their agency as they developed their translanguaging-as-social justice stance through: (a) recognizing the oppression, (b) combating feelings of powerlessness, which may vary based on low- and high-stakes contexts, (c) pushing back/transgressing, and (d) being part of a group/collective. Interestingly, doctoral students in the class expressed higher levels of autonomy and showed their strong translanguaging-as-social justice stances by sometimes challenging Masters-level students who were currently teaching.

## 3.1 Home v. school language expectations

As both teachers and students, the class grappled with ways to reconcile the often competing languaging expectations of home and school. From a student perspective, the class felt there was only one way to language correctly. Carolina, a Masters-level pre-service Spanish teacher, noted, "[Translanguaging]'s correct when you're with your friends and at your house but at school, if you want to succeed, if you want to be somebody, if you want to be taken seriously, you have to speak like a white person." Carolina's quote shows a message that many students received explicitly from various levels of influence, positioning monolingual enactments of bilingualism as the valued form of languaging in school, and other ways of languaging relegated to other, typically less formal, contexts. Here, Carolina shared her feelings of translanguaging's shortcomings in effecting social justice based on a micro-level message she had received from teachers and meso-level school language policies. Students expressed this tension as a dichotomy that precluded translanguaging from being viewed as a form of or a tool for social justice.

From a teacher perspective, students felt obligated to enforce monolingualism despite being told that dynamic bilingualism was natural and beneficial. Susie, a Masters-level middle school science teacher, shared:

> So we were saying people translanguage and people speak differently because they're pulling from different languages they know, and they're not wrong, and it's ok, and we cannot tell them they're wrong. But we're telling [students], 'well, when you're with these people, this is how you have to talk.' So, are we really doing them a favor? . . . you're still telling them [that] the better way is this [whatever is considered proper]. So, you're still saying their way is not good.

The dichotomy is manifested both within micro-level tensions as well as across micro, meso, and macro-level influences. On a micro level, whereas students' languaging practices may reflect their bilingualism, the languaging practices of teachers were characterized as monolingual. There was also tension between the individual flexible languaging practices of students and the meso-level monolingual language policies and macro-level societal monolingual expectations for languaging.

As students showed their reflexivity by grappling with this first tension as part of their translanguaging-as-social justice stance, their agentive responses highlighted a need to recognize oppression by identifying and comprehending the structures that reinforced specific languaging practices. Ana, a doctoral level former K-12 teacher, exemplifies this below in an expression of her competence:

> Each student needs to understand that in our society there are power relationships, and languaging is a way that our society uses the power relationship. The idea that the students learned not that there is a proper way–that there is a more valued way by people that are empowered in the situation. So the idea of Paulo Freire is that the students comprehend the power relationship, what is valued in each relationship. Right? So the idea that you have to make the students understand that there are not like proper way, but that society creates power relationships and values more languaging in that way, in each situation.

Cassie, a Masters-level pre-service university instructor, also expressed competence through her strong translanguaging-as-social justice stance, noting, "I think it describes translanguaging as something that . . . implements social justice by breaking the hierarchies and allowing the home and school environment to connect." In a similar vein, Veronica, a doctoral level adult TESOL instructor, highlighted that, by leveraging their agency, students can transgress existing assumptions and practices by asking why they are in school for so much time with the expectation that they learn English and, at the same time, the teacher has not learned any of the students' language/s. However, because through dynamic relations structure places certain force on agency (Palmer 2018), students still found themselves combating feelings of powerlessness (Kilgour Dowdy 2002; Ladson-Billings 2002; Purcell-Gates 2002; Wynne 2002), choosing when/whether to take actions based on their agency within those choices. As Masters-level Kindergarten teacher Mariah shared, despite feelings of competence, it may be a low level of autonomy that dictates actions (or lack thereof): "sometimes you don't repress your culture but you decide whether/where it's safe to express. So, the question of safety is valid." Veronica seems to sympathize with this comment in an attempt to boost feelings of autonomy: "So, social justice is like democracy. Right? We have democracy, so translanguaging is like the step to our social justice. But it's not like if you are translanguaging in the classroom," sighs, "social justice [just happens]." With her use of "our," she signals that social justice is not an individual act, that it requires a collective effort (Avineri and Martínez 2021).

## 3.2 Separationist v. flexible and dynamic understandings of bilingualism

The second major tension, separationist v. flexible and dynamic understandings of bilingualism, was represented across micro, meso, and macro layers of influence, manifesting itself in classroom interactions, language policies, and societal language ideology. This tension was couched in students' grappling to reconcile differences between monolingual and bilingual mindsets, which made salient a need to unlearn previous learning informed by traditional monolingual approaches to second language acquisition and to re-learn new bilingual ways of being, thinking, and languaging.

Students expressed a lower sense of purpose and autonomy but high levels of competence and reflexivity within this tension. For example, in showing a high level of competence but a low level of autonomy, shifting from a monolingual to bilingual mindset proved to be especially challenging both due to firmly formed beliefs and personal experiences that reinforced not only monolingual understandings of bilingualism, but also monolingual languaging performances. As Ana noted, "it's a process for the teachers too, right? Everybody's like in the process of learning a new perspective. And sometimes, you need so much time to be convinced. And then you need another much time to change how to act, because sometimes I'm [already] convinced about something." Ana also shared micro-level influences from interactions with other individuals: "before, when I spoke Portuguese with my son, everybody was looking at me and saying, 'Do you speak Portuguese? What is the language?' It started to make me feel that I'm doing something wrong. So they're not explicitly like, 'you are not welcome,' but there are subtle things that my language is like . . . there is something." Ana was aware of the implicit message to language in a specific way, which may have made her feel less willing to challenge that way. Additionally, Mariah shared that she is "asked all the time, 'are you from Brasil?' And I've asked a few people after I got comfortable and safe with them, 'Why would you say Brasil?' 'Oh, because you don't really speak Spanish properly.'" Carolina even put a value to this way of languaging: "[Language separation is] what I thought was right . . . I didn't like to do the whole Spanglish thing, because, you know, they had told me my whole life: not this. You don't do that, you have to keep the language pure." Again, the micro-level influence reinforces a message that languages should be kept separate and spoken in a specific way to garner respect.

Chapter 4  "If you want to be taken seriously, you have to speak like a white person" — **93**

In another show of competence, students recognized the oppression inherent in this second tension in their comparison of society's macro-level oppressive influence of monolingual language ideology with translanguaging. The following dialogue highlights several students addressing competing versions of what it means to be bilingual.

> Veronica: No but I think [translanguaging is] more about doing, not just saying, right?

> Ana: But I think that there is something else that they pointed out that it very, is a very interesting point to discuss, that is, what is to be bilingual enough? [She answers her own question.] There *is* a bilingual enough.

> Lauren: I was going to say [the] same, because to some extent, I understood that for [Carolina] being bilingual is like black and white, [either] you are, [or] you are not.

> Carolina: Right cuz . . .

> Lauren: To some extent [it] is like a continuum.

Veronica's statement broadens a traditional understanding of bilingualism by including action (i.e., doing), Ana challenges the notion of "bilingual enough," and Lauren, a doctoral level former K-12 teacher, relays the oft-stated dichotomy of being bilingual or not. Lauren's final contribution places bilingualism on a continuum when viewed from a bilingual/translanguaging perspective. Thus, through conversation the students demonstrate their understanding of how bilingualism is typically viewed while also juxtaposing that view with a more dynamic one. However, just because students stated the contrast between separationist and dynamic understandings of bilingualism did not necessarily lead to feelings of empowerment.

Students' feelings of powerlessness, or low levels of autonomy, were manifested within this tension through micro-level influences in their role as teachers who were expected to be omniscient pedagogues that modeled and policed their students' languaging. Not embodying those characteristics was viewed as a loss of power, as was expressed by Veronica: "So in addition to understand that you are giving up some of your power, you need to be willing to give up some of your authority as the person who knows everything." The fear was that if teachers could not understand students, they would not be able to be in control and support students' learning.

This notion was challenged, though, and met with thoughts for what might be required to engage in transgressive acts. Despite a low level of autonomy, even within this one class session, students showed signs of reflexivity through their shifts, or the processes of unlearning and relearning. Carolina referred to the multiple transformations that occurred for her with each course she completed and shared a specific shift she made in this class. "Teachers make sure that you only use the target language, and you're nice about [it], but then now, it's like this translanguaging and then it's like another way of teaching like, it's okay to use the first language to support and sustain." She also noted that "It's not about you have to learn the language perfectly. It's about . . . communicative competence." In these examples, students' micro-level interactions with others challenged meso-level monolingual languaging expectations. Whereas Carolina was aware of previous teachings such as only using the target language, she has recognized and seems to support key differences in a newfound flexible/dynamic understanding of bilingualism presented throughout the course.

Students' ideas related to transgressing were taken up from the role of student and teacher, showing an embodiment of purpose. In reflecting on her monolingual approach to writing (i.e., drafting a paper in only Spanish when required to be submitted in Spanish), Carolina showed a shift as she engaged in pushing back on what she saw as the monolingual status quo:

> But then now that I'm thinking this, you know, now, I don't know what to think anymore, because maybe those people are okay, maybe everybody's . . . Okay, like, nobody's wrong here. You know, it's okay, if they write in their first language and then translate it to, to English or whatever. Other than that, I guess, is just to get your point across.

She sees opportunities to leverage students' (and her own) full linguistic repertoires to support their learning rather than stymie teachers' understanding. Carolina further pushes back by problematizing the way that society has viewed the bilingualism of second and third generations. "And when we were talking about the second and third generation, how they explained that they're losing the language, are they really losing the language? Or is the language evolving?" Questioning how bilinguals already language opens space for considerations and acceptance of new generations' flexible ways of becoming and "doing being bilingual" (Gort 2015).

Mariah relates these new ways of thinking and languaging to a collective nature: "it's enabling everybody in the room to be interdependent and not independent. I think it's kind of the opposite action of independent thinking. I think it's interdependent. I think that's what they're saying is the dynamics of the communication in translanguaging. That it comes through a little bit messy and mixed in connection between people. So it's interdependence." In so doing, Mariah's expression of her translanguaging-as-social justice stance challenges the U.S.-centric notion of individuality and recognizes the need for collaboration to leverage translanguaging as a form of social justice.

## 3.3 Translanguaging theory v. translanguaging pedagogy

Students' class conversations revealed an acceptance of and alignment with the theoretical underpinnings of translanguaging (i.e., it is natural for bilinguals), but a reticence to purposefully leverage their own and/or their students' flexible languaging practices when they served in an instructor role. There were multilayered factors contributing to this third tension. With influence from both meso- and macro-levels, students' conversations revealed that they interpreted their purpose as instructors to be all-knowing and in control. Perhaps the result of meso-level school policies and expectations and a macro-level American (i.e., U.S., but certainly Latin American) belief that teachers are knowledge givers and in charge of their classroom, Susie mentioned, "as educators, we need to know where they're at, you know?", which seemed to be in conflict with creating a translanguaging space in the classroom. In this context, student translanguaging was sometimes viewed as an impediment to teachers understanding their students rather than a bridge to supporting them, thus a type of powerlessness. Putting it bluntly, Mariah asked, "what do you do in the classroom when translanguaging is putting up some kind of barrier for understanding?" This comment suggests a micro-level influence of the teacher's locus of control. That is, because teachers' own linguistic repertoire was a possible reason for precluding their comprehension of multilingual students, they feared they would not be in control of students' learning, and any interactions perceived as unsuccessful were viewed as the fault of student translanguaging (not the teacher). Susie noted,

> I feel like as an educator, though, it'll make our lives more difficult in the sense of, if we're not fully understanding what they're saying, then how are we going to know [that] ok they grasp the concept? Do they still need help with this? Do they still need help with that? It makes it that much harder to know where they're at. And that's half the battle–to know where they're at. How to know where to take it from and to move forward. I feel like it's a double-edged sword. And yes it's very social justice-y and very encompassing, for lack of a better way of putting it, but it's limiting as an educator, I feel.

However, the perceived need to always understand emergent bilingual learners may have precluded students from leveraging their learners' entire linguistic repertoire just to accommodate the teacher's less flexible linguistic repertoire. It seems to be students' high levels of competence (i.e., they understood what it means to translanguaging in classrooms as well as the current language policies and expectations of them as teachers) coupled with a lower level of autonomy (i.e., they felt that allowing learners to translanguage would prevent them from understanding and doing their jobs as teachers) that produced this tension between feeling that the idea of translanguaging was inherently good but that it could restrict their own comprehension and support of their learners.

When Ryan encouraged the class to think about this tension from a different perspective and to consider how translanguaging might not only provide access to more students but also leverage their languaging practices and knowledge that would otherwise go unnoticed ("if our new normal is knowing that we're just not going to understand everybody all of the time, how might that change our perspective, our understanding, . . . our world view?"), students began to see translanguaging as a tool for social justice. For example, Mariah stated, "I might not understand some of what you say. You may not understand some of what I say. So that kind of *puts us on equal footing*. It's saying that neither one of us has the last word, but let's *negotiate* to try to at least get learning happening" (emphasis added). She continued, noting that translanguaging also has the potential to transgress the typical micro- and meso-level power structures through student-teacher co-design: "It brings the power and responsibility into the whole group and it levels the playing field where every stakeholder in the group has power, which is wonderful."

In addressing the meso-level expectation that students must work to understand the teacher, Veronica leveraged her autonomy, pointing out that social justice needs to focus on students, not on teachers' perceived challenges. She asked,

> Why does it always have to be harder for students? Maybe we would have more balance . . . Teachers would have a little bit more challenge and students would have a little of less challenge because they could use the other features of their linguistic repertoire and it would help them to be active in the classroom, to learn more. Not to be silent. Not to be just passive in the class. So why [does] the whole workload needs to be on students? It would be more social justice-y if we give them a little bit more help.

She also pushed back on the concerns of others who thought that translanguaging could lead to lack of comprehension by focusing on leveraging all of students' skills and experiences: "If you silence all those [LOTE] features and you just keep the power language, you [the teacher] know less, because they will not tell you if they know–let's say if they know any English. They will not inform that they know anything about history and anything about biology. Because they just simply don't speak English, right?" Pushing back on this same meso-level influence, Ana showed the power of translanguaging to facilitate communication and show knowledge (i.e., not preclude it) when she shared, "When they speak in [monolingual] paragraphs, they have to have complex grammar. And they don't have that [yet in English]. But [when drawing on their full linguistic repertoire] they [can] speak in their mind the paragraph. How can I access that if they don't translanguage?" And Sam, a doctoral level student who was teaching a modern language class and developing a translanguaging stance through trying translanguaging design in class, showed her own shift in her translanguaging-as-social justice stance:

> I'm teaching a standard [language] and I have heritage students that speak a dialect and they're right. And their dialect too. And I completely understand what they mean. And I know that they are–they don't write me something odd or something away from what I ask them. Because it's not just in the standard and I don't take points off of them because it's their language that they have been using all their lives.

She continued to show criticality in her translanguaging-as-social justice stance by noting that for students who are characterized as "native" speakers of a language, despite regularly committing "errors" according to standardized rules, instructors rarely comment on or correct them.

As before, class discussion showed that, to generate more power to be transgressive or for students to develop a greater sense of autonomy, and for translanguaging to be realized as a tool for social justice, students recognized a need for both time and collaboration. Specifically, Veronica called attention to the collective nature needed to effect change in ideology and practice. She mentioned opportunities to leverage parents' languaging practices and teacher preparation programs as avenues to draw on a group approach and concluded that "We would, everybody would change a little bit. We all need to change . . . And, imagine in ten years all those students say, 'maybe it's [viewing dynamic bilingualism as a problem] not normal because it was not a norm in my classroom and in your classroom.'"

## 4 Discussion and conclusion

Based on our analysis of students' class conversations, juxtaposing students' reifying experiences with a class like the focal one–that serves as a way to unlearn and relearn–may serve as one way to develop students' translanguaging-as-social justice stances. That is, findings suggest that the class served as a space for students to safely explore existing beliefs, behaviors, and their key influences; receive critical feedback from peers and an instructor; and consider and try out new beliefs and behaviors. Our analysis of the class discussion showed that students seemed to understand their purpose, have a high level of competence, and a lower level of autonomy across all three tensions. In thinking about opportunities to leverage their autonomy by pushing back, it was primarily doctoral level students that showed reflexivity, perhaps because they were not so "deep" in the system and more eager to reimagine and challenge what could be done better. They saw the potential of translanguaging to be transgressive and to empower their own students through translanguaging. Masters students, whose talk suggested that the many meso- and macro-level influences may preclude them from seeing their micro-level classroom practices as transgressive, expressed a comparably lower level of autonomy. Perhaps having experiences in public education systems and being more entrenched in monoglossic language policies in K-12 classrooms contributed to their feeling "trapped" and that they could not effect change or transgress in the way that we teacher educators expect them to. Classes like this one provide fertile ground for multiple voices to come together to forge a mutual understanding and move forward together through reimagining while grounding ourselves in classroom realities.

Moreover, we wonder if teacher educators engage Masters students in contemplative and challenging conversations the same way that we often do with doctoral students. If those conversations already exist, do they invite Masters students to push back on existing power structures (Delpit and Kilgour Dowdy 2002), or do they serve to merely provide a set of teaching tools that might reify monolingual norms and notions of bi/multilingualism as too challenging for school contexts? As such, we invite teacher educators to explore and reflect upon their translanguaging-as-social justice stances and their alignment with how they teach and what they expect of Masters and doctoral level students.

# 5 Implications

## 5.1 Future research

This small study is evidence that a translanguaging-as-social justice stance is a complex combination of teacher purpose, competence, autonomy and reflexivity, and is influenced by micro-, meso-, and macro-level factors (Peña-Pincheira and De Costa 2021). As such, we believe the approach we have used to analyze this student conversation represents a feasible framework for investigating translanguaging-as-social justice stance. The ecological view provides a multidimensional look at the dynamic process of being and becoming that is developing a translanguaging-as-social justice stance. Researchers can use the framework as a tool to analyze, unpack, and even develop their own translanguaging-as-social justice stances.

## 5.2 Teacher education

As teacher educators, we need to provide support for both pre- and in-service teachers on how to maneuver the complex institutions and systems that are highly political and police language use (Avineri and Martínez 2021). Our research highlights the importance of having difficult conversations. In engaging in reflective conversations that question and problematize the experiences of multilinguals, TESOL student educators challenge themselves and others in embracing previously prohibited creativity and criticality (Li Wei 2011), seeing strategic pedagogical translanguaging as social justice. In addition, teacher educators must debunk myths around languaging and push student educators to move beyond translanguaging just for the sake of translanguaging. Even when intentional spaces are created to discuss the potential of translanguaging as transgressive, this study shows that developing a translanguaging-as-social justice stance involves baby steps – making adjustments (shifts) or changing mindset (stance) during/after conversation. These incremental steps–or shifts in perception of translanguaging as transgressive–are important since educators do not need to be "all in" to develop a translanguaging-as-social justice stance (Menken and Sánchez 2019). As a long-term dynamic process of unlearning and relearning, the collaborative endeavor of engaging in these open discussions may serve as a way for educators to continue to develop their own translanguaging-as-social justice stance.

Beyond identifying tensions that comprise students' translanguaging-as-social justice stances and engaging in critical conversions, we must also follow TESOL students into their classrooms to learn how/if their translanguaging-as-social justice stances manifest in their teaching (Showstack 2015). Understanding how they leverage their purpose, competence, autonomy, and reflexivity will allow us, as teacher educators, to work in partnership in developing co-stances, co-designs, and co-shifts (Tian and Shepard-Carey 2020) as we continue to engage in the transformative practices of translanguaging. Together, and with time, courage, and agency, we can continue to engage in transformative practices that comprise our critical translanguaging repertoires, including a translanguaging-as-social just stance.

## 5.3 Policy

To fully leverage the power of a translanguaging-as-social justice stance and support teachers to engage in equity-oriented teaching practices, implementing assets-based language policies may be a necessary next step. Given the meso-macro tensions identified by Masters level students, both K-12 and higher education should consider heteroglossic language policies that not only enable but also encourage dynamic languaging in instruction and assessment. These policies would offer teacher educators, pre- and in-service teachers, and K-12 students opportunities to engage in and observe language practices that represent authentic and meaningful ways to both teach and make meaning collectively and individually without worrying about possible stigmatization.

# References

Anzaldúa, Gloria. 2015. *Light in the Dark/Luz En Lo Oscuro: Rewriting Identity, Spirituality, Reality*. North Carolina: Duke University Press.
Avineri, Netta & Danny C. Martinez. 2021. Applied linguists cultivating relationships for justice: An aspirational call to action. *Applied Linguistics* 42(6). 1043–1054.
Delpit, Lisa & Joanne Kilgour Dowdy (eds.). 2002. *The Skin That We Speak: Thoughts on Language and Culture in the Classroom*. New York: The New Press.
Flores, Nelson & Jonathan Rosa. 2015. Undoing appropriateness: Raciolinguistic ideologies and language diversity in education. *Harvard Education Review* 85(2). 149–171.
García, Ofelia. 2009. *Bilingual Education in the 21st Century: A Global Perspective*. Malden: Blackwell.
García, Ofelia & Li Wei. 2014. *Translanguaging: Language, Bilingualism and Education*. Basingstoke: Palgrave Macmillan.
García, Ofelia, Kate Seltzer & Daria Witt. 2018. Disrupting linguistic inequalities in US urban classrooms: The role of translanguaging. In Piet Van Avermaet, Stef Slumbrouck, Koen Van Gorp, Sven Sierens & Katrijn Maryns (eds.), *The Multilingual Edge of Education*, 41–66. London: Palgrave Macmillan.
Gort, Mileidis. 2015. Transforming literacy learning and teaching through translanguaging and other typical practices associated with "doing being bilingual." *International Multilingual Research Journal* 9(1). 1–6.
Kilgour Dowdy, Joanne. 2002. Ovuh dyuh. In Lisa Delpit & Joanna Kilgour Dowdy (eds.), *The Skin That We Speak: Thoughts on Language and Culture in the Classroom*, 3–14. New York: The New Press.
Kroskrity, Paul V. 2000. Regimenting languages: Language ideological perspectives. In Paul V. Kroskrity (ed.), *Regimes of Language: Ideologies, Polities, and Identities*, 1–34. Santa Fe: School of American Research Press.
Kroskrity, Paul V. 2004. Language ideologies. In Alessandro Duranti (ed.), *A Companion to Linguistic Anthropology*, 496–517. Malden: Blackwell.
Ladson-Billings, Gloria J. 2002. I ain't writin' nuttin': Permissions to fail and demands to succeed in urban classrooms. In Lisa Delpit and Joanna Kilgour Dowdy (eds.), *The Skin That We Speak: Thoughts on Language and Culture in the Classroom*, 107–120. New York: The New Press.
Li Wei. 2011. Moment analysis and translanguaging space: Discursive construction of identities by multilingual Chinese youth in Britain. *Journal of Pragmatics* 43. 1222–1235.
Li Wei. 2013. Who's teaching whom? Co-learning in multilingual classrooms. In Stephen May (ed.), *The Multilingual Turn: Implications for SLA, TESOL, and Bilingual Education*, 177–200. New York: Routledge.
Li Wei & Peter Martin. 2009. Conflicts and tensions in classroom codeswitching: An introduction. *International Journal of Bilingual Education and Bilingualism* 12(2). 117–122.
Menken, Kate & María Teresa (Maite) Sánchez. 2019. Translanguaging in English-only schools: From pedagogy to stance in the disruption of monolingual policies and practices. *TESOL Quarterly* 53(3). 741–767.

Ortega, Lourdes. 2019. SLA and the study of equitable multilingualism. *The Modern Language Journal* 103(S1). 23–38.

Palmer, Deborah K. 2018. Introduction to the special issue: Teacher agency and "pedagogies of hope" for bilingual learners (in a brave new world). *International Multilingual Research Journal* 12(3). 143–144.

Pantić, Nataša. 2015. A model for study of teacher agency for social justice. *Teachers and Teaching: Theory and Practice* 21(6). 759–778.

Peña-Pincheira, Romina & Peter I. De Costa. 2021. Language teacher agency for educational justice-oriented work: An ecological model. *TESOL Journal* 12(2). 1–13.

Prada, Josh & Blake Turnbull. 2018. The role of translanguaging in the multilingual turn: Driving philosophical and conceptual renewal in language education. *EuroAmerican Journal of Applied Linguistics and Languages* 5(2). 8–23.

Purcell-Gates, Victoria. 2002. ". . . As soon as she opened her mouth!": Issues of language, literacy, and power. In Lisa Delpit and Joanna Kilgour Dowdy (eds.), *The Skin That We Speak: Thoughts on Language and Culture in the Classroom*, 121–144. New York: The New Press.

Robinson, Elizabeth, Zhongfeng Tian, Tiffany Martínez & Aybahar Qarqeen. 2019. Teaching for justice: Introducing translanguaging in an undergraduate TESOL course. *Journal of Language and Education* 4(3). 77–87.

Rodríguez, Alma D., Sandra I. Musanti & Alyssa G. Cavazos. 2021. Translanguaging in higher education in the US: Leveraging students' bilingualism. *Critical Inquiry in Language Studies* 18(4). 353–373.

Showstack, Rachel E. (2015). Institutional representations of 'Spanish' and 'Spanglish': Managing competing discourses in heritage language instruction. *Language and Intercultural Communication* 15(3). 341–361.

Tian, Zhongfeng, Laila Aghai, Peter Sayer & Jamie L. Schissel (eds.). 2020. *Envisioning TESOL Through a Translanguaging Lens: Global Perspectives*. Cham: Springer International Publishing.

Tian, Zhongfeng & Leah Shepard-Carey. 2020. (Re)imagining the future of translanguaging pedagogies in TESOL through teacher-researcher collaboration. *TESOL Quarterly* 54(4). 1131–1143.

Vogel, Sara & Ofelia García. 2017. Translanguaging. In George Noblit (ed.), *Oxford Research Encyclopedia of Education*, 1–21. Oxford: Oxford University Press.

Wynne, Joan. 2002. "We don't talk right. You ask him". In Lisa Delpit & Joanna Kilgour Dowdy (eds.), *The Skin That We Speak: Thoughts on Language and Culture in the Classroom*, 203–220. New York: The New Press.

Xenia Hadjioannou
# Chapter 5
# Starting with the teachers: Pursuing paradigmatic shift through the development of teachers' translanguaging repertoires

**Abstract:** Translanguaging pedagogy calls for strategically and systematically leveraging all students' language knowledge toward bilingualism and biliteracy; a commitment that demands critical consideration of normative practice, identifying and dismantling oppressive patterns, and angling teaching toward equity and social justice (Calabrese Barton, Tan, and Birmingham 2020; Zapata et al. 2019). Teacher education has a crucial role to play, since adopting translanguaging pedagogy requires a paradigmatic shift from common monolingually oriented approaches. Based on multi-year work with inservice teachers at a U.S. university, the chapter explores efforts to help inservice teachers develop their translanguaging repertoires and envision and implement translanguaging practices in their teaching. This involved supported, interconnected critical examinations of normalized practices in the teachers' professional contexts built around the notion of reseeing: re-seeing bilingualism and "English Learners," as well as one's own teaching and instructional contexts. These examinations were identified as promising in elucidating patterns of injustice against linguistically minoritized students and in supporting the conception of more socially just alternatives. Also promising were guided curricular re-envisionments. However, shifts toward translanguaging-informed teaching can be frustrated by systemic resistance as well as by deeply rooted monolingual ideologies that may undercut teachers' best intentions to adopt translanguaging practices.

Translanguaging conceptualizes bilinguals as having a single, unified language repertoire from which they strategically select features to make sense of the world and to communicate effectively (García and Li Wei 2014). Centering this conceptualization, translanguaging pedagogy charges educators with the responsibility to recognize emergent bilingual students as bilinguals-in-the-making and make available to them educational contexts that support them toward achieving competent and

---

**Xenia Hadjioannou,** Penn State Berks

https://doi.org/10.1515/9783110735604-006

confident bilingualism and biliteracies (Fu, Hadjioannou, and Zhou 2019; García, Johnson, and Seltzer 2017). However, meeting this charge presupposes a fundamental rehaul of normalized conceptualizations and practices in educational settings. This chapter reports on multi-year work with inservice teachers though a graduate course focused on supporting inservice teachers develop their translanguaging repertoires and envision and implement translanguaging practices in their professional contexts. The insights reported here are a distillation of what I have learned from my experience teaching about translanguaging pedagogy and are informed by analyses of student-created artifacts, course materials, and my reflective journals for the course. Central to this exploration is the framework of *reseeing*. Through their course experiences, inservice teachers responded to scaffolded invitations to critically examine (or resee) ideologies, norms, and practices, with the intention of reshaping their perceptions of bilingualism and "English Learners" toward a translanguaging orientation, and pursuing translanguaging practices in their teaching and their instructional contexts.

# 1 "Is a language other than English spoken in your home?"

In the United States, when students first enter school, a survey is sent home to be completed by the family. A key question invariably included in this survey is one that asks: "Is a language other than English spoken in your home?" Though the actual wording of this question varies across districts and states, its function is fairly standard: a positive response raises a red flag, which triggers a review of the child's proficiency in English. Typically, students who are determined to be adequately proficient in English are fundamentally treated as monolingual speakers of English, with no systemic considerations set in place to support or otherwise engage their heritage languages in the education process. On the other hand, students who are identified as not adequately proficient in English, are labeled as English Learners (EL) and the core objective of schooling becomes to help them develop native-like proficiency in English. In some situations, particularly in schools committed to culturally responsive pedagogy, home languages are acknowledged as relevant to children's schooling but, often, they are relegated to being an aid to the development of the student's proficiency in English rather than a fundamental component of their education. These practices are ubiquitous in the US educational system and represent a monolingual approach to teaching and learning.

In contrast, in educational settings that operate from a plurilingual, translanguaging perspective, bilingual students are viewed through a drastically different lens. When a family indicates that a language other than English is spoken in the home, that is not marked as a potential problem but as part of the linguistic tapestry of the school community. It is also understood as a vital part of the teaching and learning experience and of the relationship between the school and the family. If English is the target language or the primary language of instruction, the school will still ask about English proficiency, but that question will be asked differently and treated differently than in monolingually-oriented settings. In plurilingual settings, students who are proficient in English and another language are viewed and treated as experienced bilinguals and are supported in using all their languages in the process of learning. Students who are not, are understood not as English learners but as *emergent bilinguals*, individuals on the way to becoming experienced bilinguals. And the school's responsibility is to support them along this path. In this context, all of the students' languages are given a vital, voiced position in the pursuit of school learning, and the focus shifts from trying to help English learners become English knowers to facilitating the expansion of the language repertoires of all bilingual students, ultimately aspiring to experienced bilingualism and biliteracy (Fu, Hadjioannou, and Zhou 2019; García, Johnson, and Seltzer 2017; Pacheco et al. 2019; Gort and Sembiante 2015).

Despite the pervasiveness of monolingual ideologies in educational systems around the world and their decisive role in shaping the educational experiences of bilingual students in the US and beyond, recent scholarship suggests that English-only approaches to the education of bilingual students are incompatible with how bilinguals use their language resources to think, study, and learn (Flores and Schissel 2014; Fu, Hadjioannou, and Zhou 2019; García and Li Wei 2014; García et al. 2021; Herrera 2022). In addition, critical examinations of monolingual norms in education characterize monolingual frames as collusive with systems of racialized hegemony and oppression, which work to marginalize and colonize groups that speak non-preferred languages (Toh 2019; Watson and Shapiro 2018). In contrast, *translanguaging pedagogy* embraces the languages and cultures of all students, leveraging them in nurturing students' growth toward bilingualism and biliteracy (Fu, Hadjioannou, and Zhou 2019; García, Johnson, and Seltzer 2017; Pacheco et al. 2019; Gort and Sembiante 2015).

Repositioning to a translanguaging orientation from a monolingual perspective represents a paradigmatic shift (Pontier and Tian 2022). As such, it presents complex challenges for teachers in bilingual and English-centric contexts alike. Teachers operating within a translanguaging pedagogical model are called to recognize and honor students' complex cultural and linguistic identities (Creese and Blackledge 2010; Herrera 2022); engage in their teaching new and often unfamiliar linguistic practices and resources (de Oliveira, Gilmetdinova, and Pelaez-Morales 2016; Pacheco and Miller 2016); and construct plurilingual curricula and activities within the context of monolingual institutional goals (Martínez-Roldán 2015; Tian 2022). Such paradigmatic shifts to teaching praxis are not simple and they are not apolitical. A commitment to translanguaging pedagogy demands critical consideration of normative practice, identifying and dismantling oppressive patterns, reconceptualizing and redesigning curricula and instruction, and angling teaching toward an equitable and socially just educational context (Fu, Hadjioannou, and Zhou 2019; García, Johnson, and Seltzer 2017).

Moving away from long-standing, entrenched models and practices cannot be solely accomplished through top-down reform mandates or short-term professional development training (Darling-Hammond and McLaughlin 2011; Hutchinson and Hadjioannou 2019; Woodbury and Gess-Newsome 2002). Rather, practice transformation necessitates long term engagement with teachers as both learners and educators and "means providing occasions for teachers to reflect critically on their practice and to fashion new knowledge and beliefs about content, pedagogy, and learners" (Darling-Hammond and McLaughlin 2011: 82). As such, the need to prepare teachers to leverage the entirety of students' linguistic repertoires as a strategic and intentional component of their educational experience and to critically consider norms and practices is fundamental.

This chapter reflects empirical insights gained from several years of working with inservice teachers learning about translanguaging and its pedagogical implications in the context of graduate level coursework at a regional campus of a large, multicampus university in the northeastern United States. Much of this work was centered on a course on teaching literacy to linguistically diverse students, which sought to expand inservice teachers' translanguaging repertoires by introducing them to translanguaging theory and pedagogy, engaging them in critical examinations of their professional contexts and instructional praxis, and supporting them in envisioning and implementing a shift toward translanguaging practice. As the instructor, I redesigned the course to center translanguaging pedagogy, in reflection of my long-standing scholarship in the areas of linguistic diversity, language policy, and translanguaging. In addition, the course was informed by my personal journey toward translanguaging theory and a plurilingual perspective, which helped redefine how I see myself as a multilingual person, how I conceptualize the multilingual communities in which I participate, and how I envision education for young people. The data corpus considered in this analysis included reflective fieldnotes; syllabi and curricular materials; student assignments, discussion forum contributions and other written communications over the course of three semesters (from 2018 to 2020). In what follows, I will situate this analysis within García, Johnson, and Seltzer's (2017) translanguaging pedagogy framework of *stance, design, and shifts a*nd within the paradigm of justice-oriented teaching. I will then share examples of promising practices that emerged from this experience and highlight potential impediments to shifting towards a translanguaging paradigm.

## 2 Translanguaging pedagogy: Stance, design, and shifts

A translanguaging perspective on bilingualism theorizes that individuals have a single, unified linguistic repertoire, which encompasses the linguistic features of all their languages, (García and Li Wei 2014) and that, when communicating, bilinguals strategically select features from this unified repertoire to pursue effective communication in response to their audience and communicative intentions (García 2011). Indeed, García and Li Wei (2014) describe translanguaging as the natural languaging practice of bilinguals and characterize it as "bilingual norm."

Conceptualizing a unified language repertoire is a vital point, as it puts into question the long-standing, ubiquitous educational practice of treating the target language(s) of schooling as the only language(s) of relevance to the educative process. As a result, languages and nonstandard varieties besides the target language are excluded from educational contexts, and language separation policies regulate and constrain language use in bilingual education models. In contrast, the clear implication of a unified language repertoire is that "the development of proficiency in one language cannot reasonably be separated from the other languages and language tools of a speaker" (Fu, Hadjioannou, and Zhou 2019: 7). Translanguaging pedagogy purposefully and strategically engages all of students' languages in the learning process, with a focus on "making meaning, enhancing experience, and developing identity" (Li Wei 2018: 15). In addition, translanguaging pedagogy transforms power relations between teachers and students and fosters critical rethinking of "artificial and ideological divides" between such ostensibly dichotomous pairs as indigenous and immigrant, standard and nonstandard language varieties, majority and minority (Li Wei 2018: 15).

In envisioning instruction and assessment through translanguaging pedagogy, García, Johnson, and Seltzer (2017) structure their recommendations around the interrelated strands of *translanguaging stance*, the teachers' belief that all of a student's languages work together in meaning making and learning; *design*, which includes curriculum that actively encourages and integrates the use of multilingual and multimodal resources; and *shifts*, which involve the willingness to change the course of lessons to make space for student voices. According to García and her colleagues, this triptych, which is foundational to the empirical work that informs this chapter, is based upon a commitment to the purposes of translanguaging pedagogy, which include supporting student engagement with complex content and texts, creating translanguaging spaces that honor bilingual ways of knowing, developing linguistic practices for academic contexts, and supporting students' socioemotional development and confident bilingual identities (Fu, Hadjioannou, and Zhou 2019; Zhang and Hadjioannou 2022; Celic and Seltzer 2011).

## 3 Justice-oriented teaching and learning

Translanguaging pedagogy is fundamentally justice-oriented as it challenges the limiting barriers of monolingual ideologies of schooling and expands students' opportunities to use the entirety of their language repertoire in the service of learning. Calabrese Barton, Tan, and Birmingham (2020: 478) explain that "justice-oriented teaching and learning is that which is *equitable* and *consequential*." That is, teaching that "expand[s] opportunities for disciplinary engagement and learning in culturally relevant and rigorous ways" and which engages students in opportunities that encourage criticality that leads to actual change in hierarchies, patterns, and practices within and outside of school. Operating within such discourses as critical pedagogy, critical literacy, teaching for social justice, and antiracist pedagogy, "justice-oriented teachers use a curriculum that reflects students' personal and cultural identities; includes explicit instruction about oppression, prejudice, and inequity; and makes connections between curricular standards and social justice topics" (Dover 2016: 518). Pursuing these curricular objectives shapes a classroom environment that privileges student voices and multiple perspectives; encourages and instructs students questioning and deconstructing texts, discourses, and norms; allows indeterminacy and attuning to student ideas; and promotes change toward equity (Luke 2012; Dover 2016; Ciardiello 2004; Schultz 2008; Zapata et al. 2019).

Translanguaging pedagogy is inconceivable without a deep commitment to criticality and justice-oriented teaching and learning. As Li Wei (2018) argues in his articulation of translanguaging as a practical theory of language, criticality is baked into translanguaging, as its very enactment involves the ability to identify patterns of use, norms and hierarchies, and the willingness and skill to then push against conventions and counter-propose innovative alternatives.

Justice-oriented teaching is also crucially embedded in the three core beliefs García, Johnson, and Seltzer (2017) place at the heart of translanguaging pedagogy. The first belief involves the conviction that home and school language practices are both part of the language knowledge and cultural understanding of students and that they need to be leveraged synergistically as part of schooling to help students develop as knowers, learners, and meaning-makers. This belief is also central to the imperative for justice-oriented teaching to reflect "students' personal and cultural identities" (Dover 2016: 518). The second core belief involves valuing the knowledge of families and communities and engaging them as sources of knowledge, which caters to justice-oriented teaching's commitment to cultural relevance and multiple perspectives and sources of knowledge. Finally, the third core belief casts classrooms as democracies in action, a conceptualization that is also explicitly connected to justice-oriented teaching. In such a setting, it is not just the teacher who is identified as an expert, but students' expertise is also valued and involved in the co-construction of knowledge. In addition, democracy in action means taking a critical perspective to the world and to content that comes into classrooms, and engaging in the exploration of power dynamics, the identification of biases and silencing, and taking reparative action toward justice.

# 4 Shifting into translanguaging pedagogy through a re-seeing/revaluing lens

As mentioned earlier, translanguaging pedagogy represents a paradigmatic shift from the monolingual ideologies that pervasively inform approaches to and models for the education of linguistically diverse students in the United States. Monolingual ideologies permeate the very fabric of the US educational system: they are infused in ESL standards, in teacher education courses on the education of "English Learners," in the English language development models deployed to support students identified as English Leaners, in the language we use to refer to minoritized linguistic communities. As such, adopting and implementing translanguaging pedagogy cannot be accomplished but through a process of progressive, deliberate shifting of perspectives and practices.

In acknowledgment of this reality, my work on translanguaging pedagogy with inservice teachers has been informed by Yetta Goodman's (1996) invitation for teachers to (a) re-see and revalue readers by looking closely at what they do and acknowledging the complex meaning-making in which they engage while reading, and (b) to engage in practices that encourage and support readers to re-see and revalue themselves through guided reflection. Goodman's invitation to re-see and revalue offers a productive model for teacher education seeking to inspire and support teacher movement toward translanguaging pedagogy and will be used as an organizing principle in presenting my work with inservice teachers.

This involves experiences that compel teachers to re-see bilingualism by examining the languaging practices of experienced bilinguals; re-see the students schools identify as "English Learners" by getting to know their bilingual lives; re-see their own teaching through a critical eye and rethink instructional priorities and patterns; and expand their perspective to re-see their instructional contexts and consider existing structures and norms with a critical eye.

## 4.1 Re-seeing bilingualism

According to Valdés (2020: 192), "popular beliefs about bilingualism in the American context are part of a linguistic culture that is closely related to ideologies that consider monolingualism in English to be 'the crowning attribute of citizenship' (Jordan 1921: 35)."

Within this context, bilingualism occupies a peculiar position in the American imagination. Professionals who are experienced bilinguals and have been successful in English-medium contexts are admired for their ability to be proficient in more than one language. As a nonnative speaker of English who works at a U.S. university, I have often received compliments by people in my professional and personal social spheres over my English proficiency, the richness of my English vocabulary, and my ability to write in a formal academic register in a language I did not grow up speaking. Though I appreciate such compliments as well intentioned and authentic, it is also clear that they come from a monolingual view of the world, in which monolingualism is the presumed norm, and experienced, biliterate bilingualism is understood as an atypical, exceptional accomplishment instead of an ordinary outcome of a supportive, language-rich environment.

At the same time, however, as Haugen (1972: 308) notes in his classic essay titled *The Stigmata of Bilingualism* in the United States, being bilingual is often equated to being uneducated and poor, adding that "for many people, 'bilingual' is a euphemism for 'linguistically handicapped.'" Similarly, Lippi-Green (2011) observes that speaking English with an accent that distinguishes the speaker as nonnative is connected to discriminatory treatment, particularly when the accent is linked to nonwhite communities or nonpreferred countries of origin. Valdés (2020: 193) links these prejudices against bilinguals from marginalized communities to their perceived "flawed nature" when compared to the myth of "'true' or 'real' bilinguals who are the sum of two native-speaking monolinguals."

Therefore, to re-see and revalue bilingualism, it is important to help inservice teachers build their knowledge of the languaging practices of bilinguals and interrogate their assumptions about the nature of bilingualism. A practice I have found to be successful in beginning this revaluing line is inviting teachers to consider data from natural language interactions of experienced bilinguals and to explore the language work bilinguals do when interacting with each other. Particularly powerful can be transcripts of interactions between interlocutors who share more than one language. When introducing such transcripts, I always make it a point to clarify that they represent natural language interactions that demonstrate common languaging practices, not cherry-picked rare events. Table 1 presents an example of such an interaction I have shared with teachers. It is an excerpt from an instant messaging exchange with a friend who is also a college professor and with whom I share three language varieties: Modern Standard Greek (MSG), Cypriot Greek (CG), and American English (AE). The excerpt was part of a longer conversation making arrangements for a visit.

**Table 1:** Bilingual Interaction Sample.

| Speaker | Turn | Original message | English translation |
|---|---|---|---|
| Hara | 1 | Θα έρθει και η Σωτηρία από το τμήμα και σκεφτόμαστε πως θα το κάνουμε. Επίσης θέλω να οργανώσω ένα πάρτυ για την Stacey who is retiring and I do not know when | *Sotiria from the department is coming as well and we are wondering how to do this. I also want to organize a party for* Stacey who is retiring, and I do not know when |
| Xenia | 2 | είναι και η Σωτηρία ευπρόσδεκτη. Δεν την ξέρω, αλλά αυτό δεν είναι καθόλου πρόβλημα | *Sotiria is welcome too. I don't know her, but that is not a problem at all.* |
| Hara | 3 | **eisai thea** | *You rock* |
| Xenia | 4 | [Bus company name] bus baby! I can drive you down with me and then you can go back at your own time | [Bus company name] bus baby! I can drive you down with me and then you can go back at your own time |
| Hara | 5 | **tha to skefto kai tha su po!** thanks!!! | *I'll think about it and let you know!* Thanks!!! |

Notes:
a) Italics indicate English translations of expressions rendered in Greek
b) Bolded text marks the use of the Latin alphabet to represent Greek

When exploring the interaction excerpt in Table 1 in collaborative groups, the first thing my students notice is the flexible movement across named languages in the transcript. They often express surprise that this movement happens both across and within utterances and even sentences (see turns 2 and 4 for movement across utterances and turns 1 and 5 for within). Upon closer inspection, students note the presence of creative, non-standard norms of semiosis when they realize that there are occasions when Greek words are encoded using the Latin alphabet

(Turns 3 and 5). In the conversations that ensue, my monolingual students are invariably fascinated by the fact that two highly literate, experienced bilinguals are comfortably communicating by intermingling features from two named languages so fluidly. Many acknowledge that had they not known that both speakers are proficient in Greek and English, they would have assumed that this movement was the result of inadequate proficiency. And, some admit that that is how they have interpreted such translanguaging behaviors by bilingual students and families. Often this activity is coupled with other examinations such as scrutinizing signage and street art in multilingual neighborhoods, tracing the presence of languages other than English in popular music and TV, and noticing how bilingual people in their lives translanguage throughout the day. Ultimately, these discussions typically lead to the realization that, when translanguaging, bilinguals creatively leverage all their linguistic resources to pursue their communication objectives and connect with each another. This, along with scholarly texts that bring to the fore the fluid uses of language forms in bilingual communities, are often cited in reflections by the inservice teachers with whom I work as pivotal moments in their engagement with translanguaging pedagogy, as it helps them re-see bilingualism and understand translanguaging as a natural and productive bilingual practice.

## 4.2 Re-seeing "English Learners"

Another practice I find quite promising are opportunities to re-see the students the US school system identifies as English Learners. A significant preamble to this is an exploratory discussion of the different terms that have historically been used to label students who attend US public schools and who are deemed as needing specialized language support services due to limited proficiency in English. Critically examining such terms as Limited English Proficient (LEP), second language learner, English as a Second Language (ESL) student, English Language Learner (ELL), English Learner (EL), and Emergent Bilingual (EB) is a helpful exercise, as it involves teachers in interrogating the assumptions, ideologies, and values encapsulated in the terms we use (Martínez 2018; García 2009). It also encourages them to (a) consider how labels situate teachers and schooling in relation to the students we serve and our responsibilities toward them, and (b) to make informed choices about their preferred terminology/ies. In response, participants have routinely reported dismay at never having considered the different terminologies and their implications and often articulate a commitment to using empowering and valorizing terminology.

Another engagement that encourages the re-seeing and revaluing of the students U.S. schools label as "English Learners" is an assignment that asks teachers to interview and observe one of their emergent bilingual students with the purpose of developing a robust learner profile and a better understanding of their bilingual lives. In addition, the assignment involves teachers in investigating and learning about one of their student's heritage languages. In reflective comments on the assignment, teachers frequently identify this as an eye-opening experience. Common reactions involve acknowledgments of a growing awareness and respect of student and family funds of knowledge and embarrassed admissions of never thinking to learn more about the languages spoken by their students and their literacies in those languages. Several confess that, prior to this assignment, their focus when engaging with their bilingual students had centered on their English proficiency as described by their *ACCESS for ELLs* score reports (WIDA 2021) and they knew little about their bilingual status. This comment from a teacher after interviewing one of her bilingual students for the assignment is emblematic: "It's March and I never thought to find out what languages she spoke at home. She is fluent in two other languages! I had no idea." Interviewing bilingual students about their languaging practices and observing them across various communication situations at school prompts teachers to re-see their "English Learner" students and shift their perspective from one of deficit that focuses on a proficiency they do not yet have, to a perspective of valuing that focuses on the language knowledge they already have and their paths toward bi- or multilingualism.

In addition, this exploration provided teachers with actionable information regarding their students' language and literacy repertoires, which they could incorporate in their instructional design to engage all of their students' languages (and literacies) in the process of school learning. This was further supported by the project section that required teachers to compose a multimodal language profile of one of their focal students' home languages. Among other components, the projects included information about the language communities that speak the profiled language, about its phonology and writing system, and about characteristics that were pedagogically relevant. They also included bilingual pictionaries of words or phrases that would be helpful to the student they had interviewed. Encouraged to adopt a format that was meaningful and helpful to them, teachers created multimodal artifacts involving paragraphs of written text, diagrams, charts, images, and sound. Composing and sharing these profiles, yielded knowledge the teachers could employ in creating translanguaging spaces in their teaching, as well as in supporting their students' English development in more targeted ways. Later on in the semester, teachers often reported that this assignment had prompted them to take an interest in learning more about their students' home languages, casting themselves as learners, and using students and their families as resources. In one such instance, a teacher who at the beginning of the semester had related her struggles to get one of her emergent bilingual students to engage with her, sent me an update to report significant strides, adding: "I made a deal with [my student] that he needs to teach me a new word or phrase every day. He loves to see me struggle."

## 4.3 Re-seeing our own teaching: Scaffolded instructional redesign for translanguaging

Re-seeing and revaluing bilingualism and our bilingual students are fundamental to the process of stance shifting toward translanguaging pedagogy. However, a shift in beliefs and attitudes alone is unlikely to lead to transformative practice, particularly in the face of opposing forces in the form of entrenched practices and models in teachers' educational contexts and of their own long standing instructional habits (Hutchinson and Hadjioannou 2019). An engagement I have found useful in supporting teachers' adoption of translanguaging pedagogy in their teaching is a scaffolded revision of units they have taught before. This endeavor is supported by reading and discussing García, Johnson, and Seltzer's (2017) practitioner-oriented book *The Translanguaging Classroom*, in which the authors offer example-supported guidance for translanguaging design in instruction and assessment, with explicit focus on content objectives, as well as on general linguistic, language specific, and translanguaging objectives. In addition, García and her colleagues (2017: 72) encourage teachers to organize the elements of their instruction along the translanguaging design cycle which supports content integration, "bringing students' complex bilingual language practices to the surface," and students demonstrating their knowledge in multiple, authentic ways.

The process of reconceptualizing instructional units they are already teaching with a translanguaging pedagogy lens can be a productive one for teachers, as it encourages them to re-see their current instruction with a critical eye and identify blind spots as well as missed opportunities for including the perspective of minoritized linguistic and cultural communities. Along the way, the teachers intentionally work to create translanguaging spaces in their classrooms, where plurilingual content, conversations, and knowledge demonstrations are given productive, voiced positions, and where critical literacy considerations regarding power, bias and silencing are common and intentional. In addition, I believe that it sets the tone of translanguaging pedagogy as a consistent instructional frame rather than a "curricular ornament" (Siegel 1995: 473) that is to be briefly shoehorned into the "regular" curricular sequence, much like content related to African Americans often shows up in February and poetry shows up in April, only to be quickly tucked away in favor of more canonical content.

The units, which are workshopped for a number of weeks in and out of class with the support of teacher and peer conferences, represent a wide range of topics and subject areas. Admittedly a challenging assignment that requires a lot of revision and recalibration during composition, the unit revision prompts teachers to consider such unfamiliar practices as making available multimodal resources in their students' home languages, planning discussions of language choices in multilingual texts, offering language choice in student work and designing bilingual assessments. It also involves utilizing knowledge of students' home languages for targeted grammar and vocabulary explorations, and building in opportunities to investigate and interrogate multiple perspectives, identify patterns of oppression, and envision justice-oriented action.

Revised units included in the data collected have ranged from an early elementary unit on butterflies that incorporates multilingual and multimodal resources and includes bilingual charts and diagrams as assessments, to a middle grades social studies unit on human geography taking a critical perspective to the notion of regions and its use to shape and marginalize cultural identities, to a middle school unit on writing poetry with authentic voice in which students are supported through culturally and linguistically diverse mentor texts toward enhancing their authoring voice and using multiple languages in their writing. In a note the author of the latter example sent me while teaching her unit after the end of the course, she shared the story of a reading conference with two of her students:

> I wish you could have been a fly on the wall for today's meeting. Today, my EB read aloud to us from the Spanish copy of her *Bravo!* by Margarita Engle book while the other student and I followed along in our English copies. Then she shared her thinking about the poem with us – some of the sharing was in Spanish and some was in English – but knowing that the other student and I don't speak Spanish – she translated herself for us. She just had so much to say and saying it first in Spanish helped her. When she was finished, the other student shared the poem she had chosen to read – and then I listened as my EB and the other student talked about how that poem changed just a bit when translated into Spanish. I honestly had tears of joy in my eyes to hear the conversation they had.

Ultimately, it can be said that opportunities to re-see and re-envision instruction along a translanguaging framework, particularly when followed by successful implementations, can be vital in validating translanguaging pedagogy as a realistic and effective model in the eyes of teachers and in cementing its presence in their praxis.

## 4.4 Re-seeing our instructional context

Teachers and their classroom communities are not islands. They are situated within the interlinking contexts of their schools, their surrounding communities, the different levels of the educational system, and other sociopolitical contexts (Webb, Metha, and Jordan 2010; Darling-Hammond and McLaughlin 2011). Making the paradigmatic shift from monolingually oriented ideologies to a plurilingual perspective and translanguaging pedagogy should also involve a critical awareness of these ecologies and their normative structures and practices. Such awareness can be vital in better understanding the experience of emergent and experienced bilingual students and their families in relation to schooling and recognizing institutionalized affordances and biases that shape their learning opportunities and social encounters and affirm or undermine their identities as bilinguals. In addition, this awareness can be instructive both in working within the system to create spaces for the enactment of translanguaging pedagogy, but also in envisioning and carrying out action toward systemic, justice-oriented change.

A project I have found to be highly productive in supporting teachers in re-seeing their instructional contexts is a mini ethnographic case study of sorts through which teachers are invited to examine their own schools and the experience of bilingual students from minoritized communities within them. As part of this examination, teachers investigate their school demographics for information about the linguistic as well as the cultural and ethnic diversity of the student body. In addition, they take a walking tour of the area surrounding their school buildings, taking photos and fieldnotes with a focus on the presence of non-English or bilingual signage, community resources, and other elements that may be welcoming or unwelcoming to culturally and/or linguistically minoritized communities. Moving inward, the teachers then spend time conducting critical field observations within their school buildings, with a focus on the school institutional culture and overall climate, curriculum, and pedagogy. Among other considerations, through these observations, teachers attend to such issues as the existence of opportunities for bilingual students to see, hear or use their heritage languages; the groupings and socialization opportunities experienced by students identified as English learners throughout the school day; the diversity of experience represented in curricular material and bookshelves; and the types of learning engagements and performance assessments provided to English Learners. In the write up of this project, teachers report the findings of this exploration and propose specific actions for change and advocacy toward equitable learning opportunities for minoritized students and for a justice-oriented learning experience for all students.

Through these explorations, teachers get to re-see the schools in which they teach and to interrogate practices and patterns they may have thought unremarkable in the past, as well as notice students whose experience may have gone unseen. Some of their findings are hopeful and affirming and the teachers are happy to now be aware of them, whereas other findings are concerning and prompt teachers to explore avenues for change. So, for instance, several of my students are pleased to discover newcomer kits in various languages in their school counselor's office and note the presence of bilingual posters in several classrooms, and a developing school ethos for honoring student funds of knowledge through curriculum and instruction, and through expanding the diversity of the literature available to the students. Other common findings, however, include a marginalization of minoritized languages and perspectives in curricular material and in instruction, persistent privileging of English and of certain groups of students, teacher biases and prejudices against marginalized students and their families, and insidious social segregation of bilingual and other culturally minoritized students within and beyond formal learning experiences.

Many teachers report being surprised at the pervasiveness of patterns in their own schools that consistently marginalize minoritized communities and bilinguals in particular. When exploring opportunities for change and advocacy, most express a commitment to enact translanguaging pedagogy in their own classrooms, citing specific shifts they are already in the process of making. Many report already having spoken to colleagues, ESL teachers, librarians and administrators about ways they can better support the development of their students' bilingual repertoires and nurture their identities as bilingual people. Common ideas include enriching libraries and curricular resources with plurilingual materials, involving students in locally focused advocacy and change projects, engaging families by developing plurilingual family resources and by leveraging their knowledge and expertise. Beyond their buildings, teachers recognize a need for wider systemic changes at the district and state levels, proposing such ideas as rethinking state regulations, guidance and standards for working with emergent and experienced bilingual students and their families; organizing professional learning opportunities for teachers to learn about translanguaging pedagogy and explore how to bring it into their classrooms; and creating material banks and guides school personnel can use to create a plurilingually oriented, welcoming environment for the families they serve.

# 5 Resistances to shifting toward translanguaging pedagogy

Despite the generally promising information I have shared so far, this chapter would be incomplete if I did not also acknowledge that shifting toward translanguaging pedagogy is not an easy process and that there are many resistances along the way. Some of these resistances are at the institutional level, whereas others can be described as personal-level resistances though, in many ways, they are also rooted in teachers' professional contexts.

As discussed early in the chapter, the U.S. educational system, as well as many other systems around the world, are organized around monolingual ideologies that involve a resolute focus on the target language(s) of instruction and exclude or marginalize other languages and language varieties from formal educational experiences. Consequently, dominant structures and educational models are built with monolingualism as a core structural principle. For example, educational standards explicitly pursue idealized native-like proficiency (Valdés 2020) in the target languages, textbooks and instructional materials typically reflect the language of instruction with little if any acknowledgment of other languages or language varieties spoken by their target audience, and the acquisition of languages other than English is often relegated to minimal foreign language instruction in high school. In addition, the instructional models employed to support students who are not yet proficient in the language of instruction ubiquitously focus on the rapid acquisition of English, with little attention to heritage languages and the students' literacies in them (Fu, Hadjioannou, and Zhou 2019).

These dominant structures hold great gravity in all aspects of schooling and represent realities that are in many ways outside of individual teachers' control. Beyond this, when individual teachers or faculty groups push for changes consistent with translanguaging pedagogy such as the examples shared in the preceding section, and particularly when these changes pursue social justice agendas, they are often met with resistance from administrators and colleagues, who offer these structural realities as justifications for why the proposed changes are impracticable or inappropriate.

A type of resistance that challenges teachers on the personal level has to do with the powerful tag that dominant discourses and ideologies have on instructional praxis. Teachers' long-standing exposure to these frameworks means that they are deeply (and often unconsciously) rooted into their professional identities and their instructional repertoires (Hutchinson and Hadjioannou 2019). Therefore, even if teachers are theoretically committed to translanguaging pedagogy, their interpretations of teaching situations as well as their reactions and instructional decisions may still be influenced by these long-standing frames. In addition, it needs to be acknowledged that a shift to translanguaging pedagogy carries personal costs both in time and money, as it often involves locating and acquiring or creating plurilingual instructional materials and redesigning curricula to create translanguaging spaces and pursue translanguaging learning objectives. At the same time, this shift can be very fatiguing because of its time demands but even more so when teachers feel that they are alone in the effort to transform their praxis and bring about consequential change in their schools. On this point, the sustaining power of a community of translanguaging teachers cannot be understated.

# 6 Conclusion

Monolingual ideologies are a dominant force in US education, running through systemic structures and educational models, and decisively influencing the experiences of students and their teachers. In this volume, a case is made that translanguaging pedagogy is a promising approach for the education of all students. Embracing translanguaging pedagogy represents a paradigmatic shift, which cannot be reasonably accomplished through top-down reform. We must start with the teachers! To do so, we must provide "occasions for teachers to reflect critically on their practice and to fashion new knowledge and beliefs about content, pedagogy and learners" (Darling-Hammond and McLaughlin 2011: 82). Goodman's (1996) notions of re-seeing and revaluing can be a valuable heuristic in this endeavor. Opportunities for teachers to re-see bilingualism support their understanding of the languaging practices of bilinguals, and explorations that prompt them to re-see "English Learners" are important in helping teachers recognize them as individuals with complex linguistic knowledge who are bilinguals in the making. In addition, opportunities for designing translanguaging instruction can support teachers in se-seeing their own teaching and revaluing their instructional priorities and instructional patterns. Finally, looking at their own schools with a critical eye can help teachers re-see their instructional contexts and prompt them into action for justice-oriented change that honors and meaningfully engages all of their students' languages in the process of school-based learning. By starting with the teachers, teacher education can serve a crucial role in helping teachers' develop their translanguaging repertoires and in supporting them envision and implement translanguaging pedagogy in their professional contexts.

# References

Calabrese Barton, Angela, Edna Tan & Daniel J. Birmingham. 2020. Rethinking high-leverage practices in justice-oriented ways. *Journal of Teacher Education* 71(4). 477–494.

Celic, Christina & Kate Seltzer. 2011. "Translanguaging: A CUNY-NYSIEB Guide for Educators." CUNY-NYSIEB. http://www.nysieb.ws.gc.cuny.edu/files/2012/06/FINAL-Translanguaging-Guide-With-Cover-1.pdf (accessed 18 January 2016).

Ciardiello, A. Vincent. 2004. Democracy's young heroes: An instructional model of critical literacy practices. *The Reading Teacher* 58(2). 138–147.

Creese, Angela & Adrian Blackledge. 2010. Translanguaging in the bilingual classroom: A pedagogy for learning and teaching? *The Modern Language Journal* 94(1). 103–115.

Darling-Hammond, Linda & Milbrey W. McLaughlin. 2011. Policies that support professional development in an era of reform. *Phi Delta Kappan* 92(6). 81–92.

de Oliveira, Luciana C., Alsu Gilmetdinova & Carolina Pelaez-Morales. 2016. The use of Spanish by a monolingual kindergarten teacher to support English language learners. *Language & Education: An International Journal* 30(1). 22–42.

Dover, Alison G. 2016. Teaching for social justice and the common core: Justice-oriented curriculum for language arts and literacy. *Journal of Adolescent & Adult Literacy* 59(5). 517–527.

Flores, Nelson & Jamie L. Schissel. 2014. Dynamic bilingualism as the norm: Envisioning a heteroglossic approach to standards-based reform. *TESOL Quarterly* 48(3). 454–479.

Fu, Danling, Xenia Hadjioannou & Xiaodi Zhou. 2019. *Translanguaging for Emergent Bilinguals: Inclusive Teaching in the Linguistically Diverse Classroom*. New York: Teachers College Press.

García, Ofelia. 2009. Emergent bilinguals and TESOL: What's in a name? *TESOL Quarterly* 43(2). 322–326.

García, Ofelia. 2011. Theorizing translanguaging for educators. In Christina Celic & Kate Seltzer (eds.), *Translanguaging: CUNY-NYSIEB Guide for Educators*, 1–6. New York: The Graduate Center, The City University of New York.

García, Ofelia, Nelson Flores, Kate Seltzer, Li Wei, Ricardo Otheguy & Jonathan Rosa. 2021. Rejecting abyssal thinking in the language and education of racialized bilinguals: A manifesto. *Critical Inquiry in Language Studies* 18(3). 203–228.

García, Ofelia, Susana Ibarra Johnson & Kate Seltzer. 2017. *The Translanguaging Classroom: Leveraging Student Bilingualism for Learning*. Philadelphia: Caslon.

García, Ofelia & Li Wei. 2014. *Translanguaging: Language, Bilingualism and Education*. New York: Palgrave Macmillan.

Goodman, Yetta M. 1996. Revaluing readers while readers revalue themselves: Retrospective miscue analysis. *The Reading Teacher* 49(8). 600–609.

Gort, Mileidis & Sabrina Francesca Sembiante. 2015. Navigating hybridized language learning spaces through translanguaging pedagogy: Dual language preschool teachers' languaging practices in support of emergent bilingual children's performance of academic discourse. *International Multilingual Research Journal* 9(1). 7–25.

Haugen, Einar. 1972. *The Ecology of Language. Language Science and National Development*. Stanford: Stanford University Press.

Herrera, Luz Yadira. 2022. Growing critical bilingual literacies in a bilingual teacher residency program. *Journal of Language, Identity & Education* 21(3). 174–190.

Hutchinson, Mary & Xenia Hadjioannou. 2019. Fidelity of practice: The challenge of transformative change in teacher professional development. In Ann E. Lopez and Elsie L. Olan (eds.),

*Transformative Pedagogies for Teacher Education: Critical Action, Agency and Dialogue in Teaching and Learning Contexts*, 87–102. Charlotte: Information Age Publishing.
Li Wei. 2018. Translanguaging as a practical theory of language. *Applied Linguistics* 39(1). 9–30.
Lippi-Green, Rosina. 2011. *English with an Accent: Language, Ideology and Discrimination in the United States*. Florence: Taylor & Francis Group.
Luke, Allan. 2012. Critical literacy: Foundational notes. *Theory Into Practice* 51(1). 4–11.
Martínez, Ramón Antonio. 2018. Beyond the English learner label: Recognizing the richness of bi/multilingual students' linguistic repertoires. *The Reading Teacher* 71(5). 515–522.
Martínez-Roldán, Carmen María. 2015. Translanguaging practices as mobilization of linguistic resources in a Spanish/English bilingual after-school program: An analysis of contradictions. *International Multilingual Research Journal* 9(1). 43–58.
Pacheco, Mark B., Shannon M. Daniel, Lisa C. Pray & Robert T. Jiménez. 2019. Translingual practice, strategic participation, and meaning-making. *Journal of Literacy Research* 51(1). 75–99.
Pacheco, Mark B. & Mary E. Miller. 2016. Making meaning through translanguaging in the literacy classroom. *The Reading Teacher* 69(5). 533–537.
Pontier, Ryan W. & Zhongfeng Tian. 2022. Paradigmatic tensions in translanguaging theory and practice in teacher education: Introduction to the special issue. *Journal of Language, Identity & Education* 21(3). 139–43.
Schultz, Brian. 2008. Strategizing, sustaining, and supporting justice-oriented teaching. *Democracy & Education* 17(3). 8.
Siegel, Marjorie. 1995. More than words: The generative power of transmediation for learning. *Canadian Journal of Education / Revue Canadienne de l'éducation* 20(4). 455–475.
Tian, Zhongfeng. 2022. Translanguaging design in a third grade Chinese language arts class. *Applied Linguistics Review* 13(3). 327–343.
Toh, Glenn. 2019. Oppression, obscuration and ideology. In Glenn Toh (ed.), *Effecting Change in English Language Teaching: Exposing Collaborators and Culprits in Japan*, 51–71. Cham: Springer International Publishing.
Valdés, Guadalupe. 2020. The future of the seal of biliteracy: Issues of equity and inclusion. In Amy Jeineke & Kristin Davis (eds.), *The Seal of Biliteracy: Case Studies and Consideration for Policy Implementation*, 175–201. (Contemporary Language Education). Charlotte: Information Age Publishing.
Watson, Missy & Rachael Shapiro. 2018. Clarifying the multiple dimensions of monolingualism: Keeping our sights on language politics. *Forum – Conference on College Composition and Communication* 38. https://files.eric.ed.gov/fulltext/EJ1176417.pdf (accessed 30 March, 2021).
Webb, L. Dean, Arlene Metha & K. Forbis Jordan. 2010. *Foundations of American education*. Upper Saddle River: Pearson Merrill.
WIDA. 2021. "ACCESS for ELLs scores and reports." WIDA, Board of Regents of the University of Wisconsin System. https://wida.wisc.edu/assess/access/scores-reports (accessed 29 March 2021).
Woodbury, Sonia & Julie Gess-Newsome. (2002). Overcoming the paradox of change without difference: A model of change in the arena of fundamental school reform. *Educational Policy* 16(5). 763–782.
Zapata, Angie, Selena Van Horn, Daryl Moss & Misha Fugit. 2019. Improvisational teaching as being with: Cultivating a relational presence toward justice-oriented literacies. *Journal of Adolescent & Adult Literacy* 63(2). 179–187.
Zhang, Xuezi & Xenia Hadjioannou. 2022. Chinese graduate students' translanguaging practice in the context of academic writing in English. *Applied Linguistics Review* 13(3). 373–388.

Wayne E. Wright, Trish Morita-Mullaney, Woongsik Choi, and Haiyan Li

# Chapter 6
# Building bilingual teachers' translanguaging repertoires in a new immigrant destination state

**Abstract:** This case study examines the extent to which a teacher training program helped bilingual teachers develop their knowledge and practice of translanguaging pedagogies. Seven bilingual education teachers completed an ELL licensure program in addition to a new Dual Language Bilingual Education (DLBE) Graduate Certificate Program as part of a federally funded project to improve DLBE education in Indiana. The study addresses the following research questions: (1) What are teachers' views of bilingualism and translanguaging and how have they changed? (2) How do teachers describe their own translanguaging practices, and those of their students? And (3) To what extent have the teachers changed their teaching practices to engage in more translanguaging pedagogies? Data are drawn from teacher interviews, discussion board postings, audio comments on VoiceThread discussions, course assignments, and videos of teachers' classroom instruction. Findings reveal some success of the program in helping teachers build their translanguaging repertoires in the classroom and raise their consciousness about the monoglossic ideological structure in the institution. However, translanguaging instances were observed more frequently during Spanish times to benefit English-dominant students. More work is needed to help teachers develop the critical consciousness and agency needed to create a more socially just classroom space for their ELL students.

## 1 Introduction

This chapter provides a critical analysis of Indiana's Dual Language Bilingual Education (DLBE) policy and programs and presents a case study of the first cohort of in-service bilingual education teachers to complete Purdue University's English Language Learner (ELL) teacher licensure program and new DLBE Graduate Certificate Program. We argue that such training is essential to help DLBE teachers

**Wayne E. Wright, Trish Morita-Mullaney, Woongsik Choi, Haiyan Li,** Purdue University

https://doi.org/10.1515/9783110735604-007

develop their translanguaging repertoires (García and Li Wei 2014) and shift their language ideologies (Kroskrity 2004) to ensure the success of their students.

Following García's (2009) framework of dynamic bilingualism, we use the term "translanguaging" to refer to the natural and normal ways bilinguals mix and use their languages in their everyday lives without adherence to the boundaries of "named" languages to make sense of their bilingual worlds, to communicate, and to learn (see also García and Li Wei 2014). In the context of the classroom, we use translanguaging to refer to "pedagogical practices that use bilingualism as a resource rather than ignore it or perceive it as a problem" (Baker and Wright 2021: 464). Teachers' translanguaging repertoires include their developing *stances* on the appropriateness of translanguaging, ways they *design* instruction inclusive of translanguaging pedagogies, and strategic *shifts* in their instructional practices which enable students to draw on all of their linguistic resources to learn effectively (García, Johnson, and Seltzer 2017). We also view translanguaging as a form of culturally sustaining pedagogy (Paris and Alim 2017), given that students' home languages are a central element of their cultural identity. Simply put, educational approaches that fail to value and further develop students' home languages cannot be culturally sustaining.

DLBE is a broad label for a variety of models that target various student populations, separately or in combination, for purposes of developing proficiency in two (or more) languages (Wright and Choi in press). We view DLBE programs as essential for ensuring social justice for historically marginalized multilingual students, including students officially designated as ELLs,[1] heritage language speakers, and racial and ethnic minorities. Nonetheless, we acknowledge that even two-way bilingual programs, where ELLs and English majority students are purposely integrated, are often grounded in a monoglossic perspective (Baker and Wright 2021), are subject to gentrification (Cervantes-Soon et al. 2020; Delavan, Freire, and Valdez 2021; García-Mateus 2020; Morita-Mullaney and Chesnut 2022), and often cater more to the desires and needs of the "rich and white" (Flores, Tseng, and Subtirelu 2021). Thus, raising the "critical consciousness" of DLBE teachers around power relations and inequalities in the policies, practices, and pedagogy of two-way programs is essential within our teacher training programs (Palmer, Cervantes-Soon, and Heiman 2019; Cervantes-Soon et al. 2017).

---

[1] We recognize and value terms such as emergent bilingual and multilingual learners as more inclusive terms that recognize students' entire linguistic repertoire. We use the term English language learner (ELL) here to specifically focus on the subset of multilingual students who are officially designated as students in the process of attaining proficiency in English, and thus legally entitled to state and federal programs and support.

## 2 The Indiana context

Indiana is a new immigrant destination state with a history of neglect of its rapidly growing ELL population (Morita-Mullaney 2019; Morita-Mullaney and Singh 2021). DLBE programs are fairly new in Indiana, supported by recent legislation driven by neoliberal ideologies designed to provide future economic advantages through one-way DLBE programs that only serve language-majority English speakers. Indiana's legislation was directly inspired by the Utah model which has mainly served predominantly white English-speaking students learning Spanish and Chinese (Freire, Valdez, and Delavan 2017; Sung and Tsai 2019). Thus, the state's DLBE programs were not created from a social-justice perspective to right historic wrongs and address the unique linguistic, cultural and academic needs of ELLs – the students for whom bilingual education was originally intended to benefit (Wiley and Wright 2004).

Nonetheless, state support for DLBE has opened up ideological and implementation spaces (Hornberger 2005) for some districts to offer two-way DLBE programs inclusive of ELL students. Few Indiana bilingual teachers have state ELL teacher licensure, and currently there is no state bilingual licensure (Morita-Mullaney and Stallings 2018). Thus, few Indiana bilingual teachers have received ELL training, and even fewer have any training in bilingual education. Even fewer are familiar with the concept of translanguaging. At Purdue University we aim to rectify these problems with accessible ELL licensure and graduate DLBE certificate programs that are grounded in research and a social justice framework (Morita-Mullaney et al. 2020). With rich longitudinal data from multiple sources, this study makes a unique contribution to the literature on ways to build bilingual teachers' translanguaging repertoires by documenting our successes and challenges in a new immigrant destination state (Hilburn 2014).

## 3 Participating schools and in-service DLBE teachers

The participants in this study are the grant program's first cohort of seven in-service teachers who teach in DLBE education programs at two schools in different Indiana school districts. Silton Elementary School[2] is in a district of about 50,000 on the fringe of the greater Indianapolis urban area. Silton has one of the longest-running DLBE programs in the state. It began in 1994 with one-way

---

[2] Pseudonyms are used for all names of schools and school districts.

Spanish immersion programs primarily serving majority white English-speaking students in grades K-6. In 2008 the school began moving towards a two-way DLBE model inclusive of the growing number of Latinx students in the district. ELLs now account for about 10% of the school district's total student population. In grades K-2, instruction follows an 80/20 model (e.g., 80% in Spanish, 20% in English), moving to a 70/30 model in grade 3. The upper grades (4–6) follow a 50/50 model with paired classrooms, meaning students spend half the day with a teacher providing instruction in English and the other half with a teacher providing instruction in Spanish. Students have the option of continuing with the DLBE program through middle school and high school.

In contrast, Mapleton Elementary School is in a small town of about 35,000 in Northern Indiana, which has also recently experienced a demographic shift. Latinx ELLs now make up about 22% of students in the school district. Mapleton's DLBE program was established in 2017 and was just in its second year at the time this study began. Kindergarten and first-grade students were in a 50/50 model supported by the state's grant program. At the time, Mapleton was one of the two-way programs in Indiana, made possible by state funding. Mapleton uses a 50/50 paired classroom model, with one English and one Spanish classroom in grades K – 2. The school plans to slowly grow the program to grade 5 as the students move up in grade level. The district plans to open up another DLBE strand in another elementary school.

Among the seven participating teachers, four teach both Spanish and English in the same classroom, and three teach in English as part of a paired-classroom model with a Spanish-speaking partner[3] (see Table 1).

**Table 1:** Participating DLBE Bilingual Teachers.

| Teacher | School | Grade | Language(s) of Instruction |
|---|---|---|---|
| Emily | Silton | K | Spanish & English |
| Connie | Mapleton | K | English |
| Cherise | Silton | 1st | Spanish & English |
| Jill | Mapleton | 1st | English |
| Teresa* | Silton | 2nd | Spanish & English |
| Lorena | Silton | 3rd | Spanish & English |
| Sofia* | Silton | 6th | English |

*Sofia previously taught 1st grade (Spanish & English) and Teresa previously taught 3rd grade (Spanish & English) the prior school year when they began the grant program. Others remained in the same grade level.

---

[3] Some Spanish speaking-partner teachers were part of the original group of participants, but withdrew for reasons not directly related to the project.

Sofia, Lorena, and Teresa are Latina Spanish speakers, though Sofia describes herself as a heritage speaker who reclaimed her Spanish language in college. Emily and Cherise are white non-native Spanish speakers. Connie and Jill are white English majority speakers who are making an effort to learn some Spanish. In the findings section below we will further discuss their evolving linguistic identities.

Both Silton and Mapleton began their DLBE programs from a monoglossic ideology insisting on the strict separation of the languages. Most of the participants were experienced teachers. However, prior to participating in this grant program, only three had previously completed an ELL teacher licensure program, and none had received formal bilingual education teacher training beyond short-term professional development workshops sponsored by their districts. The Mapleton teachers, for example, were sent on a short trip to Utah to visit dual language schools and learn about the model that adheres to strict language separation. The Silton teachers have many more years of experience with dual language, and some had attended conferences such as La Cosecha in New Mexico and participated in professional development trainings that got them thinking more about ways to help students "bridge" or make cross-language connections between their separated English and Spanish instruction time (Beeman and Urow 2012).

## 4 Professional development and data sources

A five-year National Professional Development Grant from the U.S. Department of Education was awarded to Purdue University to help dual language teachers earn state ELL teacher licensure and complete a new DLBE Graduate Certificate program developed with support from the grant.[4] Teachers participated in seven online, asynchronous courses that were highly interactive with up-to-date readings, video lectures, text- and voiced-based discussions, collaborative group assignments, and field experiences (see Morita-Mullaney et al. 2020 for details on the development of the program).

During this 18-month program, dual language teachers moved through the foundations of linguistics, English language development, second language teaching and learning, assessment, and content area instruction, culminating with two

---

[4] The Indiana Department of Education has embraced our programs by provided funding for teachers to complete our ELL licensure program and have helped advertise our DLBE Graduate Certificate Program.

courses on the foundations and methods of bilingual education. All courses focused on the constructs of oral language, vocabulary in use, and small group instruction. Participating teachers also received instructional coaching six times over the 18-month period from a highly experienced dual language, bilingual coach. Coaching sessions focused on fostering sustained interaction among students and teachers and other issues.

In this chapter we share the findings of a qualitative case study focused on the case of the seven DLBE teacher and their developing translanguage repertoires. We address the following research questions: (1) What are the teachers' ideologies of bilingualism and translanguaging stances and how have they changed? (2) How do teachers describe their own and their students' translanguaging? And (3) To what extent have the teachers developed their translanguaging repertoires and shifted their classroom instruction practices to include translanguaging design?

We focus primarily on data collected in Fall 2019, after teachers had completed the 2018–2019 school year, the five online courses in the ELL Licensure Program, and four coaching sessions. In Fall 2019, the teachers took the two bilingual education courses needed to complete the DLBE Graduate Certificate. While the ELL licensure courses are taught from a bilingual lens and introduced the teachers to the concepts of translanguaging and translanguaging pedagogies, these concepts were of greater focus in the two bilingual education courses. Also in Fall 2019, the teachers received two additional coaching sessions, and the research team conducted one final classroom observation, video recording the teachers' English language arts (ELA) and Spanish language arts (SLA) blocks near the end of the semester.

In their final semester in our project, teachers took the DLBE courses. In the Foundations of Bilingual Education course, the teachers read chapters from *Foundations of Bilingual Education and Bilingualism* (Baker and Wright 2021)[5] and from *Dual Language Essentials for Teachers and Administrators* (Freeman, Freeman, and Mercuri 2018). They discussed these readings via traditional text-based discussion boards and also via VoiceThread, a cloud-based platform which enables audio and video discussions in an asynchronous format. Assignments included a bilingual proficiency self-assessment, and a bilingual program observation (conducted in their own schools and classrooms).

For the Bilingual Education Teaching Methods course, the teachers read chapters from *Biliteracy from the Start: Literacy Squared in Action* (Escamilla et al. 2013), and *Teaching Reading and Writing in Spanish and English in Bilingual and Dual Language Classrooms* (Freeman and Freeman 2006). They discussed these

---

5 At the time of the course, students read the 6th edition of Baker and Wright published in 2017.

readings via the discussion boards and VoiceThreads. Using the Literacy Squared framework, they conducted observations within their own classrooms and developed a biliteracy lesson plan. The Literacy Squared framework contributes to the development of teachers' translanguaging repertoire with a focus on methods to bridge Spanish and English literacy instruction, to use cross-language strategies (e.g., cognates), and to develop students' metalanguage. The Freeman and Freeman text also emphasized cross-language connections, pushing back against traditional models that insist on the strict separation of languages. As a cumulative and culminating project, the teachers worked in school-teams to evaluate their programs using the Center for Applied Linguistics' *Guiding Principles for Dual Language Education* (Howard et al. 2018).

Each of the six coaching sessions involved a debrief and discussion following the coach's observation of the teacher's classroom instruction. The coaching sessions were designed to focus on classroom interaction, oral language development, and vocabulary, and thus were not specifically focused on translanguaging. However, given that translanguaging pedagogy is conducive to each of these areas, the topic came up in several of the sessions.

Video recorded classroom observations were conducted by members of the research team focused on each teacher's language arts instructional block in English and/or Spanish. To fully capture instruction and classroom interactions, two video cameras were used – one focused on the teacher and the other focused, when appropriate, on pairs or small groups inclusive of ELL students. Digital audio recorders were also placed on the teacher and near the students.

Cumulatively, the data collected for this study include the following: Coursework from the two bilingual education courses including (a) 5 assignments, (b) 23 discussion board postings, and (c) transcriptions of teachers' audio comments on 36 VoiceThread discussions; Coaching data including (d) transcriptions of 34 coaching sessions interviews, (e) 42 coach-teacher reflections, (f) 6 coach reflections; and (g) over 25 hours of video recordings (and corresponding audio recordings) from classroom observations conducted in 2019.

Analysis of online course data was informed by the framework developed by Paulus and Wise (2019) for analyzing online talk for evidence of transformation and learning. Under this framework, we defined the "object of interest" as *teacher statements about translanguaging* including statements of their views, descriptions of their own and their students' use of translanguaging, and the teachers' descriptions of their pedagogical uses of translanguaging in the classroom. This object of interest is conceptualized as a characteristic of individual teachers, rather than the group collectively. That is, we first looked at each teacher individually to understand their translanguaging repertoire, including their stance, design, and shifts, before drawing any conclusions about the group as a whole. Our assumption is that the teacher's online talk represents their inner-psychological states, that is, their current understandings and development of their translanguaging repertoires. While the online talk was naturally occurring, we as researchers had some measure of control over the environment itself. While we did not teach the bilingual courses or participate in the discussions, the first author designed the courses and supervised the course instructor. The first and second authors also recorded video lectures for several of the course modules. Thus, the teachers' coursework and interactions constitute what Paulus and Wise classify as "researcher-influenced ('designed') online talk." Specifically, we designed these courses and opportunities for "online talk" to include attention to the development of bilingual teachers' understandings and effective classroom uses of translanguaging.

Data handling and analysis were informed by the approach outlined by Richards (2021). All course data and coaching data were imported into NVivo 12 for Teams for organization and analysis. We created case codes for each teacher, recording attributes such as school, grade-level, and language of instruction. Thematic codes were then created and closely aligned to each research question to capture ideologies of bilingualism and translanguaging (RQ#1), teachers' and students' own uses of translanguaging (RQ#2), and use of translanguaging pedagogy (RQ#3). All course assignments and two discussion boards that had an explicit focus on translanguaging were manually coded. Given the large amount of data, we used NVivo's search features to identify other locations in the data record containing teachers' talk about translanguaging, using terms such as translanguage/translanguaging, codeswitch/codeswitching, bridge/bridging, cross-language/linguistic, mix, metalanguage, and Spanglish. Relevant matches were carefully reviewed and coded. A matrix highlighting the number of coded passages for each thematic code by teacher case code enabled us to dive deeper by reviewing the thematic coding unique to each teacher. We then created detailed memos for each teacher to summarize each of the thematic codes. These memos were also used to capture our findings of the video analysis. Each instance of translanguaging observed in the teacher's classroom during English and/or Spanish language arts instruction was timestamped and described. After multiple readings we did a second cycle of coding within the memos and other codes to capture patterns and themes. Review and discussion of the teacher memos enabled us to answer the research questions relevant to each teacher and draw conclusions about the group of teachers as a collective whole.

## 5 Teachers' ideologies of bilingualism and translanguaging stances

All teachers expressed positive views of bilingualism, meaning in general they valued the idea of children and others knowing two (or more) languages, and bilingual teachers valued their own bilingualism. Course readings and assignments enabled them to reflect on and validate their own experiences as bilinguals of various types (Baker and Wright 2021), and to examine and further develop their understanding and views related to translanguaging.

Lorena, a simultaneous bilingual, is a first-generation Mexican American who grew up in a Spanish-speaking home in a bilingual Latinx community in New York City and was educated herself through bilingual education. Teresa described herself as a sequential bilingual who grew up in Puerto Rico and moved to the U.S. mainland in 10$^{th}$ grade. Sofia's family returned to Texas from Mexico when she was four years old. Due to what Sofia described as "subtractive bilingualism" she quickly lost proficiency in Spanish as she was educated in English-only Texas classrooms. She began to reclaim her Spanish language – and her identity – as a heritage learner in college. Emily and Cherise are sequential bilinguals who grew up in monolingual English-speaking homes but gained proficiency in Spanish in high school, college, and through extensive experiences in Ecuador and Spain respectively. Connie and Jill grew up in English-speaking homes, and initially considered themselves to be monolinguals. However, after completing the initial readings in the foundations of bilingual education course, and after reflecting on their own efforts to learn some Spanish, they now describe themselves as "incipient bilinguals," recognizing their ability to understand and produce some Spanish as they continue their attempts to learn more and use it with their students.

All teachers are passionate about their programs and helping all students to become bilingual and biliterate. However, in their detailed descriptions and reflections of their school's bilingual program there is little mention of ELLs, and little evidence of social justice framing of bilingual education for Latinx students, though there was a brief mention of DLBE goals to support cross-cultural understanding. Silton's long history of starting out as a one-way immersion program for English speakers, and Mapleton's adoption of the Utah model indicate these are not programs stemming from grassroots civil rights efforts within the Latinx community and were founded from a firmly monoglossic perspective, privileging English majority speakers. However, throughout the program, the teachers developed greater critical consciousness around notions of culture. Most noted the need to involve students in cultural activities and conversations to learn not only language, but also to develop deeper cultural understanding. For example, as

Teresa, a sequential bilingual, reflected, "It's not just the language, but they can see how their culture is represented, or the connection and differences between two cultures as they're seeing the connections between the languages." Throughout the course discussions and in a detailed analysis of their programs in the final course, the teachers acknowledged much need for improvement in the area of cross-cultural understanding. As Connie, an incipient bilingual, stated, "[we] want to show that we honor and value all cultures and that we don't prioritize a different culture over another and that all people matter. . . . It definitely is an area that I would love to have more instruction or guidance in my own classroom."

In contrast, there was a major shift in the teacher's ideologies of translanguaging. Taken collectively, their perspectives on translanguaging have shifted to a much more positive stance. Prior to this program, some had never even heard the word *translanguaging*, but most had negative views of mixed language use, believing it was a result of low proficiency in the target language. Some had viewed translanguaging as interference in learning the target language. Lorena, a simultaneous bilingual, recalled her own experience, "Growing up it was frowned upon to mix the two languages. We would constantly get corrected or reminded to stop translanguaging." Sofia used to believe bilingual books or translation "would prevent [students] from learning the target language." Jill, an incipient bilingual, shifted from believing in the strict separation of the two languages to translanguaging and commented, "If our goal is bilingualism, then why can't the students and parents hear a teacher speak in two languages?"

The teachers' development of a positive translanguage stance opened them up to loosening the strict separation of languages in their programs and creating more opportunities for students to showcase and draw upon their entire linguistic repertoire, as we will illustrate in the following sections. The bilingual foundations and methods courses led to much active reflection and discussion about past, current, and future efforts to incorporate translanguaging design through bridging, use of cognates, developing metalanguage, and modeling and helping students make cross-language connections.

## 6 Teacher and student translanguaging

The course readings, assignments and discussions gave teachers opportunities to reflect on their own and their students' translanguaging, and further develop their translanguaging stance. These included ways the teachers on the "English-side" could also effectively engage in translanguaging pedagogy. The teachers' accounts of varying patterns of personal translanguaging practices reveal their varied views and perceived appropriateness of translanguaging in their immediate social contexts. Cherise, a sequential, English-dominant bilingual, and Sofia, a heritage Spanish speaker, reported translanguaging constantly in different contexts and consider translanguaging as a more "natural" and the "simplest" way to fully use their linguistic repertoire. Teresa and Lorena reported they translanguage more in social settings than in the formal educational context. Lorena claims that while she translanguages frequently in these social contexts, she does not do so with her own family in order to maintain her daughters' Spanish language development. Connie and Emily believed themselves to translanguage more educationally than socially, that is, more in school than outside of school. Jill identified herself as a receptive Spanish speaker, rarely translanguaging and incapable of modeling translanguaging in class. The teachers identified that interlocutors and context are significant factors impacting their translanguaging.

The teachers' developing translanguaging stance was reflected in their positive views and descriptions of their students' translanguaging practices. They indicated that their students translanguage in diverse patterns. Emily, an English-majority and sequential bilingual, observed her kindergarten students translanguaging more in general communication than during academic tasks. She further noted "they can listen to directions and a story completely in Spanish, yet give a detailed, correct answer in English." Sofia, a heritage Spanish speaker, noticed her native Spanish-speaking students translanguage more than their native English-speaking peers. Cherise, Lorena, and Jill mentioned their students translanguage all the time, even without realizing they are doing it. Cherise and Lorena also shared that students often translate for each other and their parents.

Teachers identified similar factors affecting students' translanguaging: interlocutors and context. For example, Jill indicated that translanguaging happened more frequently during student interaction than in student-to-teacher interaction. Connie observed that her ELLs' translanguaging depends on "what friends they are around." Emily suggested students' diversity and heterogeneous pairing could encourage more translanguaging in class. Cherise attributed natural translanguaging to a solid base in language proficiency; therefore, she finds that upper elementary grade students tend to translanguage more naturally and frequently. Emily found that her kindergarten students used translanguaging at times for substitution of unknown words and for reporting the speech of other people. Overall, the teachers were impressed with students' growing translanguaging capability as a result of the bilingual programs.

# 7 Enactment of translanguaging pedagogies in the classroom

As shown above, as teachers moved through the program, they developed a positive translanguaging stance, accepting and valuing the role translanguaging should be playing in their DLBE classrooms and programs. To understand the extent to which they began to include translanguaging design in their instructional practices, we first look at their descriptions of such practices in their coursework and their discussions with the coach. We then share the findings of our analysis of the videos of their classroom instruction on the extent to which they engaged in translanguaging shifts.

## 7.1 Coursework and coaching

All teachers shared their experiences of incorporating translanguaging designs in their lessons and classrooms. Common across all teachers were descriptions of their bridging lessons to make explicit connections between what the students were learning during separate English and Spanish instruction times. Emily, Sofia and Teresa mentioned doing their bridging lessons at the end of each week or unit. Lorena commented that bridging lessons are really beneficial and that "the kids enjoyed [them] a lot." Overall, the teachers saw positive impacts of translanguaging on their students' engagement and learning.

Four teachers highlighted their use of cognates in bridging lessons. Sofia commented, "It is so neat to see students make connections between the two languages" and described how identifying cognates also "affirms students' cultures, identities and bilingualism." Three teachers described creating cognate word walls and charts, and other metalinguistic charts. Cherise described a bridging lesson she taught during her ELA block where students created a side-by-side academic vocabulary list in English and Spanish, compared the words to find the cognates, and then referred to the list as they composed a paragraph with her in English through shared writing. Teresa also mentioned her use of a bilingual anchor chart to engage her students in a discussion about the differences in capitalization and punctuation in English and Spanish. Emily emphasized that such bilingual charts allow "for the Spanish students to connect it back to something they know in their native language and help to bridge that knowledge and encourage translanguaging."

The "incipient bilingual" teachers at Mapleton, who originally adhered to strict language separation, collaborated with their Spanish partner teachers for bridging. Connie noted a bridging lesson she coordinated with her Spanish partner teacher, centered around the English and Spanish versions of the book *Brown Bear, Brown Bear*. Students learned colors and engaged in story retelling tasks on both the English and Spanish sides. The teachers created a single bilingual anchor chart which they passed back and forth across the hall so that they could build off of – and make connections with – things students learned in their other language. And Jill described co-teaching a bridging lesson with her Spanish partner teacher at the end of the prior school year by bringing both classes together for a lesson about animal habitats. Students learned a song about habitats in both Spanish and English. The teachers then did a parallel read-aloud of a *Magic School Bus* book about animal habitats, each alternating reading pages from the English and Spanish versions. Students then worked in groups to discuss things animals need in a habitat (food, shelter, water, space/air) and were encouraged to translanguage as they discussed while both teachers rotated to provide support in their respective teaching language.

Teachers describe using a few other translanguaging strategies. Lorena and Connie, for example, mentioned providing quick explanations in the non-target language (e.g., in English during Spanish time). Sofia, Teresa, and Jill noted efforts to add bilingual books to their classroom libraries to support cross-language connections. Teresa reported these bilingual books are very popular with her students. Emily and Sofia made use of the "*como se dice*" strategy from Literacy Squared. As Sofia explained, "this is a speaking frame which allows students to say '¿Como se dice, my mom is coming to volunteer at 11?' I then will support them in saying it in Spanish." Sofia also made daily announcements in her classroom in both languages. Jill described her students making cards for a local church in both English and Spanish. Cherise paired students bilingually so they could support each other.

Finally, the five teachers at Silton each described instances of just loosening the strict separation rules and allowing themselves and/or the students to translanguage during lessons and activities. Emily declared, "Allowing my students to translanguage has really transformed my classroom into a more interactive learning environment with higher engagement than ever before!"

Despite these promising examples of translanguaging designs and strategies, all teachers expressed to the coach their frustrations and concerns that their efforts are insufficient. Most of these conversations occurred in coaching sessions 4 and 5, which took place while the teachers were taking the bilingual education courses. This provides evidence that these courses led the teachers to reflect deeply as they developed their translanguaging stance. Concerns about shortcomings were also evident in the coursework discussions.

The coach praised a few of the teachers for the bridging and other translanguaging strategies she observed and gave specific recommendations on how to increase them. However, some of the teachers were very honest about their struggles. Lorena told the coach that, at Silton, they "aren't really doing the bridging" and other translanguaging strategies they learned about in their courses: "None of what we're learning with Purdue, we're doing, honestly. . . . But we definitely need to start it." She claims they cannot do it "the Purdue way . . . what we're learning" at Silton because "we have our own [school] framework." Teresa also told the coach that they "aren't really doing the bridging stuff" at Silton because "it doesn't go with . . . how we're planning our instruction." On the discussion board, Emily similarly noted challenges to plan for and implement cross-language strategies because "a lot of our curriculum is so specifically dictated." Likewise, Cherise lamented Silton's curriculum goes against what they learned in their course readings, and finds the mandated curriculum makes it difficult to find time to bridge to the other language. Cherise and Teresa also noted another challenge at Silton is that not all teachers share a similar translanguaging stance. As Teresa stated,

> There's some division with that in our building still, and we're trying to work on making the bridging [happen] in both classrooms. It happens in the Spanish classrooms, but it's not happening in the English classrooms the way they should.

The two Mapleton teachers in the 50/50 model on the English side also noted challenges coordinating with their Spanish partner teachers. Connie said, "Right now translanguaging is used sporadically and it is not planned for by my partner teacher and I." She also finds teaching cross-language connections is difficult because she is not proficient in Spanish. Jill likewise expressed concern about the lack of bridging, noting her team's practices are just "scratching the surface, dabbling on the surface."

## 7.2 Video observations of translanguaging shifts

We found signs of translanguaging shifts in the videos of teachers' classroom teaching. The videos of the final observations were conducted in each teacher's classrooms towards the end of the Fall 2019 semester as students were finishing up the bilingual methods course and completing the program. Videos for the four teachers who teach in both English and Spanish (Emily, Cherise, Lorena and Teresa) included both ELA and SLA lessons, while only ELA observations were video recorded for the three who only teach in English (Sofia, Connie, and Jill). Each translanguaging instance was counted using a very simple classification of three general purposes for classroom translanguaging: (1) *instructional* refers to any translanguaging by the teacher or students for purposes of teaching and learning; (2) *classroom management* refers to translanguaging to address student behavior or personal needs; and (3) *interpersonal* refers to any translanguaging between students or between the teacher and students for general communication not directly tied to teaching or learning. We defined a "translanguaging instance" as a switch in language (a word, a phrase, or longer connected discourse) that occurred in a clearly defined context or time period, and sufficiently separated in time or space from a prior or subsequent instance. Thus, a single "instance" could range from less than one second to several minutes.

As shown in Table 2, we identified a total of 77 translanguaging instances, most of which were for instructional purposes (n = 44), followed by classroom management (n = 21) and interpersonal (n = 12) purposes. Note that for the three teachers on the "English side," no instances were observed for Connie or Jill at Mapleton, and only one brief classroom management instance was observed for Sofia at Silton. Thus, all but one of the translanguaging instances occurred in the four Silton classrooms where the teachers are proficient bilinguals and teach in both languages. It should be acknowledged that the research team did observe some translanguaging in these teachers' classrooms in the prior school year, particularly for Sofia who previously taught $1^{st}$ grade in both Spanish and English, and for Jill whose co-teaching bridging lesson described above was captured on video. Nonetheless, only one translanguaging instance occurred among the three "English side" teachers in the final observation. We acknowledge the limitation that these videos provide just a single snapshot of an hour or two of a single school day.

**Table 2:** Number of Translanguaging Instances by Teacher and Purpose.

|  | Instructional | Classroom Management | Interpersonal | Total |
|---|---|---|---|---|
| **Spanish & English Teachers** |  |  |  |  |
| Lorena | 16 | 4 | 8 | 28 |
| Emily | 11 | 8 | 2 | 21 |
| Teresa | 13 | 7 | 0 | 20 |
| Cherise | 4 | 1 | 2 | 7 |
| **"English-side" Teachers** |  |  |  |  |
| Sofia | 0 | 1 | 0 | 1 |
| Connie | 0 | 0 | 0 | 0 |
| Jill | 0 | 0 | 0 | 0 |
| **Total** | 44 | 21 | 12 | 77 |

**Table 3:** Number of Translanguaging Instances During English and Spanish Instruction Time.

|  | During English Time | During Spanish Time |
|---|---|---|
| Instructional | 13 | 31 |
| Classroom management | 7 | 14 |
| Interpersonal | 0 | 12 |

Given these programs maintain separate and distinct English and Spanish instruction times, it was possible to count the number of translanguaging instances during these times. As shown in Table 3, more translanguaging, for all three purposes, occurred by far during Spanish time (74%), than during English time (26%), and no instance of translanguaging for interpersonal purposes was observed during English time.

Nearly all instances were quick. Most were single words or phrases in the non-target instructional language by the teacher and students. All four teachers accepted and affirmed student comments and answers that were partially or entirely in the other language, but kept instruction in the target language, typically modeling how to say the student's utterance in the target language. All four occasionally switched to the non-target language to provide a quick translation of a word or phrase. Some instances of teacher translanguaging may have been subconscious and natural. In all but one instance, accepting students' translanguaging responses happened during Spanish time and appeared to always be to accommodate English-dominant students. Likewise, nearly all of the teacher's translanguaging for quick explanations were in English during Spanish time, again to the benefit of the English-dominant speakers.

During English time, Cherise made some quick cross-linguistic comparisons related to the use of commas and capitalization in Spanish. Lorena and Teresa made cross-language connections using cognates. Only Teresa had an extended instance of a short bridging lesson. During an ELA lesson on the water cycle, Teresa purposefully made cross-language connections with what students had learned about the water cycle in Spanish. She reviewed several cognates with the students (evidencia/evidence, evaporación/evaporation; vapor/vapor; ciclo/cycle) along with other water cycle words in Spanish (agua/water; nubes/clouds) which she and the students added to a comparison chart. As Teresa built students' metalanguage through these cross-language comparisons, one of the students noted the difference in the use of *de/of*. Teresa affirmed and explained:

> De . . . Yes. In English, we don't say, "cycle of water," we just say "water cycle." But, here we say **"ciclo de agua."** But remember what we talked about in **español, como se dice**, my **favorito** color, **y me dice mi color favorito** . . . so we switch it, right?

Thus, she affirmed the student's observation, but also reminded the class of what they learned in Spanish time about how *de* is not required in an adjective phrase like *mi color favorito* [my favorite color], and how the order of the adjective and noun are switched in Spanish.

During Spanish time when teaching a connected lesson about water and clouds, Teresa provided a quick explanation with a phrase in English:

> Teresa: Que son los stratos, los cieros y los cumulos? Son que? Mark?
> [What are the stratus, cumulos, and the cirrus? Are what? Mark?]
>
> Mark: Clases de nubes.
> [Types of clouds].
>
> Teresa: Gracias. Clases de nubes . . . **they're types of clouds. OK**? Hay tres nombres . . . tres diferentes de nubes . . . .
> [Thank you. Types of clouds . . . **they're types of clouds. OK**? There are three types . . . three different kinds of clouds].

Mark, an English-dominant student, was the only student to raise his hand to answer the question. Thus, Teresa's use of translanguaging ensured students – particularly the English-dominant – understood the concept.

Lorena had the only other observed longer stretch of translanguaging. During ELA she read aloud a book about a secret school for girls in Afghanistan. She paused frequently to explain unknown words and phrases in English. After reading the line, "the school closed for a long winter recess," a student asked about the word *recess*, noting it was not the same as when they go out to recess. Lorena smiled and drew on the students' knowledge of Spanish and cognates to help students understand the difference. She asked students about the difference between *recesso* [recess (a break)] and *recreo* [playtime]. Through the discussion Lorena helped the students understand that the cognate *recesso/recess* has the broader meaning of *a break*.

Instances of student-to-student translanguaging for instructional purposes were observed in the classrooms of Emily and Lorena, all of which took place during Spanish time when students were working in pairs or groups. In Emily's class, two girls – one ELL and one English-dominant – worked together on a worksheet in Spanish, and the English-dominant student helped her partner with the task but spoke in English. In Lorena's classroom, lots of English can be heard among the chatter of students as they work in small groups on a Spanish lesson task. In at least three instances, English-dominant students asked their ELL partner or group member how to say a certain word in Spanish.

Nearly all classroom management translanguaging instances were short words or phrases to get the class or individual students to settle down (e.g., "Hey, please listen"), or using English proper nouns for objects or curriculum during Spanish instruction time that may not have a standard Spanish equivalent (e.g., iPad, Smartboard, AR [Accelerated Reader], Raz Kids). A couple of more extended translanguaging instances were observed when teachers interacted one-on-one with students in private. For example, during English time, Lorena spoke in Spanish to an ELL boy who was not feeling well, and in English during Spanish time to calm down an upset English-dominant student.

The interpersonal translanguaging instances all occurred in English during group and independent work time when instruction time was in Spanish. We could only make out little snippets here and there, but most were between students with interjections by the English dominant students, for example: "Why?" "No, we're doing this." "Hey! That's not yours." "Oh shoot!" and "Can't copy!" A couple of Lorena's students requested her assistance in English: "Can you come here?"

# 8 Conclusion

Indiana's DLBE policy and programs were established and grounded in ideologies of neoliberalism and monoglossic views of bilingualism (Delavan, Freire, and Valdez 2021). Few DLBE teachers in the state have completed ELL licensure programs, and even fewer have formal training in bilingual education. This study of the first cohort of seven in-service bilingual education teachers to complete Purdue University's ELL licensure program and DLBE Graduate Certificate Program provides evidence of the importance of this training to help DLBE teachers shift their ideologies away from monoglossic views of bilingualism and develop their translanguaging repertoires to ensure the success of their students (García and Li Wei 2014).

Most of the teachers began the program with limited knowledge and understanding of translanguaging and held monoglossic views reinforced by their program's emphasis on strict separation of English and Spanish instruction. We found that through our program's coursework and instructional coaching, all teachers developed a more positive translanguaging stance and increased their translanguaging designs and shifts in their classrooms. However, the teachers expressed frustration and concerns that their model's prescribed curriculum and separate language instruction times/classrooms leave little room for bridging lessons and other forms of translanguaging. We also found that translanguaging is most common in the classrooms of proficient bilingual teachers who teach in both languages, and that translanguaging is more common during Spanish instruction than during English instruction. The classroom video evidence suggests that translanguaging may be used more often by, and for the benefit of, the dominant English-speaking students during Spanish instruction. This pattern is consistent with Hamman's (2018) finding that English was "more likely to be integrated into Spanish instruction than vice versa" in her study of a Midwest DLBE program (32). More work is needed to turn teachers' attention to the needs and full use of ELLs' linguistic repertoires during English instruction and power dynamics among the language-dominant and language-minority students.

While we view bilingual education and translanguaging from a stance of social justice and culturally sustaining pedagogy (Paris and Alim 2017), the teachers' development of critical consciousness is just beginning (Cervantes-Soon et al. 2017). At the very least, the teachers recognize that they are still struggling just to promote cross-cultural understanding within their programs (Howard et al. 2018). However, there are positive signs that they are beginning to recognize how the neoliberal and monoglossic ideological underpinnings of their programs are limiting their own agency in making greater shifts in their implementation spaces (Hornberger 2005).

These findings point to the need for even greater focus in bilingual teacher education programs and professional development trainings on developing teachers' critical consciousness as part of their translanguaging stance. Such focus can empower teachers as leaders who can push back against neoliberal and monoglossic ideologies, and work with their school administrators to make needed structural and curricular changes to ensure their programs are culturally sustaining, equitable, and centered on ELL students.

# References

Baker, Colin & Wayne E. Wright. 2021. *Foundations of Bilingual Education and Bilingualism*, 7th edn. Bristol: Multilingual Matters.

Beeman, Karen & Cheryl Urow. 2012. *Teaching for Biliteracy: Strengthening Bridges Between Languages*. Philadelphia: Caslon Publishing.

Cervantes-Soon, Claudia, Lisa Dorner, Deborah Palmer, Daniel Heiman, Rebecca Schwerdtfeger & Jinmyung Choi. 2017. Combating inequalities in two-way language immersion programs: Toward critical consciousness in bilingual education spaces. *Review of Research in Education* 41. 403–427.

Cervantes-Soon, Claudia, James Gambrell, G. Sue Kasun, Wenyang Sun, Juan A. Freire & Lisa M. Dorner. 2020. "Everybody wants a choice" in dual language education of El Nuevo Sur: Whiteness as the

gloss for everybody in media discourses of multilingual education. *Journal of Language, Identity, and Education* 20(6). 394–410. https://doi.org/10.1080/15348458.2020.1753201.
Delavan, M. Garrett, Juan A. Freire & Verónica E. Valdez. 2021. The intersectionality of neoliberal classing with raciolinguistic marginalization in state dual language policy: A call for locally crafted programs. In Nelson Flores, Amelia Tseng & Nicholas C. Subtirelu (eds.), *Bilingualism for All? Raciolinguistic Perspectives on Dual Language Education in the United States*, 19–39. Bristol: Multilingual Matters.
Escamilla, Kathy, Susan Hopewell, Sandra Butvilofsky, Wendy Sparrow, Lucinda Soltero-González, Olivia Ruiz-Figueroa & Manuel Escamilla. 2013. *Biliteracy from the Start: Literacy Squared in Action*. Philadelphia: Caslon.
Flores, Nelson, Amelia Tseng & Nicholas C. Subtirelu. 2021. Bilingualism for all for just for the rich and white? Introducing a raciolinguistic perspective to dual language education. In Nelson Flores, Amelia Tseng, & Nicholas C. Subtirelu (eds.), *Bilingualism for all? Raciolinguistic Perspectives on Dual Language Education in the United States*, 1–18. Bristol: Multilingual Matters.
Freeman, Yvonne S. & David E. Freeman. 2006. *Teaching Reading and Writing in Spanish and English in Bilingual and Dual Language Classrooms*. Portsmouth: Heinemann.
Freeman, David E., Yvonne Freeman & Sandra Mercuri. 2018. *Dual Language Essentials for Teachers and Administrators*, 2nd edn. Portsmouth: Heinemann.
Freire, Juan A., Verónica E. Valdez & M. Garrett Delavan. 2017. The (dis)inclusion of Latina/o interests from Utah's dual language education boom. *Journal of Latinos and Education* 16(4). 276–289.
García, Ofelia. 2009. *Bilingual Education in the 21st Century: A Global Perspective*. Malden: Wiley/Blackwell.
García, Ofelia, Susana Ibarra Johnson & Kate Seltzer. 2017. *Translanguaging Classrooms: Leveraging Student Bilingualism for Learning*. Philadelphia: Caslon Publishing.
García, Ofelia & Li Wei. 2014. *Translanguaging: Language, Bilingualism, and Education*. New York: Palgrave Macmillan.
García-Mateus, Suzanne. 2020. Bilingual student perspectives about language expertise in a gentrifying two-way immersion program. *International Journal of Bilingual Education and Bilingualism*. 1–16. https://doi.org/10.1080/13670050.2020.1797627.
Hamman, Laura. 2018. Translanguaging and positioning in two-way dual language classrooms: A case for criticality. *Language and Education* 32(1). 21–42. https://doi.org/10.1080/09500782.2017.1384006.
Hilburn, Jeremy. 2014. Challenges facing immigrant students beyond the linguistic domain in a new gateway state. *Urban Review* 46. 654–680. https://doi.org/10.1007/s11256-014-0273-x.
Hornberger, Nancy. 2005. Opening and filling up implementational and ideological spaces in heritage language education. *The Modern Language Journal* 89(4). 605–609.
Howard, Elizabeth R., Katherine J. Lindholm-Leary, David Rogers, Natalie Olague, José Medina, Barbara Kennedy, Julie Sugarman & Donna Christian. 2018. *Guiding Principles for Dual Language Education*, 3rd edn. Washington, DC: Center for Applied Linguistics.
Kroskrity, Paul V. 2004. Language ideologies. In Alessandro Duranti (ed.), *A Companion to Linguistic Anthropology*, 496–517. Malden: Blackwell.
Morita-Mullaney, Trish. 2019. At the intersection of bilingual specialty and leadership: A collective case study of district leadership for emergent bilinguals. *Bilingual Research Journal* 42(1). 31–53. https://doi.org/10.1080/15235882.2018.1563005.
Morita-Mullaney, Trish & Colleen Chesnut. 2022. Equity traps in the deselection of English learners in dual language education: A collective case study of school principals. *NABE Journal of Research and Practice* 12(2). 49–68. https://doi.org/10.1080/26390043.2022.2079390.

Morita-Mullaney, Trish, Jennifer Renn, Annie M. Garcia & Wayne E. Wright. 2020. Preparing K-12 teachers for effective instruction of English learners: The transformation of a Purdue University online language teacher education program. In Hyun-Sook Kang, Dong S. Shin & Tony Cimasko (eds.), *Online Education for Teachers of English as a Global Language* 19–38. New York: Routledge.

Morita-Mullaney, Trish & Malkeet Singh. 2021. Obscuring English Learners from state accountability: The case of Indiana's language blind policies. *Educational Policy* 35(4). 621–645. https://doi.org/10.1177/0895904818823751.

Morita-Mullaney, Trish & Lynn Stallings. 2018. Serving Indiana's emergent bilingual immigrant (EBI) youth: A collective case study of EBI teacher education. *The Teacher Educator* 53(3). 293–312. https://doi.org/10.1080/08878730.2018.1462422.

Palmer, Deborah, Claudia Cervantes-Soon & Daniel Heiman. 2019. Bilingualism, biliteracy, biculturalism, and critical consciousness for all: Proposing a fourth fundamental goal for two-way dual language education. *Theory into Practice* 58(2). 121–133. https://doi.org/10.1080/00405841.2019.1569376.

Paris, Django & H. Sami Alim (eds.). 2017. *Culturally Sustaining Pedagogies: Teaching and Learning for Justice in a Changing World*. New York: Teachers College Press.

Paulus, Trena M. & Alyssa F. Wise. 2019. *Looking for Insight, Transformation, and Learning in Online Talk*. New York: Routledge.

Richards, Lynn. 2021. *Handling Qualitative Data: A Practical Guide*, 4th edn. Thousand Oaks: SAGE.

Sung, Ko-Yin & Hsiao-Mei Tsai. 2019. *Mandarin Chinese Dual Language Immersion Programs*. Bristol: Multilingual Matters.

Wiley, Terrence G. & Wayne E. Wright. 2004. Against the undertow: The politics of language instruction in the United States. *Educational Policy* 18(1). 142–168. https://doi.org/10.1177/0895904803260030.

Wright, Wayne E. & Woongsik Choi. in press. DLBE programs types for different target populations. In Juan A. Freire, Cristina Alfaro & Ester J. de Jong (eds.), *Dual Language Bilingual Education Handbook*. New York: Routledge.

Nihal Khote
# Chapter 7
# A teacher's perspective of translanguaging *corrientes*: Contextualizing power and control in the translanguaging stance

**Abstract:** García and Li Wei (2014: 3) suggest that in fostering translanguaging in classrooms, teachers endorse "shifts in orders of discourses, bringing the voices of the Other to the forefront," thus enacting a social justice agenda. However, within traditional asymmetrical pedagogical relations between teachers and students in US classrooms, teachers control discursive parameters limiting *what* and *how* statements can be made. Fostering a translanguaging classroom is thus largely a function of teachers' stance, as within stance lies the authority to validate, or not, students' use of non-dominant languages. In this chapter, I explore the epistemological orientations of the translanguaging stance in terms of embedded relations of power and control in teacher-student interactions. The data consists of translanguaging dialogs in Spanish and English between I, author and teacher, and my students in a sheltered 9th grade class with Latinx bilingual learners in rural North Georgia. In my analysis of our interactions, I used Bernstein's (1990) conception of classification and framing rules to conceptualize power relations in the teacher's stance. The findings demonstrate micro shifts in translanguaging *corriente* within a stance comprising waves of strong classification and framing followed by weak classification and framing to set up the groundwork for the translanguaging moment. The study provides new insights into micro/local dimensions of the translanguaging stance and on the discursive ecology of the classroom.

## 1 Introduction

During 13 years of teaching Mexican and Central American immigrant English learners (ELs) in a sheltered 9th grade ESOL (English for Speakers of Other Languages) language arts class in a school district in rural North Georgia, translanguaging in Spanish and English was an important feature of my classroom. I initially encouraged student translanguaging as a means to break down barriers

**Nihal Khote,** Kennesaw State University

https://doi.org/10.1515/9783110735604-008

between home and school knowledge, to implement a permeable curriculum (Dyson 1993). García and Li Wei (2014: 3) suggest translanguaging practice endorses "shifts in orders of discourses, bringing the voices of the Other to the forefront, thus relating translanguaging to criticality, critical pedagogy, social justice and the linguistic human rights agenda". In effect, García and Li Wei indicate that translanguaging is about breaking boundaries, pushing the limits of the dominant cultural paradigm of what is permissible in linguistic and pedagogical terms, to support and influence the collective educational and social consciousness of the classroom. However, whether translanguaging practice happens in a classroom or not is largely a function of the teacher's stance comprising the choice to foster (or not) students' use of non-dominant codes and 'home languages' and by doing so, open up, or restrict *heteroglossia* and its consequent multivoicedness of ideology and beliefs within the official space (Bakhtin 1981). It is in this respect that a teacher's translanguaging stance is central to the critical outcomes of translanguaging, especially in the context of limited discursive parameters of a classroom that dictate what can be said, and how one can appropriately say what can be said.

Much work has been done on the use of translanguaging repertoires in educational contexts as a tool for literacy (García, Johnson, and Seltzer 2017). However, there is a need for more investigation into the translanguaging stance, in relation to the teacher's power over regulation of the discursive aspects of the interaction, or control over *what* is being transmitted, along with *how* the message is being transmitted. García and colleagues (2017), identify three components of translanguaging educational practices: stance, design, and shifts. A teacher's *stance* refers to their beliefs and ideologies about emergent bilingual students and their language practices that positions translanguaging as "a right of the child to fully bring themselves into the classroom to achieve academically . . . to disrupt hierarchical structures of power" (73). Inherent in this conception of the teacher stance are embedded power relations between teacher and students, what Foucault (1982) calls "government," or the ways in which the conduct of individuals or of groups is directed in non-confrontational ways. The assumption is that the teacher sets up affordances that privilege the act of translanguaging, allowing for certain flexibility in the boundaries and discursive limits of the classroom. Theorizing the teachers' translanguaging stance implies understanding the extant power relations that mediate control over these boundaries, or over what is being transmitted along with how the message is being transmitted. Garcia and colleagues (2017: 21) suggest that translanguaging pedagogical practices include *shifts*, or moves a teacher makes in response to their students. I conceptualize shifts in terms of transfer of power relations from person to person within the translanguaging *corriente*, or the dynamic and continuous alterations of discursive parameters in the linguistic landscape of the classroom. In other words, I investigate the role that teachers and students play in power shifts and moves within the translanguaging corriente and explore the affordances and limitations of the teacher's translanguaging stance.

I use Bernstein's (2000) sociological theories to theorize power relations embedded in the translanguaging stance. Bernstein's conception of classification and framing track contextually appropriate, in-the-moment options and discursive micro-moves afforded to the teacher and the multilingual learners in the class. The data consists of transcribed interactions and dialogues between the teacher (author) and the students to demonstrate the play of translanguaging moves (invite, acknowledge, respond). The findings show that the teacher's stance comprised strong classification and framing followed by weak classification and framing to set up the groundwork for the translanguaging moment and that the translanguaging stance takes the form of ripples or waves corresponding to the embedded strength of power and control dynamics in the corriente.

My work as translanguaging 'teacher-researcher' along with my students, as insiders and active negotiators of the discursive ecology of classroom, positioned me with an emic view into the dynamics of stance. The findings from this work provide insights into the embedded power relations in the translanguaging stance. The chapter outlines a framework which can shed light on links between the macro/global and the micro/local dimensions of translanguaging repertoire.

## 2 Context of study

The classroom site for this study was my 9th grade classroom where I taught language arts in a rural school district in Northwest Georgia. The school enrolled 65% Latinx students, 31% Caucasian, and 4% African American and Asian, with 76% of the students on free or reduced lunch. There was a high number of bilingual learners of intermediate English language proficiency, many who were categorized as Long-Term English Language Learners" (LTELLs) (Menken 2008; Menken and Kleyn 2010) because they had been in ESOL classrooms for more than 6 years. This particular class had 16 students mostly from Mexico and Central America, whose parents worked in the local carpet mills. Students like Domingo, Roberto, and Karen (pseudonyms used) were seemingly proficient in communicating orally in English and Spanish but were unable to pass the annual gateway language proficiency tests in reading and writing in English. Juan and Sofía, on the other hand, had been in the country for little more than a year and were considered to be newcomers. Although most of the students translanguaged in Spanish and English frequently, they had emerging proficiency in their home languages. The data in this study comprised 40 hours of audio-recordings of classroom activities and interactions. From the larger dataset, I transcribed sections where the students or I translanguaged that were representative of power moves made by either teacher or students. I present three of these dialogues analyzed to illuminate aspects of translanguaging stance and pedagogy

# 3 Theoretical framework

To do school literacy, be it reading or writing, Latinx bilinguals should engage with texts using their full meaning-making repertoires, and the teachers need to develop what García and colleagues (2017) have called a translanguaging stance. According to the authors, instructional design is planned so that it incorporates authentic student input and multilingual ecology to advance the translanguaging corriente and validate dynamic bilingualism in the classroom.

## 3.1 Locating power in stance

When students' translanguaging and the teacher's pedagogical stance are in harmony, the translanguaging corriente manifests itself in all its dynamism and complexity. García, Johnson, and Seltzer (2017: 25), suggest that "by weaving together the two dimensions – the students' linguistic performances and the teacher's pedagogy, [the translanguaging corriente] creates the dynamic flow, the *movimiento*, between these two dimensions." The authors suggest that the translanguaging stance be in sync with the emergent and moment-to-moment nature of the translanguaging corriente and adjust to its shifts. However, theorizing translanguaging stance should necessarily take into consideration the location of power and control over classroom discourse, particularly because traditional pedagogic relationships between teachers (the transmitters of knowledge) and students (the acquirers of knowledge) are asymmetrical. It is largely up to the teachers to decide what is to be learned, what shape, form and sequence the knowledge will take, and how the learning will be assessed. Teachers control the nature of knowledge imparted (what comprises curriculum), the mechanisms of distribution (how it is transmitted) and endow the knowledge authority and value by evaluating students' understandings of this knowledge based on pre-determined standards. Infusing the translanguaging stance in classroom discourse interrupts traditional teacher-student hierarchies of knowledge production and distribution as students' translanguaging repertoires mediate and construct meanings and messages that "shift orders of discourse, bringing voices of the

Other to the forefront" (García and Li Wei 2014: 3). The translanguaging stance co-constructs knowledge *juntos,* or together, with students, in an intentional design in which students' language practices incorporate their culture, family, and community as resources (García et al., 2017: 58). However, final control on the nature of the translanguaging corriente rests in hands of teachers who can accept or not, non-dominant language use, and acknowledge or not, ideologies or minoritized knowledges that may not be appropriate to their class. They can restrict what Bakhtin (1981) defines as *heteroglossia,* or the presence of different voices that impart various evaluations, conceptions and experiences of the world in language. Therefore, it is key to consider the location of the teacher's power and control *during* the translanguaging event. In effect, the translanguaging stance is conceptualized as a function of the location of power and control over the discursive parameters of the classroom. Bernstein's (1996/2000) sociological theories on pedagogical practice provide useful insights into understanding power relations in the classroom and thus offer a framework to theorize translanguaging stance and shifts. In particular, the perspective of power relations embedded in the translanguaging stance would also shed light on the potential and regulation of criticality in the classroom. In the next section, I describe the concepts of classification and framing and explain how these serve as analytical tools for understanding the inner power dynamics of the translanguaging stance.

## 3.2 Classification and framing

Bernstein's conceptualization of symbolic codes of "classification" and "framing" applied to pedagogical practice between teacher and students are useful theoretical instruments to track shifts in power relations in terms of opening and restricting discursive boundaries of classroom talk. Classification refers to the strength of the boundaries *between* categories, such as between agencies, agents, discourses or practices. For example, strong classification (C+) is particularly seen in the marked separation of school subjects – e.g., physics, American history, language arts, etc. Strong classification, therefore, refers to separation or insulation between bodies of knowledge as seen in curriculum that is highly differentiated into traditional subjects. In this case, strong classification refers to strict separation between academic knowledge of the content areas and home learning borne from community and family's lived experiences. On the other hand, weak classification (C-) refers to a curriculum that is integrated and in which the boundaries between subjects and knowledge frames are elastic and negotiable. Weak classification implies that the insulation between categories is diffused, and the categories are thus in danger of losing their specialized identity as, for example, in interdisciplinary studies.

According to Bernstein, whatever maintains the strength of the insulation or separation, maintains the relations *between* the categories and their distinct voices. For example, content area teachers tend to remain strictly within the normative dictates of prescribed standards and "stick to the topic" and hence preserve the specialized nature of their subject, thus maintaining strong classification. However, a translanguaging stance should be flexible and permeable, allowing for discursive and linguistic inroads made by students. Operationalizing the translanguaging stance would thus require pedagogical relations with a relaxed or weakened classification reflected in a willingness to integrate student-driven co-construction of knowledge and also so-called 'diversions' and apparently off-topic discussions that would constitute con-textual shifts in the flow of the curriculum.

While classification refers to the *what* is being transmitted, framing refers to the *how*. Framing is the location of control over the rules of communication in interactional pedagogic relations between parents/children or teacher/student. According to Bernstein (1973: 88), framing refers to "the degree of control teacher and pupil possess over the selection, organization, pacing and timing of the knowledge transmitted and received in the pedagogical relationship." If classification regulates the voices within pedagogical relations, then framing regulates the form of its message and who takes control over the sequencing and pacing of the lesson. In other words, classification refers to what is taught (e.g., disciplinary knowledge), while framing is concerned with how meanings are to be put together and relayed. The teacher's framing most often transmits to the students how the extant discursive parameters are configured, providing contextualized indicators that would signal to the students whether it is propitious to translanguage or not. In other words, strong framing indexes exclusive teacher control over interactional patterns of classroom discourse, perhaps operationalized by an English-only classroom rule or represented by fast-paced lectures without appropriate scaffolds to intentionally support bilingual learners. On the other hand, weak framing would acknowledge and encourage students to use their translanguaging repertoires and codes and incorporate discursive mechanisms that communicate sharing authority over class management, pacing and the sequencing of the lesson. Thus, Bernstein's conceptualization of pedagogic practice provides theoretical instruments to measure translanguaging potential from the teacher's perspective based on classification and framing indicators transmitted within the context of on-going interactional moments. The relative strength or weakness of classification in the teachers' stance would signal a corresponding increase or constriction of control over the subject area. That is, strong classification (C+) in the teachers' stance communicates that students will be permitted to make only relevant contributions to the topic at hand, C+ representing a stance with stronger classification and control over classroom discourse, and C- signifying a stance with weaker classification and willingness to integrate students' views and beliefs on the subject. Similarly, fluctuating values of framing (F+, F-) represent the teachers' stance on interactional patterns like the degree of control over students' translanguaging and their autonomy to control what is discussed first and what next and the pacing of the lesson or the time needed to deliberate each topic. F+ represents strong framing and F- weak framing over such interactional parameters. Criteria for C and F values are presented in the next section with examples.

Bernstein makes it clear that classification and framing provide the rules of the pedagogic practice, that is, the embedded pedagogic relations between teacher and students, and consequently, of the nature and source of knowledge being constructed in pedagogic relations. Thus, I believe it is both possible and expedient to situate this study within Bernstein's concepts to explore the dynamics of the translanguaging stance by theorizing how relations of power and control are negotiated in the translanguaging event. Unmistakably, the translanguaging stance is not limited to this conception as there may be other frameworks to describe it. Another important note to mention here is that since I am the teacher (participant) and the researcher, this analysis was conducted a few years after this data was collected. I had assumed then that fostering translanguaging would potentially lead to positive engagement and academic outcomes. It was at a later stage, after my study of Bernstein, that I came to an understanding of the central role of power in orchestrating teacher-student translanguaging events.

## 3.3 Related studies

For further clarification, I refer to some studies which have used classification and framing values to analyze pedagogical relationships. Hasan (2001) highlights shifting classification and framing values in various interactions between a British mother and her 5-year child Kristy. The study sheds light on the mother's changing classification and framing that communicates consequent shifts in power relations embedded in statement to statement. In the "eating your tea" breakfast episode, the mother hurries her child to get ready for school in the morning. Kristy, the daughter, is distracted and finds ways to extend breakfast time, apparently to avoid the next step of changing into school clothes. In response, the mother forces her agenda with a stance characterized by strong classification and framing, disregarding the diversions proposed by the child and escalating the regulation till it borders on serious threats. After analyzing various episodes, Hasan found that the mother's intentional use of strong or weak classification was contingent to the contextualized pedagogical needs of the situation. What is particularly relevant to the teachers' stance in educational contexts is that Hasan showed that the mother's weak classification of contexts in the subsequent dressing up for school episode, where she allows the child to digress, did not imply an absence of control, but instead, was a mechanism for disarming the resistance of the child and exercising "control by stealth" (p. 65). Thus, Hasan provides relevant insights into how weak classification and framing structures (that are necessary for translanguaging practice) are not synonymous with the absence of power and control, "but are indicative of a different kind of power and a different mode of control" (p. 65). Both episodes attend to local contextualized and tacit messages transmitted through shifting classification values that are central to conceptualize and understand the translanguaging stance.

In another review, Morais, Neves, Davies, and Daniels (2001) summarize how Bernstein's theory was used to characterize school pedagogic practices that involved problem solving and concept understanding in science classrooms. They refer to various studies that implemented a model with a range of four classification (C++, C+, C-, C--) and framing (F++, F+, F-, F--) values to represent the ebb and flow of teacher's power and control instantiated in empirical data of teacher-student interactions. The studies focused on how students completed pedagogical tasks in relation to teacher's responses to student questions and the explicitness of assessment criteria. The findings showed that children from disadvantaged social groups had differential access to *recognition* rules (students' understanding of the conceptual and linguistic demands of the literacy task) and *realization* rules (students' ability to satisfactorily produce and complete the assessments). A discussion on recognition and realization rules is beyond the scope of this chapter; however, the model used in these studies of shifting classification and framing values to situate and track fluctuating power and control relations at a micro-level within classroom interactions is relevant and useful for my goal of theorizing the translanguaging stance. I use this model to analyze power relation shifts in teacher student interactions in translanguaging data taken from my classroom. The tables below illustrate the symbolic representation and meanings of fluctuating values of classification and framing values in the translanguaging data. The columns indicate the range of strong to weak classification (C++, C+, C-, C--) and strong to weak framing (F++, F+, F-, F--). Strong classification would comprise:

**Table 1:** Classification Criteria: Discursive Control.

| C++ | C+ | C- | C-- |
|---|---|---|---|
| Teacher chooses topic to be discussed ignoring students' propositions | Teacher chooses to continue discussion of his choice with students making relevant contributions | Student adds to the discussion adding personal insights and experiences | Student introduces topic of their choice that is not related to on-going class discussion |

And framing values would comprise:

**Table 2:** Framing Criteria: Translanguaging.

| F++ | F+ | F- | F-- |
|---|---|---|---|
| Teacher or student choose to use English only. The discursive parameters are restricted | Teacher or student choose to use English slang or 'street lingo' | Teacher or student choose to translanguage using both English and another language | Teacher or student choose to switch to using only a language other than English. Contextual discursive parameters offer choices |

# 4 Data analysis

## 4.1 Applying Bernstein to translanguaging corrientes

Translanguaging is a social activity that comprises negotiated communication of meanings. Embedded within the interactions are embedded discursive parameters and rules that are relayed and recognized (or not) by the participants, who respond dynamically to changing C and F from moment to moment. For example, a science educator may choose to hold strong classification throughout the class with the intent of inculcating scientific habitus among students. On the other hand, my classroom stance was flexible, comprising shifts in classification and framing, with the critical intent to provide affordances for increasing translanguaging potential. The translanguaging data below show how the students responded in different ways to changes in C and F rules. To provide some background, the dialog below took place in my ESOL sheltered language arts class during the last period of the day. As I took attendance, students (Roberto, Sofia, Domingo, Miguel, Juan, Veronica and

Karen) shared interesting events of the day as they entered the class. On the day this interaction was recorded, there was a blood drive in the school and students were discussing if they could donate blood at the start of the class. The table below tracks shifts in C (changes in who controls the discussion) and corresponding F shifts (shifts to translanguaging in Spanish and English).

**Table 3:** Translanguaging data 1.

|  |  | C+/- | F+/- |
|---|---|---|---|
| 1 | JUAN: *Ey, Khote! Pueden donar si tienen un tatuaje?* [Hey Khote! Can you donate if you have a tattoo?] | C-- | F-- |
| 2 | ROBERTO: *Si guey, yo tengo en mi espalda.* [Yes dude, I have one on my back.] | C-- | F-- |
| 3 | SOFÍA: No you can't if. | C- | F- |
| 4 | DOM: Yes, you can. | C- | F-- |
| 5 | NIHAL: . . . if you have recent tattoos. then I don't know | C- | F- |
| 6 | DOM: How come *Conejo* did? (*Conejo* is the name of another student) | C-- | F-- |
| 7 | NIHAL: Like if you've done it recently maybe they won't allow you. | C- | F- |
| 8 | MIGUEL: I did it like a month ago. | C-- | F-- |
| 9 | SOFÍA: And you have earrings! | C-- | F-- |
| 10 | JUAN: *Eso no tiene nada que ver*! [That has nothing to do with it!] | C+ | F+ |
| 11 | NIHAL: OK. Let's go back to what we did yesterday. | C- | F- |
| 12 | VERONICA: (softly) Noooo. | C++ | F++ |
| 13 | NIHAL: (directed at Veronica) What did we do yesterday? | C+ | F++ |
| 14 | VERONICA: Oooh, we talked about . . . | C++ | F++ |
| 15 | NIHAL: We talked about 'How to Remove the I' right? . . . by using reporting verbs, right? | C- | F- |
| 16 | JUAN: *No va poder. Tienes tatuajes*. [You won't be able. You have tattoos.] | C++ | F++ |
| 17 | NIHAL: (gestures with hand to Juan to stop) We'll go over the examples. We'll go over it quickly first. | C- | F- |
| 18 | KAREN: *Cuanto sangre le sacan?* [How much blood do they take out?] | C++ | F++ |
| 19 | NIHAL: ShHHH . . . SHHHHH. (The class becomes quiet). | C++ | F++ |

The class translanguaged as they discussed the criteria for being ineligible for donating blood. Juan and Roberto entered the classroom speaking in Spanish in line 1 and 2, immediately signaling to the class and to me that they were taking control of the discourse. As the classroom had previously been established as a hospitable space for translanguaging, Juan and Roberto initiated the discussion addressing me directly in Spanish using the informal "Ey, Khote!". Students had control in weak classification (C--) as the discussion centered around who was eligible to donate blood and the criteria under discussion were student-centered (i.e., having tattoos or earrings). Since they translanguaged freely in Spanish and English in the official space of the classroom, the framing values were also weak (F--). Translanguaging continued as students controlled the flow and included me in their discourse. I allowed the banter to continue to a point until I decided to retake control in line 11 ("Let's go back to what we did yesterday"), steering the discussion away from the students' topic to the academic domain of language arts. At this point, teacher classification got stronger (C+) as I navigated the transition to the schoolwork at hand. There was some resistance from Veronica ("nooooo") which was quickly checked, as I directed my attention to her and asked her in line 14, "What did we do yesterday?". The question signaled to the class that I was wresting control away from them to return to the task of teaching and that they reorient themselves to the new stronger classification values that I was imposing. Juan was not aware of this change in dynamic and translanguaged in Spanish and I had to physically gesture with my hand to get his attention. Karen continued to disregard the shifting classification and framing rules and tried to prolong the weaker framing by translanguaging, *"Cuanto sangre le sacan?"*. At this point, I had to make it evident that I was in charge and shushed them into silence, in effect raising the classification and framing values to their highest strength in the dialogue. No words were spoken, in English or Spanish; the multimodal translanguaging continued as my unmoving body posture and raised-hand gesture, and more serious expression communicated the point of strongest classification (C++) and framing (F++) strength.

What was important here from a classification perspective was that the stronger classification values represented a marked discursive separation from the previous C-- values when students' home knowledge was expressed in the debate on blood donation, and C++ values were communicated in the teacher's contextual shift to school academic knowledge about erasing subjectivity in writing (Removing the I). At this point, framing values shifted from translanguaging in Spanish and English (F--) to the teacher's strong framing represented by speaking in English only. Unfortunately, both Juan and Karen did not seem to attend to the shift in classification from C-- to C++ and framing from F-- to F++ and were out of phase with the shifting terrain of *invisible* control and needed *visible* forms of restraint. With the teacher's strong classification and framing, his stance had changed as he chose to maintain the boundary between home and academic knowledge and separation of home language and official English.

The sample dialog revealed the underlying shape of the corriente and shifting dynamics in stance before, during and after the translanguaging moment, represented by tacit, invisible and changing values of the distribution of power relations and control that governed the translanguaging stream. The corriente was shaped as a flat line as long as changing values of C and F were shared and acknowledged and remained invisible in so far as the rules were recognized and responded to appropriately. However, the corriente that was somewhat flat was transformed into a more pronounced wave shape as the undulating classification and framing values shifted from weak to strong (i.e., from – to ++), following the movement of power from students to teacher. At this point, when the corrientes were mis-recognized or disregarded by the students, the teacher responded with visible forms of control to re-establish his authority at the cost of suppressing the potential terrain for further translanguaging. In effect, the translanguaging moment had eclipsed with the change in teacher's stance, replaced by new discursive rules, which indexed a markedly restrictive stance.

In the next sample translanguaging dialog, I investigate the affordances of the wave nature of the translanguaging corriente in a pedagogical interaction.

## 4.2 Affordances of translanguaging wave corrientes

The previous sample dialogue above explored the location of power relations and control in the teacher's stance and its effects on the potential for translanguaging in a classroom. The interaction uncovered shifts over embedded classification and framing that flowed from students to teacher in the form of a wave as values shifted from weak to strong. Using the same analytical instruments, I explore the course of the wave and how it was transformed within interactions of a pedagogical nature. The dialog below is longer in length in order to track the changing values in C and F.

As I discussed how to manage subjectivity in writing by using the third person passive "it" construction, I had tight control over both C and F. I provided examples of the "it" construction, *It is true that people who exercise usually have more energy*, and compared it to the subjective structure, *I believe that people who exercise usually have more energy*. It is notable that I used imperative sentences as I spoke to the students, *look at this one* and *see the difference* (line 3). Embedded in these utterances was what Bernstein called the *regulative discourse* and the *instructional discourse* (Bernstein 1990, 2000). The regulative discourse transmits moral values,

**Table 4:** Translanguaging data 2.

| | | C+/- | F+/- |
|---|---|---|---|
| 1 | NIHAL: You don't have to use the I in the essays. You have to remove the I . . . Remove yourself. The one on top, look at the top also. | C++ | F++ |
| 2 | Look at this one. (reads from whiteboard) *It is true that people who exercise usually have more energy. I believe that people who exercise usually have more energy.* See the difference? This one is a clear opinion. This is how you speak; but this is how you write. OK? | C++ | F++ |
| 3 | Any questions on this? We will practice this a lot you'll get it. I'll make sure you get it. | C++ | F++ |
| 4 | Can I move on? | C+ | F- |
| 5 | SOFÍA: No! | C+ | F- |
| 6 | KAREN: Yes. | C- | F- |
| 7 | NIHAL: But you should have copied all this yesterday. | C+ | F- |
| 8 | DOMINGO: Oh, I lost the paper I lost it. | C+ | F- |
| 9 | KAREN: The dog ate it, I guess. | C- | F- |
| 10 | NIHAL: You didn't lose it! I made you file it! | C- | F- |
| 11 | DOMINGO: No, but . . . xxx (inaudible comment. Students laugh) | C- | F- |
| 12 | NIHAL: Ready? Sofía? | C- | F- |
| 13 | SOFÍA: *Espereme*! [wait a bit!] (Pause 5 secs) | C-- | F-- |
| 14 | ROBERTO: *Metele turbo!* [Come on! Faster!] | C-- | F-- |
| 15 | SOFÍA: *Yaaaa!* | C-- | F-- |
| 16 | DOMINGO: *Yaa guey*! (everyone laughs) [Yeesss dude!] | C-- | F-- |
| 17 | NIHAL: *El gordo que cae al agua*! [The fat kid who falls in the water!] | C-- | F-- |
| 18 | DOMINGO: *Asi era el Becerra cuando era chiquito*! [That's Becerra when he was little!] | C-- | F-- |
| 19 | BECERRA: *Naaa! Cuando yo era chiquillo, yo estaba come este.bien flaquillo!* [Noo! When I was little, I was like him . . . very skinny!] | C-- | F-- |
| 20 | NIHAL: *Si?* [Yes?] | C-- | F-- |
| 21 | BECERRA: *Verdad, de Dios*! [God's truth!] | C-- | F-- |
| 22 | KAREN: *Trae una foto pues*! [Bring a photo!] | C-- | F-- |

**Table 4** (continued)

|  |  | C+/- | F+/- |
|---|---|---|---|
| 23 | NIHAL: OK, OK. Are you done? (Sofía nods her head). | C+ | F+ |
| 24 | OK. An example of an "it" sentence is . . . this is very important. You need to know all of this. These are used to stress, to stress something. OK? These are used to . . . when something is a fact. You want to give an opinion. You want to say, "I think that" . . . no you can't say that. So, what do you say? You say, "it is certain that" . . . Or you can say, "it is evident that" . . . OK? | C++ | F++ |

behavior corrections, messages about identity and attitudes, in most cases tacitly contained within interactions. Regulative discourse has to do with how students are expected to interact and what behaviors are appropriate in a classroom. On the other hand, instructional discourse denotes what is usually referred to as content knowledge or the curriculum that the teacher is teaching. Bernstein suggests that the regulative discourse and the instructional discourse are interlinked as the instructional discourse is always embedded within the regulative discourse. The implication is that a teacher's curriculum comprises content knowledge communicated in the instructional discourse, mixed in with cultural rules of appropriate socialization and behavior rules transmitted in the regulative discourse. My tone communicated my firm resolve that students should focus on the content knowledge being imparted; within the instructional discourse, I was also communicating a regulatory message that there was no space for diversions, comprised by strong classification and framing. In effect, my stance signaled to the students that that was not the time nor the place for translanguaging. In lines 3, I asserted, "I'll make sure you get it," further strengthening classification and framing. However, in line 4, I relaxed control, asking students, "Can I move on?". Framing values were weakened ever so slightly as I was offering them a choice, and Sofía responded to the offer and requested that the class wait for her to finish copying the work. Framing is power over the sequencing and pace of the lesson and Karen took control by overriding Sofía, countering with a "Yes." When I argued that this work should have been copied the day before, classification values were also weakened as the topic of discussion had changed. Domingo retorted that he had lost his notes from the day before (line 8) and Karen assumed that he was lying and made a sarcastic comment that the dog must have eaten his notes. At this point, classification and framing were further weakened as we had deviated from the topic of controlling subjectivity in writing and transitioned to dogs eating students' notes. Domingo cracked a joke and students laughed and my tight focus and control of the previous moments had considerably dissipated. In line 12, I asked Sofía again if she was ready to move on (weak framing) and Sofía replied in Spanish, *"espereme!"*. The translanguaging by Sofía prompted Roberto to acknowledge the moment and continue in Spanish, in addition to assuming some of the authority of teacher as he urged her to hurry up in *"metele turbo!"* (line 14). Sofía, exclaimed *"yaaa"* which signified her irritation and Domingo associated the *"yaaa"* to a funny video of a chubby adolescent who was unable to balance on a fallen log only to fall into the stream as he shouted *"Ya guey!"* (Domingo had shared this video with the class the day before). Translanguaging provoked spontaneous intertextuality and by this point, students had control over classification and framing as the class laughed. Remembering the funny video, I too acknowledged the translanguaging moment and responded in Spanish *"El gordo que cae al agua!"*. It is important to note here that I joined in their hilarity instead of enforcing the regulatory discourse. Domingo noted the weak classification and framing and proceeded to poke fun at Becerra (another student who is chubby) and Becerra defended himself saying that he actually was skinny as a child (line 19). Once again, I joined in the jesting and Karen reinforced the humorous corriente asking for photographic proof that Becerra was once skinny. Both classification and framing were at their lowest value as students had control over the class proceedings, at which point I decided to change the dynamics and rein in the class, redirecting the discussion back to the topic of controlling subjectivity in writing. The change in my stance was represented by strong classification (return to school topic) and strong framing (back to English) as I emphasized that "this is very important" (line 24).

Thus far, the data represented shifts in the location of power relations in two directions. The first demonstrated the corriente moving from students to teacher and the second depicted the corriente from the teacher to the students and then redirected back to the teacher. In both instances, the translanguaging events happened outside of the instructional discourse. In the second example, students' translanguaging and intertextuality took the discussion to unexpected jesting and ribbing among themselves. In the next section, I explore teacher stance and shifts in translanguaging pedagogy *within* the instructional discourse. In dialog 3 below, I ask the participating students (Juan, Veronica, and Domingo) to provide examples of their opinions to teach them how to disguise subjectivity and elide agency in their writing.

The dialog began with weak framing as I asked students for their participation and that they furnish a statement that would serve as an example of their opinion. Right away, in line 2 Juan recognized the weak framing and saw the opportunity to inject the academic discussion with a *counterscript*, displaying his local knowledge in an attempt to displace the teacher's academic script (Gutierrerz, Rhymes, and Larson 1995: 447). He was still within the domain of school, neither harmonious nor resistant, but leveraging the inherently flexible, multi-voiced and dialogic

**Table 5:** Translanguaging data 3.

| | | C+/- | F+/- |
|---|---|---|---|
| 1 | NIHAL: Veronica, can you give me an example of a fact, any fact – about the population or about Mexico. Give me a fact. | C++ | F++ |
| 2 | JUAN: Mexico is full of *zetas*. | C- | F- |
| 3 | NIHAL: What? I believe that Mexico has what? | C- | F+ |
| 4 | JUAN: *No nada solo zetas*. [No, nothing, only zetas.] | C-- | F-- |
| 5 | VERO: *Dile*! [Tell him!] (laughs) | C-- | F-- |
| 6 | NIHAL: OK. How would you express that as an opinion? | C+ | F+ |
| 7 | VERO: I think that . . . . | C++ | F+ |
| 8 | NIHAL: Good! (writes on the board). I *think that Mexico is full of gangs*. | C++ | F++ |
| 9 | JUAN Yeah! | C++ | F-- |
| 10 | NIHAL: OK? But I want to remove the "I". So how do I do it? I would say: It is certain that Mexico has a lot of gangs. | C++ | F++ |
| 11 | DOM: Oh yeah! | C++ | F++ |
| 12 | NIHAL: You remove the "I". So now it seems very objective. Or you can say: It is clear that Mexico has a lot of gangs. It is evident that Mexico has a lot of gangs. | C++ | F++ |
| 13 | VERO: It is obvious . . . | C++ | F++ |
| 14 | NIHAL: It is OBVIOUS that Mexico has a lot of gangs. All these are used very often in essays | C++ | F++ |

nature of the classroom. My surprise in line 3 was evident as I asked for clarification. Juan somewhat backed down as he perceived that the framing could get stronger ("*No nada solo zetas*"). Veronica insisted that he pursue what Gutierrez, Rhymes, and Larson (1995), have characterized as "underlife" of the classroom, or students' local construction of power and identity in the discursive practices of the classroom. In effect, Veronica was trying to weaken framing and classification by challenging Juan to push the discussion away from the official script. My reaction in line 6 ("OK. How would you express that as an opinion?") is key, because what I was doing was appropriating the counterscript into the academic discussion. I did not choose to disregard the input of the students and consequently restrict the heteroglossia of voices in the classroom, which was the critical benefit and upshot of translanguaging pedagogy in the first place. Instead, I acknowledged the validity of the response and countered the counterscript in a move that legitimized the resistance but subdued its incipient rebellious intent. After some micro fluctuations in classification and framing (from ++ to – and then back to ++), the discussion returned to strong classification and framing, i.e., back to the official academic script.

## 5 Findings and discussion

In the above examples of translanguaging dialog, students initiated and responded in different ways to on-going changing C and F rules, their responses hinging on whether they recognized the fluctuating dynamics or not. What was clear was that the discursive rules that were communicated through the teacher's stance triggered appropriately contextualized responses from the students. In dialog 1, students initiated the translanguaging, took charge of classification and framing and I, the teacher, regained control from them to redirect the class back to the curriculum. The translanguaging corriente was relatively flat as students translanguaged and I accepted their invitation to join in. However, when I decided to re-take control of the class and some students disregarded my change in stance, I had to enforce classification and framing, and the translanguaging corriente took the shape of a more pronounced wave. In dialogue 2, I had initial control over classification and framing, but when I relaxed my framing stance and offered Sofía the choice to slow down the pacing of the lesson, the in-context dynamics changed, and students proceeded to wrest control over both classification and framing and began to translanguage and make jokes about each other. I joined in their jesting, but when it was time to get back to the lesson, classification and framing became stronger and translanguaging potential was dispersed. In dialog 3, I offered the opportunity to weaken framing and students responded by attempting to further weaken classification and framing. In all cases, translanguaging potential was greatest when classification and framing values were weak; that is, when the teacher relinquished control and the students recognized the propitious moment to translanguage. From this data, I make a few points to understand the translanguaging stance in my particular classroom context and explore its inner dynamics.

## 5.1 The translanguaging moment has to be mutually recognized

Translanguaging is a social activity. It is not pre-planned or rehearsed but is triggered in the spontaneous moment when conditions are propitious for its emergence. In the dialogues above, translanguaging happened because the participants, both students and I, the teacher, recognized the precise moment that was both appropriate and suitable for its development. The weaving in and out of contexts or changes in classification is not unilateral but done in partnership with all the participants, as if it were an unrehearsed, but harmonious dance.

## 5.2 Translanguaging is initiated by an 'invite' move

The timing of the translanguaging moment is key, and in the three cases, the trigger to initiate was the moment when framing values were weak. It was then that one of the students sent out a 'feeler' or 'an invite' to translanguage (dialogue 1: Juan entering the class; dialogue 2: Sofia in line 13, Juan in line 2). In the data, the invite typically occurred when teacher's framing was weak. Further studies will be required to investigate if translanguaging can occur if initiated during a stance with strong classification and framing. If translanguaging did occur during strong classification and framing, this would imply that students were translanguaging in concert with the on-going literacy goals and that the translanguaging was working productively towards attaining the literacy goals of the classroom. Such an occurrence would represent an ideal manifestation of the translanguaging corriente as the teacher's stance and teaching and learning activities would all be harmoniously constructing disciplinary habitus- wherein translanguaging is normalized, not as a counterscript, but as a constructive event that is fruitful and beneficial to both teacher and students. I propose that this would be a desirable and attainable objective, but teachers would have to previously set up discursive parameters for such an outcome to happen, for it to get uptake from other participants or not be silenced as 'inappropriate' by the teachers themselves.

## 5.3 The invite followed by response defines the shape of the translanguaging corriente

Once the invite is made, the group has the option to take on and build on the moment or reject it. In all of the dialogs presented as data in this chapter, the invites were recognized and acknowledged by all. That is, the participants were all in tune with the on-going weakening of classification and framing values. However, in the third dialog, the intention may have been to infuse counterscripts into the dialog, and the teacher's pedagogical stance recognized and appropriated the move by framing it as a legitimate response. The dissonance of participants caused the classification and framing values to fluctuate up and down in the form of a wave. The same dynamics were seen in dialog two when interacting participants were not in accordance, or out of phase, and classification and framing values became stronger. In this case, the translanguaging corriente also assumed the shape of a wave. However, in the instance when participants were in phase, then the translanguaging corriente took the shape of a softer ripple, or the shifts from ++ to – were smoother and less pronounced.

## 5.4 Teacher stance assumes embedded power relations

Bernstein (2000) notes that in asymmetrical pedagogical relations, the acquirer of knowledge, in this case, the students, only have *apparent* control as it is the teacher who grants this capacity to students and can at any time take it away or clamp down on the heteroglossia of the classroom. In dialog 1, as I tried to re-direct the class to return to the lesson, some students (Juan and Karen) seemed to disregard the changing and strengthening classification and framing and I had to leverage visible mechanisms to re-take control of the class. The implication is that weaker framing values did not correspond to absence of control or complete control of the class by the students. Weak framing only implied a different kind of *invisible* control, which was tacitly relaxed or tightened, contingent to the needs of the on-going moment. The invisibility of the control was at its most precarious in dialog 3 when the translanguaging infused counterscripts, and the teacher regained control, not by utilizing visible regulative mechanisms (as in dialog 1) but appropriated the resistance by including it as a legitimate feature of the classroom. This is what Hasan (2001: 65) refers to as "control by stealth," where weak framing acts as a mechanism for "disarming opposition by (*apparently*) entertaining the other's need" (emphasis in original). The implication is that power rests and is wielded in the teachers' stance.

## 5.5 A flexible teacher stance lays the ground rules

The data above shows that students were comfortable to initiate translanguaging or change classification, as long as the moves were initiated within highly contextualized 'appropriate' moments. Students took control over the class in moments as the translanguaging corriente shifted and students made jokes or poked fun at each other. For this to happen, the teacher had to have set the ground rules previously. Though the regulative discourse was omnipresent as the teacher had final authority over classification and framing, there was space for students to contribute to the discourse or to add what they deemed fit in the moment. The students knew (based on previous similar events) that they could joke and infuse some hilarity during an on-going lesson and invited the teacher to join in their jesting. The question then is, what are the ideal classification and framing values for a teacher's translanguaging stance to be effective and productive in a classroom? Overly relaxed framing may lead to excessive and 'aimless' chatter and diversions in which high school students typically revel, but conversely, can also lead to productive agentic discussions. On other hand, excessively strong framing implies strict control over the class and probable separation of home v/s school knowledge and consequently, the construction of a simplistic binary with seemingly lesser affordances for translanguaging may restrict authentic student engagement. I propose that the true potential of translanguaging rests in its organic integration into the disciplinary habitus of the classroom discourse and this key facet will be the subject of forthcoming studies.

The examples above seem to suggest that there is need for a highly regulated pedagogy which alternates between strong classification of discourse and strong framing over teacher/student relations alternating with weakened classification over discourses and weakened framing over pacing. In both dialogs, relaxed framing on pacing and sequencing (and allowance for the use of diverse codes and languages) with weakened classification between school and community knowledge afforded the most promise for translanguaging moments to spontaneously emerge, be recognized and shared. However, to accommodate the teacher's pedagogic objectives, the teacher also adopted a stance that comprised strong classification and framing to redirect the class back to the topic after the translanguaging moment had passed. The upshot is that contextualized flexibility and awareness of ongoing discursive shifts and moves made by *all* participants are key for setting the terrain for translanguaging to be efficacious and productive.

# 6 Conclusion

I have theorized the location of power and control in teacher's translanguaging stance using Bernstein's (2000) conceptualization of classification and framing to locate power within translanguaging pedagogy. I do not claim that the translanguaging stance, as described here, has universal application as the translanguaging activity is highly contextualized and its complex embedded dynamics of power and control are specific to each spatial, multimodal or linguistic instant and context. The analysis here indicates that translanguaging potential is high during weak classification and framing. However, considering the dynamic and extemporaneous nature of translanguaging, more work is needed to corroborate this finding, specifically to explore affordances of translanguaging within strong classification contexts.

I do wish to caution future teacher candidates about simplistic views that characterize translanguaging pedagogy as a panacea. There is no doubt that translanguaging has its benefits for literacy and social justice as so much research has demonstrated. García and colleagues (2017) have indicated that translanguaging pedagogy has the potential to shift orders of discourse and empower student voices, making it the cognitive, democratic and critical avenue and rationale for inclusion and construction of multiple forms of knowing. Moreover, students' empowerment is also embedded in the latitude to negotiate and push the discursive limits they are afforded by the teacher. However, the key to a successful translanguaging stance is negotiating extant power relations in productive ways, the aspect in need of further study.

More explorations are also warranted to understand whether one set of rules and configurations of classification and framing that conceptualize the translanguaging stance in a particular context may or may not be applicable to a different context with another teacher and a different set of teacher/student relations. Much of the control and authority of the teacher is tacit and invisible, as long as the discursive rules of engagement are mutually recognized and accepted from moment to moment by both teacher and students. However, any dissonance between the recognition of classification and/or framing that results in the pronounced wave-like, up and down shape of the corriente, could lead to the dissipation and restriction of translanguaging potential. More work that focuses on application of classification and framing in translanguaging practice outside the classroom would greatly increase our understanding of this complex practice. Finally, Bernstein does suggest that regulation and control (and teacher's power) are always embedded within pedagogic relations. The upshot is that the potential for translanguaging in a classroom setting is largely a function of the teacher's stance. Within such structured, but reflexive spontaneity, the bigger question of how much agency is afforded to students offers much promise and expectation but has yet to be fully theorized and analyzed.

# References

Bakhtin, M. Mikhail. 1981. *The Dialogic Imagination* (Caryl Emerson & Michael Holquist, Trans.). Austin: University of Texas Press.
Bernstein, Basil. 1973. *Class, Codes and Control, Vol. 2*. London: Routledge and Kegan Paul.
Bernstein, Basil. 1990. *Class, Codes and Control, Vol. 4. The Structuring of Pedagogic Discourse*. London: Routledge.
Bernstein, Basil. 2000. *Pedagogy, Symbolic Control and Identity: Theory, Research, Critique*. New York: Rowman & Littlefield Publishers.
Dyson, Anne Haas. 1993. *Social Worlds of Children Learning to Write in an Urban Primary School*. New York: Teachers College Press.
Foucault, Michel. 1982. The subject and power. In Hubert L. Dreyfus & Paul Rabinow (eds.), *Michel Foucault: Beyond Structuralism and Hermeneutics*. 2nd edn. Chicago: University of Chicago Press.
García, Ofelia, Susana Ibarra Johnson & Kate Seltzer. 2017. *The Translanguaging Classroom: Leveraging Student Bilingualism for Learning*. Philadelphia: Calson.
García, Ofelia & Li Wei. 2014. *Translanguaging: Language, Bilingualism and Education*. New York: Palgrave Macmillan.
Gutierrez, Kris D., Betsy Rymes & Joanne Larson. 1995. Script, counterscript and underlife in the classroom: James Brown versus Brown v. The Board of Education. *Harvard Educational Review* 65 (3). 445–471.
Hasan, Ruqaiya. 2001. The ontogenesis of de-contextualized language: Some achievements of classification and framing. In Ana Morais, Isabel Neves, Brian Davies & Harry Daniels (eds.), *Towards a Sociology of Pedagogy: The Contribution of Basil Bernstein to Research*. New York: Peter Lang.
Menken, Kate. 2008. *English learners left behind: Standardized testing as language policy*. Clevedon, UK: Multilingual Matters.
Menken, Kate & Kleyn, Tatyana. 2010. The long-term impact of subtractive schooling in the educational experiences of secondary English language learners. *International Journal of Bilingual Education and Bilingualism* 13(4). 399–417.
Morais, Ana., Isabel Neves, Brian Davies & Harry Daniels (eds.). 2001. *Towards a Sociology of Pedagogy: The Contribution of Basil Bernstein to Research*. New York: Peter Lang.

Peter Sayer
# Afterword
Teacher education and the development of a translanguaging stance

> *Los científicos dicen que*
> *estamos hechos de átomos,*
> *pero a mí un pajarito me contó que*
> *estamos hechos de historias.*
> *- Eduardo Galeano*

## Narrative knowledging of translanguaging pedagogy in teacher education

A significant thread that runs through this volume is Barkhuizen's (2011) notion of *narrative knowledging*. Ceballos-Zapata and Kim (Chapter 2) use narrative knowledging when they evoke the Korean opera performance *pansori* to frame and interpret their stories of translanguaging from the classroom. Henderson, Fallas-Escobar and Lindahl (Chapter 3) share the language portraits that their pre-service teachers (PSTs) created to represent their relationships with their multilingual repertoires. Likewise, most of the authors employ self-study or case study methodologies, and thus lean heavily into narratives as the mediational means through which teacher candidates can *re-see and re-hear* their students (Seltzer 2019). So let me start with a little story of my own as I think about how to connect the dots across the chapters.

I'm spending the summer here in Oaxaca, in the mountains of southern Mexico. Last Sunday I visited the *tianguis* market in Tlacolula, a town about an hour down the central valley. On my way through the valley, I stopped first at Mitla, a major archaeological site built by the Zapotecs and Mixtecs, the two ethnolinguistic groups that have inhabited the areas for millennia, and still do. I have visited Mitla many times, and it is fascinating not only because of the exquisite geometric stone facades of its well conserved buildings, but also because the site was never abandoned. It was a thriving city in the 16th century when the Spaniards and Aztecs arrived, and the people living in the current town which surrounds the ruins are the descendants of those who built it.

**Peter Sayer**, The Ohio State University

https://doi.org/10.1515/9783110735604-009

I had been working on this afterword the night before, and so as I walked amongst ancient buildings, I had translanguaging on my mind. I was mulling over Ofelia García's (2009) metaphor of the banyan tree. Like translanguaging, she argues, the banyan tree is a collage of roots and trunks that twist together to form a coherent and beautiful whole. At Mitla, however, I saw another metaphor for translanguaging. At the site, a large Catholic church was built by the Spaniards using the same stones taken from the original city; across Mexico they were intentionally not-subtle about building their churches on top of the prior site of the Indigenous people's holiest temples. The curved dome of the church's steeple juxtaposes the diagonal lines of part of the ancient temple still standing right next to it. And just beyond the temple, outside the fence of the archaeological site, I could see some workers were repairing a wall of a contemporary house, also I suspected with stones that had originally been quarried a thousand years earlier to build the original city.

**Figure 1:** The temple and church at Mitla, Oaxaca (source: Wikipedia).

Our linguistic resources, García and others (García and Li Wei 2014) argue, are like those stones at Mitla: they are part of a unitary system that we are able to shape, stack, and re-work as needed into new resources: the *translanguaging repertoires* of the title of this book. Like the ancient temple, the colonial church, and the modern-day dwellings, these language resources can coexist, serving different purposes at different points across time and space.

I arrived at the market in Tlacolula and sat down at a small stand to get a bite to eat. Two women wearing colorful embroidered *huipiles* sat down next to me. They had a large plastic bucket heaped with *chapulines*, the tasty grasshoppers fried in chile and lime that Oaxaca is famous for. They were chatting in Zapoteco, but moving back and forth with Spanish so that I could eavesdrop just enough words to get the gist of the conversation about an upcoming wedding they were going to attend. Despite my fascination in hearing how they seamlessly combined Zapoteco (or Didxsaj as the variety in Tlacolula is called), a Mesoamerican language, with Spanish, it reminded me that the language practice that we educational linguists call *translanguaging*, the women in Tlacolula call *talking*. While the scholarly term "translanguaging" adds reverence and recognition for how remarkable it is that they can mesh two languages that are so distinct (both phonologically and syntactically; Zapoteco is both tonal and VSO) together so effortlessly, in fact for most multilinguals – like the chapulines sellers in the market – this bilingual blending is wholly unremarkable and the most quotidian way of using language.

I should qualify that: For multilinguals, translanguaging is unremarkable talking . . . until those same multilinguals enter school. Upon entering school, the colonial structures that divide, order, and hierarchize languaging into languages come into force, what Kroskrity (2004) refers to as *regimes of language*, and the translanguaging repertoires and identities of multilinguals are rendered invisible and moot. Pontier and Tian (Chapter 4) pose a key question: "Who gets to control what type of languaging we're supposed to use [in schools]?" On the one hand, the answer is obvious: control is how an ideology exerts its power, and control over the language(ing) of school is one of the most basic exercises of discursive power. The ideology at work here is variously called Standard Language Ideology (Wiley 1996) or Monolingual Ideology (Heller 1996), and it often permeates the monolingual stance that educators adopt, albeit unwittingly. It is enshrined in our curricula, state standards, textbooks, and assessments (Hadjioannou, Chapter 5). On the other hand, the authors of this volume make clear that teachers have agency, and with a critical consciousness they can adopt a multilingual stance that allows them to design and shift their teaching to leverage their students' translanguaging repertoires.

## Developing a translanguaging pedagogical stance

Adopting a translanguaging pedagogy that leverages students' multilingual repertoires sounds promising, but it's no easy task. Barros, Domke, Symons, and Ponzio (2020) discuss the resistance teacher candidates encounter when confronting language hierarchies and monolingual language ideologies. As Wright, Morita-Mullaney, Choi, and Li (Chapter 6) document, even in dual language programs where there is an explicit objective of developing students' bilingualism, biliteracy, and biculturalism, there are the broader constraints and language hierarchies that conspire against languaging that does not conform to standard/monolingual norms. Li Wei (2018) argues that a key aspect of flexible languaging in the classroom is for the teacher to open up *translanguaging spaces t*hat allow for previously stigmatized language practices to gain currency. However, we must be realistic in recognizing that these translanguaging spaces are not created out of a linguistic vacuum. Rather, they must be very deliberately carved out of the spaces that the dominant language ideologies now occupy. That is why the authors in this volume (Pontier and Tian, Chapter 4; Hadjioannou, Chapter 5) refer to translanguaging as transgression, evoking the title and overarching thesis of the late bell hooks' (1994) *Teaching to Transgress.* When teachers are able to open up the classroom's discursive spaces to flexible languaging, then the translanguaging *corriente* can flow, as Khote (Chapter 7) so effectively demonstrates.

What becomes key then for teacher candidates is the development of a *translanguaging pedagogical stance.* Seltzer (2019) defines translanguaging stance as a teaching philosophy that views students' families and communities as holders of information for the co-construction of knowledge and frames the classroom as a democratic space for collaborative work towards social justice. Stance, as Hadjioannou (Chapter 5) explains, is the foundational aspect of García, Johnson, and Seltzer's (2017) *stance-design-shift* translanguaging pedagogy framework. Henderson, Fallas-Escobar, and Lindahl (Chapter 3) explain that:

> A translanguaging stance is a critical aspect of translanguaging pedagogy which is comprised of three collaborative joint/juntos beliefs: a) students bring linguistic and cultural practices from their homes and communities to school, which work juntos in student meaning making; b) students bring knowledge from their homes and communities that is valuable for instruction and curriculum; and c) classrooms are spaces for teachers and students to co-construct knowledge and actively work juntos for a more just society.

Khote (Chapter 7) maintains that "Fostering a translanguaging classroom is largely a function of teacher's stance as within stance lies the authority to validate, or not, students' use of non-dominant languages." Across the chapters, the authors highlight several different central concerns in developing teacher candidates' translanguaging stance. Ceballos-Zapata and Kim (Chapter 2) draw upon the similar concept of *translingual dispositions (*Lee and Canagarajah 2019), which include three key elements: language awareness, social values, and learning strategies. Pontier and Tian (Chapter 4) center the notion of translanguaging-as-social-justice stance, drawing on Peña-Pincheira and De Costa (2021) to argue that it emerges from the Venn intersection of purpose, autonomy, competence and reflexivity. Musanti (Chapter 1) includes an honest account of how she herself had to confront her own bilingual training and ingrained language ideologies: "Like many of us in the field of bilingual education, I have taught about the need to keep language separated and I have advocated for the negative effects of translation in bilingual education." This reminds us that the need for reflexivity and self-critique in teacher education starts with ourselves as teacher educators. She continues by acknowledging: "My teaching then contributed to legitimize only standard forms of either Spanish or English rendering students' language use and the variation of Spanish spoken in the region incorrect or inappropriate." This reminds us that translanguaging pedagogy has to cross not just named language boundaries, but also the linguistic boundaries that govern standard/vernacular, as well as the discursive boundaries that regulate the interactional structures of the classroom (cf. Khote, Chapter 7), or what Tyack and Tobin (1994) referred to as the *grammar of schooling*.

## Conclusions

This collection is an effort to show how teacher educators and teacher education programs can support the development of a stance that strongly embraces translanguaging, not just as an approach for teaching language, but as one that is tightly interwoven with a pedagogy based on students' linguistic and cultural identities. As García (Foreword) reminds us: "sometimes more attention is paid to teaching language than to teaching bilingual students." A translanguaging stance puts bilingual students front and center. The editors set the vision for this volume at the outset (Tian and King, Introduction): "This volume argues that it is important to develop teachers' *translanguaging repertoires* in teacher education so that we have more competent and caring . . . teachers who could enact culturally and linguistically sustaining practices to transform U.S. schooling in ways that advance a social justice agenda." Within teacher education programs, we are increasingly realizing the strong integration of translanguaging into educators' professional development coursework and experiences; as it provides a foundation for teachers to build a pedagogical approach around the interrelated principles of social justice and students' multilingual identities.

# References

Barkhuizen, Gary. 2011. Narrative knowledging in TESOL. *TESOL Quarterly* 45(3). 391–414.
Barros, Sandro, Lisa M. Domke, Carrie Symons & Christina Ponzio. 2020. Challenging monolingual ways of looking at multilingualism: Insights for curriculum development in teacher preparation. *Journal of Language, Identity & Education*. 1–16. DOI: 10.1080/15348458.2020.1753196
García, Ofelia. 2009. *Bilingual Education in the 21st Century: A Global Perspective*. Malden: Blackwell.
García, Ofelia, Susana I. Johnson & Kate Seltzer. 2017. *The Translanguaging Classroom: Leveraging Student Bilingualism for Learning*. Philadelphia: Caslon.
García, Ofelia & Li Wei. 2014. *Translanguaging: Language, Bilingualism and Education*. Basingstoke: Palgrave Macmillan.
Heller, Monica. 1996. Legitimate language in a multilingual school. *Linguistics and Education* 8(2). 139–157. https://doi.org/10.1016/S0898-5898(96)90011-X.
hooks, bell. 1994. *Teaching to Transgress: Education as the Practice of Freedom*. New York: Routledge.
Kroskrity, Paul V. 2004. Language ideologies. In Alessandro Duranti (ed.), *A Companion to Linguistic Anthropology*, 496–517. Malden: Blackwell.
Lee, Eunjeong & Suresh Canagarajah. 2019. The connections between transcultural dispositions and translingual practices in academic writing. *Journal of Multicultural Discourses* 14(1). 14–28. https://doi.org/10.1080/17447143.2018.1501375.
Li Wei. 2018. Translanguaging as a practical theory of language. *Applied Linguistics* 39(1). 9–30.
Peña-Pincheira, Romina & Peter I. De Costa. 2021. Language teacher agency for educational justice-oriented work: An ecological model. *TESOL Journal* 12(2). 1–13. https://doi.org/10.1002/tesj.561.
Seltzer, Kate. 2019. Reconceptualizing "home" and "school" language: Taking a critical translingual approach in the English classroom. *TESOL Quarterly* 53(4). 986–1007.
Tyack, David & William Tobin. 1994. The grammar of schooling: Why has it been so hard to change? *American Educational Research Journal* 31(3). 453–479. https://doi.org/10.3102/00028312031003453.
Wiley, Terrence G. 1996. Language policy and planning. In Sandra Lee McKay & Nancy Hornberger (eds.), *Sociolinguistics and Language Teaching*, 103–148. Cambridge: Cambridge University Press.

# Index

(in)equity 2, 13, 29, 99, 103, 108

acquisition XIII, 92, 118
advocacy 13, 61, 116–117
agency 5–6, 7, 26, 66, 81, 84, 89–91, 99, 123, 141, 159, 165, 169
assessment(s) 2, 24, 53, 61, 83, 86, 99, 107, 114–116, 127–128, 152, 169
attitudes 55, 62, 114, 158
autonomy 81, 84, 88–93, 95–99, 151, 171
awareness
– critical 3, 28, 62, 116
– critical language 16, 62, 65, 71, 77
– critical multilingual 14–15, 20, 24, 28
– cultural 71
– language 13, 24, 38, 67, 170
– linguistic 72
– metalinguistic 20, 29
– self 35
– sociolinguistic 16

background(s)
– cultural 28, 36, 39, 48, 53–54, 88
– diverse 36, 55, 65
– linguistic 65, 88
– minority 55
– multicultural 38
– multilingual 38
– socioeconomic 87–88
belief(s) 3, 11–13, 26–27, 29, 53, 55, 61–62, 82, 84, 92, 95, 97, 106–110, 114, 119, 146, 151, 170
bilingual
– children XI
– courses 130
– education IX, XII, 6, 12–13, 15, 17–18, 22–23, 29–30, 63, 66, 74, 86–87, 107, 123, 125, 127–129, 131, 135, 140–141, 171
– identity/ies 5, 27, 77–78, 88, 108
– Latinx XIII, 14, 18, 30, 60–61, 131, 145, 148
– program(s) XI, 124, 128, 131, 133
– teacher XI, XII, 36–7, 11–17, 20, 22, 24, 26, 28–30, 39, 60–61, 123, 125, 130–131, 141
– teacher candidates 3, 11, 13–15, 20, 24, 29

– teacher education programs 60, 141
– teacher education 3, 13, 60, 141
– teacher educator(s) 3, 11–14, 16–17, 30, 61
– teacher preparation 3, 7, 11, 14–16, 22, 28–30
bilingualism XIII, XIV, 1–35, 6, 11–16, 18, 26–29, 61, 66, 73, 77, 81–83, 88, 90–94, 97, 103–105, 107, 110, 112, 114, 119, 123–124, 131–132, 134, 140, 148, 170
biliteracy 13, 23, 29, 103, 105, 129, 170
bridge 26, 95, 127, 129–130, 134, 136

case study 6, 11, 116, 123, 128, 167
classification 6, 89, 136, 145, 147, 149–153, 155–156, 158, 160–165
coding 4, 20, 64–65, 89, 130
collaboration IX, 2, 39, 94, 97
collaborative 4–5, 42–44, 47, 50, 53, 59, 61, 64, 99, 111, 127, 170
competence 16, 29, 81, 84, 88–95, 97–99, 171
cultural
– assets 2, 54
– awareness 71
– background(s) 28, 36, 39, 53–54, 88
culture(s)
– black 50–51, 54
– dominant 4, 55
– minority 54
curriculum, curricula 6, 16, 52, 62, 83, 106–108, 116–117, 119, 136, 140, 146, 148–150, 158, 161, 169–170

deficit 4, 20–21, 27, 29, 37, 44, 60, 63, 72, 77, 113
discourse(s) 3, 11, 14, 16, 27, 29, 43, 53, 64, 108, 118, 137, 145–146, 148–150, 155–156, 158–159, 164–165
diversity
– cultural 30
– linguistic 14, 16–17, 29–30, 61, 106
dominant 4, 6, 11, 13, 21, 27, 36–37, 51, 54–55, 65, 118–119, 138–141, 145–146, 149, 170

empirical 85, 106–107, 152
English Language Learner(s) 6, 42, 44, 112, 123, 147

https://doi.org/10.1515/9783110735604-010

English learners  6, 86, 105, 116, 145
English-dominant  6, 123, 133, 138–140
ethnicity  65, 68

family/ies  XI, XIII, 4, 18, 23–25, 46, 59, 64, 66–69, 71, 84, 104–105, 109, 112–114, 116–117, 131, 133, 149, 170
fluidity  3, 12, 26, 42
framework  XIII, 5, 20, 38, 40, 46, 50, 55, 62, 81, 84, 88–89, 98, 104, 106, 115, 124, 129, 136, 147–149, 170
framing  2, 4, 6–7, 16, 60, 131, 145, 147, 149–153, 155–156, 158–159, 161–165
funds of knowledge  1, 113, 117

gender  XII, 51, 63, 67

hegemonic  3, 12–13, 17, 28–29, 61, 66
hegemony  14, 105
heritage
– cultural  27, 36
– language  IX, 5, 83, 124
– Spanish  63, 71, 133
hybrid  39, 43

identity/ies
– bilingual  5, 27, 77–78, 88, 108
– cultural  26, 55, 108–109, 115, 124, 171
– cultural and linguistic  13, 66, 105
– Latinx  11
– linguistic  39, 59, 78, 127
– multilingual  171
– work  78
ideological  IX, 3, 12–13, 27, 61, 84, 107, 123, 125, 141
ideology/ies
– bilingual  128, 130–131
– hegemonic  13, 17
– heteroglossic  5
– language  3, 6, 12–13, 16, 38, 66, 83, 86, 88, 92–93, 124, 170–171
– monoglossic  XII, 22, 127, 141
– monolingual  5–6, 14, 83, 103, 105, 108–109, 116, 118–119, 169
– neoliberal  125, 140
– raciolinguistic  XIII, 67

– standard language  169
– translanguaging  130–132
immigrant(s)  XI, 6, 29, 41–42, 107, 125, 145
inclusive(ness)  3, 11, 14, 20–22, 26–27, 88, 124–126, 129
– linguistic(ally)  11, 14–17, 19, 24, 27, 29
integration  20, 114, 164, 171
interview(s)  XIV, 5–6, 113, 123, 129

knowledging  XIV, 4, 35–36, 42–43, 167

*la frontera*  3, 11, 13, 15
language portrait(s)  XIV, 4, 59–60, 62–66, 69, 71–77, 167
Latinx
– bilingual  XIII, 14, 18, 30, 60–61, 131, 145, 148
– identity/ies  11
– pre-service teacher(s)  4, 59–60, 63, 72, 77–78
levels of influence  89–90
literacy  17, 23, 38, 61, 113, 129, 146, 148, 152, 162, 165
– critical  108, 114
– Spanish  16
– teaching  106

majority language  35
marginalization  3–4, 26, 43, 117
marginalized  IX, 1–2, 4, 53, 63, 110, 117, 124
metalanguage  129–130, 132, 138
metalinguistic  20, 23, 28–29, 83, 134
migrant  24
minoritized
– bilinguals  XIII, 117
– communities  6, 52, 116–117
– knowledges  149
– languages  117
– multilingual speakers  1
– speakers  1, 83
– students  1, 4, 8, 37, 103, 116–117
minority language  35
monolingual bias  83
multilingual
– identity/ies  171
– students  XIII
multimodal analysis  64

native speaker(s) 12, 83
native speakerism 73, 77
newcomer(s) 117, 147

observation(s) XIII, 46, 116, 128–129, 136–137, 139
oppression 5, 26, 29, 51–52, 71, 81, 90–91, 93, 105, 108, 115

*Pansori* XII, XIII, 35–41, 43, 46–47, 50–55
pedagogy/ies IX, 1–2, 3, 5, 11, 13, 28, 39, 55, 82–83, 85, 106, 116, 119, 124, 148, 164, 171
– antiracist 52, 108
– critical 108, 146
– critical language awareness 13
– culturally responsive 104
– culturally sustaining 15–16, 124, 141
– language learning 30
– linguistic 14, 16, 30
– monoglossic 29
– *Pansori* 4, 37–38, 40–41, 43, 47, 51, 53, 55
– socially just 11, 14–15, 22, 28
planning 14–15, 17, 19–20, 23, 28, 115, 136
plurilingual 105–106, 114, 116–117, 119
policy 61, 84, 106, 123, 140
political IX, XIII, 1, 3, 13, 15, 77, 84, 99
politics 4, 43
power
– dynamics 39, 109, 141, 149
– powerlessness 81, 90–91, 93, 95
– relations 7, 91, 107, 124, 145–147, 149, 151, 156, 159, 163, 165
– structures 5, 96, 98
pre-service teacher(s) XII, XIII 4–17, 35, 4159, 60, 65, 167
– Latinx 4, 59–60, 63
purpose 5, 7, 60, 68, 81, 84, 88–89, 92, 94–95, 97–99, 113, 171

qualitative 3, 7, 63, 128
questionnaire(s) 18, 20, 22, 26–27

race XII, 51–52
recording(s) 88, 128–130, 148
reflection IX, 2, 20, 29, 36, 38, 42, 62, 69, 78, 81, 86, 89, 106, 109, 132

reflexivity 84, 88–93, 97–99, 171
repertoire(s)
– bilingual 24, 28–29, 117
– cultural and linguistic 14, 30, 83
– linguistic 4, 7, 14–17, 19, 23–24, 29, 53, 59–66, 71–72, 74–75, 77–78, 83, 87, 94–96, 106–107, 124, 132–133, 141
– multilingual 16, 167, 169
– multilinguistic 13
– translanguaging IX, 1–2, 3, 4, 5, 6, 7, 8, 13–15, 20, 24, 27–28, 83, 99, 103–104, 106, 119, 123–125, 128–130, 140, 146–148, 150, 168–169, 171
resources
– cultural and linguistic 44, 83
– linguistic 35, 38–40, 61, 76, 112, 124, 168

shift(s) IX, XI, XII, 24–5, 6, 12, 14, 16, 27, 43, 46, 52, 59–60, 62, 67, 78, 83, 93–94, 96, 99, 103, 105–107, 109, 113–114, 116–117, 119, 124, 126, 129, 132, 140–141, 145–156, 159, 163–165, 169–170
social justice IX, 1–2, 3, 4, 5, 7, 13, 15–16, 22, 24, 29–30, 59, 63, 68, 71, 78, 81–86, 88–91, 94–99, 103, 108, 118, 124–125, 131, 141, 145–146, 165, 170–171
– agenda(s) 2, 7, 118, 145, 171
– framework 125
– lens 5
– orientation(s) 1, 66, 88
– stance(s) 5, 81–85, 89–91, 94, 96–99
– turn 2, 7
sociopolitical XII, XIV, 116
stories 35–37, 40–44, 46–47, 51, 53, 55, 167

teacher candidates IX, 7, 11, 13–16, 20, 24, 26, 28, 61, 72, 165, 167, 169–170
teacher preparation XII, 14, 16, 26, 60–61, 63, 72, 97
TESOL IX, XI, XII, 57–8, 39, 81–85, 87, 89, 91, 99
thematic analysis 64
training 37, 46–47, 106, 123, 125, 140, 171
– teacher 6, 123–124, 127
transcript(s), transcriptions 89, 111, 129
translanguaging
– corriente(s) XI, 4, 6, 35, 43, 54, 145–149, 153, 156, 159, 161–165, 170

- design(s)  6, 35, 96, 114, 128, 132, 134–135, 140
- pedagogical practices  XI, XIV, 146
- pedagogy/ies  2–3, 4, 5, 7, 13, 15–16, 24, 26, 53, 59, 61–62, 77, 81, 90, 95, 103–109, 112, 114–119, 123–124, 128–130, 132, 159, 161, 164–165, 167, 169–171
- practice(s)  XI, XII2–1115, 16, 17, 29, 61, 103–104, 106, 123, 133, 146, 152, 165
- repertoire(s)  IX, 1–2, 3, 4, 5, 6, 7, 8, 13–15, 20, 24, 27–28, 83, 99, 103–104, 106, 119, 123–125, 128–130, 140, 146–148, 150, 168–169, 171
- shift(s)  54, 134, 136

- space(s)  XI, 15, 95, 108, 113–114, 119, 170
- stance(s)  XI, XII, 3–4, 6–7, 11, 14–15, 17–18, 23, 53, 59–63, 68, 71–72, 77–78, 88, 96, 107, 128, 132–136, 140–141, 145–152, 161, 164–165, 170–171

translingual
- approach  39, 44, 52
- disposition(s)  4, 35–42, 53–55, 61, 170
- framework  52
- practice(s)  35, 39, 43

video analysis  20, 130